A CANYON VOYAGE

The Grand Canyon

Looking south from the Kaibab Plateau, North Rim, near the head of Bright Angel Creek, the canyon of which is seen in the foreground. The San Francisco Mountains are in the distance. On the South Rim to the right, out of the picture, is the location of the Hotel Tovar. The width of the canyon at top in this region is about twelve miles with a depth of near 6000 feet on the north side, and over 5000 on the south. Total length, including Marble Canyon division, 283 miles. Sketch made in colour on the spot by F. S. Dellenbaugh, June 4, 1903.

A CANYON VOYAGE

The Story of John Wesley Powell and the Charting of the Grand Canyon

Frederick S. Dellenbaugh

SKYHORSE PUBLISHING

Visit our website at www.skyhorsepublishing.com.

10 9 8 7 6 5 4 3 2 1

Library of Congress Cataloging-in-Publication Data is available on file.

Cover design by Tom Lau

Print ISBN: 978-1-5107-2449-5

Ebook ISBN: 978-1-5107-2451-8

Printed in the United States of America.

CONTENTS

List of Illustrations   ix

Introduction   xv

CHAPTER I

PAGE

A River Entrapped—Acquaintance not Desired—Ives Explores the Lower Reaches—Powell the Conqueror—Reason for a Second Descent—Congressional Appropriation—Preparation—The Three Boats—The Mighty Wilderness—Ready for the Start   1

CHAPTER II

Into the Wilderness—The Order of Sailing—Tobacco for the Indians Comes Handy—A Lone Fisherman and Some Trappers—Jack Catches Strange Fish—The Snow-clad Uintas in View—A Larder Full of Venison—Entrance into Flaming Gorge   9

CHAPTER III

The First Rapid—Horseshoe and Kingfisher Canyons—A Rough Entrance into Red Canyon—Capsize of the *Nell*—The Grave of a Bold Navigator—Discovery of a White Man's Camp—Good-bye to Frank—At the Gate of Lodore   19

CHAPTER IV

Locked in the Chasm of Lodore—Rapids with Railway Speed—A Treacherous Approach to Falls of Disaster—Numerous Loadings and Unloadings—Over the Rocks with Cargoes—Library Increased by *Putnam's Magazine*—Triplet Falls and Hell's Half Mile—Fire in Camp—Exit from Turmoil to Peace   34

CHAPTER V

A Remarkable Echo—Up the Canyon of the Yampa—Steward and Clem Try a Moonlight Swim—Whirlpool Canyon and Mountain Sheep—A Grand Fourth-of-July Dinner—A Rainbow-Coloured Valley—The Major Proceeds in Advance—A Split Mountain with Rapids a Plenty—Enter a Big Valley at Last   49

Contents

CHAPTER VI

A Lookout for Redskins—The River a Sluggard—A Gunshot! —Someone
Comes!—The Tale of a Mysterious Light—How, How! from Douglas
Boy—At the Mouth of the Uinta—A Tramp to Goblin City and a
Trip down White River on a Raft—A Waggon-load of Supplies from
Salt Lake by Way of Uinta Agency—The Major Goes Out to Find a
Way In . . . . , . . . 61

CHAPTER VII

On to Battle—A Concert Repertory—Good-bye to Douglas Boy—The Busy,
Busy Beaver—In the Embrace of the Rocks Once More—A Relic of the
Cliff-Dwellers—Low Water and Hard Work—A Canyon of Desolation
—Log-cabin Cliff—Rapids and Rapids and Rapids—A Horse, whose
Horse?—Through Gray Canyon to the Rendezvous 72

CHAPTER VIII

Return of the Major—Some Mormon Friends—No Rations at the Elusive
Dirty Devil—Captain Gunnison's Crossing—An All-night Vigil for Cap.
and Clem—The Land of a Thousand Cascades—A Bend Like a Bow-
knot and a Canyon Labyrinthian—Cleaving an Unknown World—Signs
of the Oldest Inhabitant—Through the Canyon of Stillwater to the Jaws
of the Colorado 94

CHAPTER IX

A Wonderland of Crags and Pinnacles—Poverty Rations—Fast and Furious
Plunging Waters—Boulders Boom along the Bottom—Chilly Days and
Shivering—A Wild Tumultuous Chasm—A Bad Passage by Twilight
and a Tornado With a Picture Moonrise—Out of One Canyon into
Another—At the Mouth of the Dirty Devil at Last 115

CHAPTER X

The *Cañonita* Left Behind—Shinumo Ruins—Troublesome Ledges in the
River—Alcoves and Amphitheatres—The Mouth of the San Juan—
Starvation Days and a Lookout for Rations – El Vado de Los Padres—
White Men Again—Given up for Lost—Navajo Visitors—Peaks with a
Great Echo—At the Mouth of the Paria 135

CHAPTER XI

More Navajos Arrive with Old Jacob—The Lost Pack-train and a Famished
Guide—From Boat to Broncho—On to Kanab—Winter Arrives—Wolf
Neighbours too Intimate—Preparing for Geodetic Work—Over the
Kaibab to Eight-mile Spring—A Frontier Town—Camp below Kanab
—A Mormon Christmas Dance 152

Contents

CHAPTER XII

Reconnoitring and Triangulating—A Pai Ute New Year's Dance—The Major Goes to Salt Lake—Snowy Days on the Kaibab—At Pipe Spring —Gold Hunters to the Colorado—Visits to the Uinkaret County— Craters and Lava—Finding the Hurricane Ledge—An Interview with a Cougar—Back to Kanab 174

CHAPTER XIII

Off for the Unknown Country—A Lonely Grave—Climbing a Hog-back to a Green Grassy Valley—Surprising a Ute Camp—Towich-a-tick-a-boo —Following a Blind Trail—The Unknown Mountains Become Known —Down a Deep Canyon—To the Paria with the *Cañonita*—John D. Lee and Lonely Dell 195

CHAPTER XIV

A Company of Seven—The *Nellie Powell* Abandoned—Into Marble Canyon —Vasey's Paradise—A Furious Descent to the Little Colorado—A Mighty Fall in the Dismal Granite Gorge—Caught in a Trap—Upside Down—A Deep Plunge and a Predicament—At the Mouth of the Kanab 215

CHAPTER XV

A New Departure—Farewell to the Boats—Out to the World Through Kanab Canyon—A Midnight Ride—At the Innupin Picavu—Prof. Reconnoitres the Shewits Country—Winter Quarters in Kanab—Making the Preliminary Map—Another New Year—Across a High Divide in a Snow-storm—Down the Sevier in Winter—The Last Summons . 242

Index 269

ILLUSTRATIONS

FACING
PAGE

THE GRAND CANYON . . . . . *Frontispiece*
> Looking south from the Kaibab Plateau, North Rim, near the head of
> Bright Angel Creek, the canyon of which is seen in the foreground.
> The San Francisco Mountains are in the distance. On the South
> Rim to the right, out of the picture, is the location of the Hotel
> Tovar. The width of the canyon at top in this region is about
> twelve miles, with a depth of near 6000 feet on the north side, and
> over 5000 on the south. Total length, including Marble Canyon
> division, 283 miles.
> Sketch made in colour on the spot by F. S. Dellenbaugh, June 4, 1903.

THE TOLL 2
> Unidentified skeleton found April, 1906, by C. C. Spaulding in the
> Grand Canyon 300 feet above the river, some miles below Bright
> Angel trail. There were daily papers in the pocket of the clothes
> of the early spring of 1900.
> Photograph by Kolb Bros. 1906, Grand Canyon, Arizona.

RED CANYON 3
> Photograph by E. O. Beaman, 1871.

BEFORE THE START AT GREEN RIVER CITY, WYOMING . 8
> The dark box open. Andy, Clem, Beaman, Prof. Steward, Cap.,
> Frank, Jones, Jack, the Major, Fred, *Cañonita*, *Emma Dean*,
> *Nellie Powell*.
> Photograph by E. O. Beaman, 1871.

FLAMING GORGE 20
> The beginning of the Colorado River Canyons, N. E. Utah.
> Photograph by E. O. Beaman, 1871.

HORSESHOE CANYON 21
> Photograph by E. O. Beaman, 1871.

ix

FACING
PAGE

RED CANYON 24
    Photograph by E. O. Beaman, 1871.

RED CANYON 25
    Ashley Falls from below.
    Photograph by E. O. Beaman, 1871.

IN RED CANYON PARK 30
    Photograph by E. O. Beaman, 1871.

THE HEAD OF THE CANYON OF LODORE 34
    Just inside the gate.
    Photograph by E. O. Beaman, 1871.

CANYON OF LODORE 35
    Low water.
    Photograph by J. K. Hillers, 1874.

THE HEART OF LODORE 42
    F. S. Dellenbaugh.
    Photograph by E. O. Beaman, 1871.

CANYON OF LODORE—DUNN'S CLIFF 43
    2800 feet above river.
    Photograph by E. O. Beaman, 1871.

CANYON OF LODORE 48
    Jones, Hillers, Dellenbaugh.
    Photograph by E. O. Beaman, 1871.

ECHO PARK 49
    Mouth of Yampa River in foreground, Green River on right.
    Photograph by E. O. Beaman, 1871.

WHIRLPOOL CANYON 56
    Mouth of Bishop Creek—Fourth of July camp.
    Photograph by E. O. Beaman, 1871.

SPLIT MOUNTAIN CANYON 57
    Photograph by E. O. Beaman, 1871.

CANYON OF DESOLATION 80
    Steward.
    Photograph by E. O. Beaman, 1871.

Illustrations

FACING
PAGE

COLORADO RIVER WHITE SALMON 102
Photograph by the Denver, Colorado Canyon and Pacific Railway
Survey under Robert Brewster Stanton, 1889.

DELLENBAUGH BUTTE 103
Near mouth of San Rafael.
Photograph by E. O. Beaman, 1871.

LABYRINTH CANYON—BOWKNOT BEND 110
The great loop is behind the spectator.
Photograph by E. O. Beaman, 1871.

STILLWATER CANYON 111
Photograph by E. O. Beaman, 1871.

CATARACT CANYON 118
Clement Powell.
Photograph by E. O. Beaman, 1871.

CATARACT CANYON 119
Photograph by E. O. Beaman, 1871.

NARROW CANYON 132
Photograph by Best Expedition, 1891.

MOUTH OF THE FREMONT RIVER (DIRTY DEVIL). . . 133
Photograph by the Brown Expedition, 1889.

GLEN CANYON 140
Photograph by E. O. Beaman, 1871.

LOOKING DOWN UPON GLEN CANYON 141
Cut through homogeneous sandstone.
Photograph by J. K. Hillers, U. S. Colo. Riv. Exp.

TOM 148
A typical Navajo. Tom became educated and no longer looked like
an Indian.
Photograph by Wittick.

GLEN CANYON 149
Sentinel Rock—about 300 feet high.
Photograph by E. O. Beaman, 1871.

THE GRAND CANYON 162
From Havasupai Point, South Rim, showing Inner Gorge.
From a sketch in colour by F. S. Dellenbaugh, 1907.

Illustrations

FACING
PAGE

THE GRAND CANYON 163
    From South Rim near Bright Angel Creek.

THE GRAND CANYON 186
    From part way down south side above Bright Angel Creek.

WINSOR CASTLE, THE DEFENSIVE HOUSE AT PIPE SPRINGS . 187
    Photograph by H. Arthur Pomroy, 1903.

LITTLE ZION VALLEY, OR THE MOOKOONTOWEAP, UPPER
    VIRGIN RIVER 187
    Photograph by H. Arthur Pomroy, 1903.

IN THE UNKNOWN COUNTRY 194
    Photograph by J. K. Hillers, 1872.

NAVAJO MOUNTAIN FROM NEAR KAIPAROWITS PEAK . . 200
    Photograph by J. K. Hillers, 1872.

EXAMPLE OF LAKES ON THE AQUARIUS PLATEAU . . 201
    Photograph by J. K. Hillers.

TANTALUS CREEK 206
    Tributary of Fremont River.
    Photograph by J. K. Hillers.

THE GRAND CANYON 218
    Near mouth of Shinumo Creek. The river is in flood and the water is
    "colorado."
    Sketch made in colour on the spot by F. S. Dellenbaugh. July 26, 1907.

MARBLE CANYON 219
    Thompson.
    Photograph by J. K. Hillers, 1872.

CANYON OF THE LITTLE COLORADO 222
    Photograph by C. Barthelmess.

THE GRAND CANYON 223
    From just below the Little Colorado.
    Photograph by J. K. Hillers, 1872.

THE GRAND CANYON 226
    Running the Sockdologer.
    From a sketch afterwards by F. S. Dellenbaugh.

THE GRAND CANYON 227
    From top of Granite, south side near Bright Angel Creek.

THE GRAND CANYON 238
    Character of river in rapids.
    Photograph by F. S. Dellenbaugh, 1907.

Illustrations

FACING
PAGE

THE GRAND CANYON 242
    At a rapid—low water.

THE GRAND CANYON 243
    At the bottom near foot of Bass Trail.

THE GRAND CANYON 254
    From north side near foot of Toroweap Valley, Uinkaret District.
    Photograph by J. K. Hillers.

THE GRAND CANYON 255
    Storm effect from South Rim.

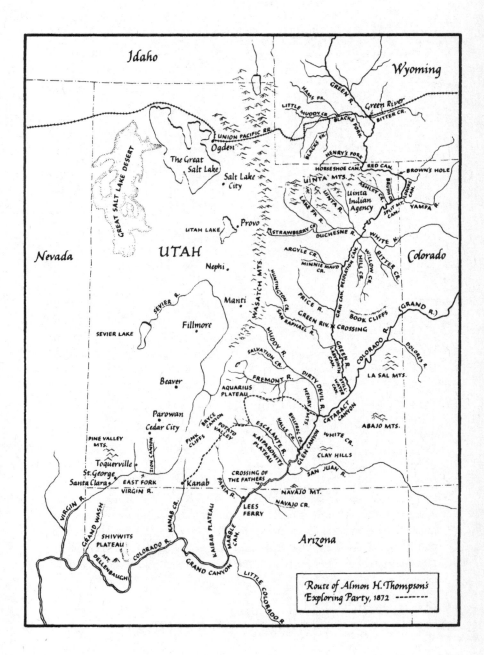

Idaho

Wyoming

Nevada

UTAH

Colorado

Arizona

Route of Almon H. Thompson's
Exploring Party, 1872 --------

INTRODUCTION

ALMOST four hundred years ago, in 1540 to be exact, Don Garcia Lopez de Cardenas discovered the Grand Canyon of the Colorado River of the West in what is now Arizona.

With twelve companions he stood on the South Rim, doubtless in awe at the singular magnificence of the scene and the magnitude, the first Europeans ever to look upon it. What were his exact feelings cannot be stated, for no writing of his on the subject is known and the notes made by Petro de Sotomayor, the chronicler of this particular sub-expedition, and given to the general, Coronado, have never been seen in our time.

Therefore historical data concerning this important exploratory event must be derived from the manuscript copy made in 1596 of the record written by Pedro de Castañeda, another chronicler of the Coronado gold-hunting foray to which Cardenas was attached. Now, thanks to the foresight and the generosity of James Lenox, Castañeda's account is in the manuscript department of the New York Public Library. This manuscript in old Spanish is not easy to read, even by the most accomplished Spanish scholar, for not only has the language changed considerably since the time of its writing but the manuscript has no punctuation and few capitals; it just runs on and on page after page.

A translation of this document into French was made years ago by Henri Ternaux-Campans for his well-known *Collection de Voyages*, and for a long period it was the only available translation. A much better one has been made by George Parker Winship and is published in the *Fourteenth Annual Report of the U. S. Bureau of Ethnology, 1896*. This gives also the Spanish text and some facsimile examples of the writing.[1]

Ternaux-Campans stated that the Spaniards declared the chasm to be three or four leagues *deep*, whereas what they actually re-

[1] *The Coronado Expedition—1540-1542*, by George Parker Winship. Extract from the Fourteenth Annual Report of the U. S. Bureau of Ethnology, Washington, 1896.

corded was that at the place where they were the gorge was three
or four leagues across in an air line (*por el ayre*) from brink to
brink. This is almost exactly a description of the Grand Canyon in
the vicinity of El Tovar Hotel, as well as in some other parts. It is
clear then that the Spaniards did not exaggerate but on the contrary
were quite exact. At the time Ternaux-Campans made his translation
little or nothing was known of this canyon and he evidently supposed
it must be a narrow, dark slit in the earth; and that the remark as
to three or four leagues must refer to depth.

Some of the party tried to reach the water but after descending
about one third of the way they were completely foiled and gave it
up.

Then for 329 years after this brief but memorable first visit all
efforts to penetrate into the mysteries of the mighty chasm likewise
failed and a superstition finally grew up that the river itself was
absolutely impassable, even that it disappeared underground in
places, making navigation not only hazardous but impossible. It must
be noted that to an observer gazing down from a height upon the
plateau through which the Marble Gorge, the upper portion of the
Grand Canyon, carves its sinister, narrow course, it appears entirely reasonable to imagine that the fierce torrent should lose itself
beneath the ponderous walls or even cut through them for gloomy
distances. So sharply defined is the gorge on the surface that its
outline is extremely forbidding in its dark and mysterious cleaving
westward into the upward slope of the land.

For a long time approach to the canyons of the Green and the
Colorado was exceedingly difficult and hazardous. The region on
both sides of the thousand miles of canyons for a wide area is arid;
the heat is great; the natives were not too hospitable, especially
after they began to learn the white man's deceptive ways. The aridity,
however, was one of the main obstacles. A man can go a long period
without food, but without water in the burning air he soon collapses.
And along these mighty canyons even an experienced frontiersman
might die of thirst within sight of the rushing torrent even in this
day of improved transportation.

E. L. Berthoud, a frontiersman of Colorado, once wrote me that
his friend Jim Bridger, who probably knew the country better than
any other white man, "would tell in camp of the Cañon of the

Colorado and Green River and of the almost utter impossibility of getting water from either cañon, although in full sight of an abundance of it—which I bitterly experienced when trying to explore down Green River south of White River in Utah in 1861."

Lansford W. Hastings in his *Guide to Oregon and California,* 1845, writes: "The greater portion of this river from its source lies through a very broken, mountainous country, breaking through lofty mountains, pouring over high cliffs, down vast perpendicular cataracts, and into deep chasms with perpendicular basaltic walls, five hundred feet in height."

Because of the immense difficulty of penetration, all the trappers and frontiersmen, with the exception of several who ventured into the upper canyons of Green River, steered wide of these canyons. All below the mouth of the Duchesne as far as the end of the Grand Canyon at the Grand Wash was *terra incognita.* Escalante in 1776 had crossed at the Ute Ford, since known as *El Vado de los Padres* or, in English, The Crossing of the Fathers, and this ford was probably known to a few frontiersmen after that. Jacob Hamblin crossed there in 1858 and after. He also found that a crossing by boat could be made at the mouth of the Paria River a few miles below El Vado—a place where Escalante first tried to get over. In a distance of many hundreds of miles these, with Gunnison Crossing of Green River, were the only known points of crossing for 329 years after the first view of the Grand Canyon by Cardenas.

There is a claim that one James White in 1867 descended through the Cataract, the Glen, and the Grand Canyons on a raft tied together with buckskin strings and a pack rope. As he knew absolutely nothing about the conditions within these canyons after the alleged descent the story may be dismissed—even granting that anyone on such a frail raft could make the descent through the many furious rapids.

At last Major John Wesley Powell, a Civil War veteran, then thirty-five years of age, descended with nine companions (eight after Uinta Valley, five after Separation Rapid) in boats from Green River, Wyoming, to the mouth of the Virgin River in 1869, and for the first time made known the character of the interior of the long line of canyons and the general conditions of the country through which they are carved. Thereby he rounded out the cycle of exploration begun 329 years before by Don Garcia Lopez de Cardenas. This volume presents the account of his second descent through the line of canyons—a descent which enabled him to couple with the narrative of the first the necessary data regarding the course of the river, the altitudes, the general geography of the region, the geology, and the first maps.

This first expedition of Major Powell's was his own private venture, aided by funds from several educational institutions, and rations from the U. S. Government. It was, therefore, not a government affair at all, except as to the rations supplied. It was not too well equipped and the loss of one boat and its contents at Disaster Falls in the Green River canyon of Lodore, almost at the outset of the voyage, compelled a more hasty progress than at first was contemplated. By the first plan about a year was to be consumed; conditions reduced the time of the voyage to three months.

In order to make clear the causes which led to a second expedition I must give here a brief résumé.

The worst portions of the Grand Canyon so far as rapids are concerned are in the Granite Gorges, of which there are three: Upper, Middle, and Lower. The party of 1869 conquered every fall in the Upper and Middle Granite Gorges successfully, and as far as Diamond Creek, notwithstanding the gruelling work, the short rations of wet, spoiled food, and the fading physical vigor of the men. Then suddenly, to their dismay, up rose the black granite once more before them, a portent of another stretch no one knew how long, of huge and fierce rapids which tax any man's full strength. Possibly they might be even worse than any above. A very bad place came into view; not only bad but in such shape that its quality could not be well seen.

There is no doubt in my mind that all the men were somewhat taken aback by this new threat of the river. Three, O. G. Howland, Seneca Howland, and W. H. Dunn, declared they meant to proceed no further. The whole expedition was at a crisis. The three were the only ones, however, who deserted or who had intention of deserting, though one man, Hawkins, states in a pamphlet printed not long ago that the Major declared to them that if only one man would stand by him he would go on to the end.

He took observations which indicated that they were not many miles from the end of the Canyon (45 in a straight line from the

Virgin River), but the three adhered to their purpose. They climbed
out on the north to reach the Mormon settlements and were killed a
day or two after by the Shewits Indians near Mt. Dellenbaugh.
Two days after their desertion the river party emerged safely from
the Grand Canyon. They were soon at the mouth of the Virgin River,
where several Mormons were encamped who gave them food and
assistance. I understand these Mormons were directed by the foresight of Brigham Young to be on the watch for the Powell party and
to be ready to aid them.

Naturally the scientific data collected under these adverse conditions were meager and unsatisfactory. Part were lost with the men
who deserted. But Major Powell was a man of extraordinary per-
tinacity, of great originality of mind, and of tremendous will.
Having determined to explore these canyons and map them he was
not to be satisfied with this halfway success. He took immediate
steps to continue the work to the finish by a second expedition.

The fact that he was lacking a right arm, lost at the battle of
Shiloh, was no hindrance to him; in fact it appeared to spur him on.
He applied to Congress for an appropriation, which was granted,
and the second expedition (the first United States Colorado River
Exploring Expedition) came into being. Professor Almon Harris
Thompson was made chief geographer and general associate manager
with Major Powell himself. It was a condition similar to the associa-
tion of Lewis and Clark. The year 1870 was devoted to planning
the second expedition and in May, 1871, it started as related herein.

This narrative of the second expedition is the only account of it
ever written for publication, or published, barring a few letters in
newspapers at the time from me and from several others of the
party, the printing of a lecture of mine in the Bulletin of the American Geographical Society, and a couple of chapters in my *Romance
of the Colorado River*.

This volume consequently is in sort an appendix to the Government Report.[1] In that Report there is no mention of the second expedition down the river, nor are any details given in a little pamphlet
Report published in 1873.[2] The narrative of the Report was largely

[1] *Exploration of the Colorado River of the West and Its Tributaries Explored in 1869, 1870, 1871 and 1872.* Washington, 1875.

[2] *Report of Explorations in 1873 of the Colorado of the West and its
Tributaries.* Washington, 1874.

based on the diaries of Jack Sumner and Professor Thompson, as well as Powell's own.

Professor Thompson in a letter to me of May 10, 1902, says:

"Jack Sumner's diary (not over six pages of foolscap) was the most complete record kept of it. Everything we know of the Colorado River except the fact that it could be passed down in boats was secured by the second voyage and subsequent explorations, a part of which you were."

Although the Major did not include a narrative of the second expedition in his Report, or write of it elsewhere himself, he had no objection to my publishing anything I pleased about it. From the start he was always friendly, kind, and considerate towards me. He took a deep interest in my future and endeavored to have me remain permanently with him as one of his aids in the execution of plans for the future which he visioned and which were developed to success.

He left Professor Thompson out of his Report, which was not quite fair, for Professor Thompson was largely responsible for the success of the second expedition. Professor Thompson felt much hurt but while feeling so he spoke in high terms of the Major's many fine qualities.

In one of the Major's letters to me in 1901, the year before he died, he says, "Now my dear Dellenbaugh, I always delight in your successes and your prosperity and I ever cherish the memory of those days when we were on the great river together." Another time when I spoke of preparing a book on the Colorado he wrote, "I hope that you will put on record the second trip and the gentlemen who were members of that expedition." This was my *Romance of the Colorado River*. He did not live to see it.

Professor Thompson frequently told me he considered me the historian of that expedition. He gave me every assistance and when he died he bequeathed to me his diaries and all his Colorado River material. These diaries I have deposited in the Manuscript Department of the New York Public Library together with my own diary of that time, and with those of other members of the expedition through the courtesy and generosity of their heirs.

Congress caused a memorial monument to be erected to Major Powell and his men on a promontory of the South Rim of the Grand Canyon not far from the Hotel Tovar. A bronze tablet bears the names of all the members of the two parties who navigated the Grand Canyon, except the three who deserted.

There has been some adverse criticism of the omission but it seems very clear that three men who refused to finish the journey and hampered the progress and success of the undertaking by backing out at a critical moment deserve no honorable mention. They are fully and justly recorded in the Report and in other places. They were men of fine quality and plenty of courage, but two of them were temporarily demoralized—the third, Seneca Howland, reluctantly went with his brother.

Jack Sumner, the dean of the first party and a most intelligent, straightforward, and level-headed man, writes of the separation: "Howland and Dunn told me at noon that they did not care about taking any more chances on the river and proposed to leave and try to make the Mormon settlements to the north of the river. I done what I could to knock such notions out of their heads but as I was not sure of my own side of the argument [safety of going on] I fear I did not make the case very strong. . . . O. G. Howland appeared to be the leader of the three and had fully made up his mind to quit. As the rapids had become a holy terror to him I saw that farther talk was useless and so informed Major Powell." Hawkins in his pamphlet (which contains some absurd misstatements) says, "Dunn, O. G. Howland and Seneca Howland had made up their minds to go and Dunn said he hated to leave Hall and myself as we had been together a long time and that we would perish in the river."

I never heard Major Powell say a word in condemnation of any of these men; on the contrary he always spoke of them affectionately.

I must repeat here a paragraph from the former edition of this book: "Major Powell was a man of prompt decision with a cool, comprehensive, far reaching mind. He was genial, kind, never despondent, always resolute, resourceful, masterful, determined to overcome every obstacle. To him alone belongs the credit for solving the problem of the great canyons, and to Professor Thompson that for conducting most successfully the geographic work under difficulties that can hardly be appreciated in these days when survey work is an accepted item of government expenditure and Congress treats it with an open hand. . . . Professor Thompson possessed invaluable qualities for this expedition: rare balance of mind, great cheerfulness, and a sunny way of looking on difficulties and obstacles as if they were mere problems in chess. His foresight and resourcefulness were phenomenal and no threatening situation found him without some good remedy."

In the preface to the first edition I expressed the opinion that anyone who wished to could use this book as a guide for navigating the river as far as Kanab Canyon (where we left it) and I am pleased to state that this has been done by my friends Emery and Ellsworth Kolb. They carried the book in their successful descent in 1910. That priceless volume, tattered and battered and filled with sand by exposure to the elements during consultation in the boat by day and by the fire at night, they presented to me with fine consideration at the Powell Monument on the day in May, 1921, when I unfurled there the flag of Major Powell's boat, the *Emma Dean*, to celebrate the fiftieth anniversary of our start from Green River "City," Wyoming.

In their interesting and valuable book, *Through the Grand Canyon from Wyoming to Mexico* (p. 249), they say, "This book [*A Canyon Voyage*] had been our guide down to this point [Kanab Canyon]: we could not have asked for a better one."

Many times since our expedition the canyons have been entered with boats. The well-equipped parties generally have gone through with success and it is my opinion that it can be done repeatedly if the equipment and personnel are adequate. The latest descents have been those of the parties of the United States Geological Survey in 1921, 1922, and 1923. These were admirably and successfully conducted, achieving all the desired results with no loss of life. Emery Kolb was chief boatman and gave most valuable direction. Colonel Claude Birdseye and Mr. E. C. La Rue, as well as the other members, are to be congratulated on their skill and on the results of the descents; accurate surveys and levelling of the river from Green River, Wyoming, to the Virgin River and below.

Their measurement of the now famous Sockdologer Rapid was a disappointment to me and something of a shock. This fall had been estimated all the way from 30 feet to 130. The latest figures are 19 feet! But this 19 feet is almost all at the beginning, in the first 100 yards. In about a mile the fall of the river is some 25 feet, and looking down from above at high water, or with the brief glimpse we had from below after running it, it certainly looked extremely high to us.[1] In a letter of mine written Sept. 19, 1872, just after we emerged, I find that I stated the fall to be 40 feet in half a mile. Distance lent enlargement and as we looked backward in time the place grew in height. It surely is a terrific descent at high water with its sharp fall and it made on us a profound impression, knowing it had to be run no matter what happened. Julius Stone in 1909 levelled what he considered to be the Sockdologer very carefully and made it 34 feet 6 inches. It must have been another fall. There are several similar falls of more descent in a short distance. I do not remember that Major Powell ever gave an opinion about it except his statement of 75 or 80 feet (p. 82) in his Report, but his diary gives it no more than 30 feet. R. B. Stanton also levelled it in 1890 but lost his notes. He ridiculed the idea that it was more than 30 or 40 feet in a mile. The current is headlong and the waves are huge and vicious.

Many dam sites are now laid out for conserving the enormous amount of water which descends through the canyons. If these projects are carried out the rapids will disappear for long stretches—perhaps the Sockdologer will—and the tourist in a motor boat will speed along up or down the canyons, viewing the towering heights with comfort.

The country which in 1871 was so inaccessible that we had to fetch our supplies by wagon and by pack train from Salt Lake City is now easily reached by railway on both sides of the Grand Canyon: on the south by the Santa Fé and on the north by the Union Pacific. The latter railroad has also opened a way into the extraordinary Cedar Breaks, Bryce Canyon, and Zion National Park by automobile from the end of the line at Cedar City. The North Rim of the Grand Canyon is accessible as well by this route.

The government at last is to build a suspension bridge across Marble Gorge near its head—five miles below Lee Ferry—where the span is only about 600 feet with a depth of 400 feet of canyon.

---

[1] The first boat of the 1923 party to run the Sockdologer seen from above "was glimpsed only at intervals. The boat was out of sight most of the time, but finally appeared below right side up, and one by one, the other boats successfully made the descent."—Colonel Birdseye.

This will make it possible to pass at this place from one side of the long canyon barrier to the other, without a ferry.

Maps and profiles of the river through the canyons may be obtained by addressing the Director, U. S. Geological Survey, Washington, at a nominal cost, and those interested in the reservoir and conservation questions should secure U.S.G.S. Water Supply Paper 556, by E. C. La Rue, which admirably presents all the data. For the region around Navajo Mountain, *The Navajo Country*, U.S.G.S. Water Supply Paper 380, by H. E. Gregory, is accurate.

I must again express my appreciation for assistance from Professor Thompson, John K. Hillers, Robert Brewster Stanton (whose diaries of his 1889-1890 descent have been given to the New York Public Library by his widow), Brigadier General Mackenzie, The U.S. Geological Survey, Julius Stone, the Kolb Brothers, Colonel Birdseye, and others.

William H. Holmes in conversation with me once aptly designated the Grand Canyon region as the "Geologist's Paradise." Nowhere else in the world are the pages of Time so clearly opened up. Millions of years are there discovered to be little more than the tick of a clock in the everlasting scheme of the universe, and while the Grand Canyon, with all its millions of years, is but a young thing in geological history, nevertheless as one looks down upon it he feels that he stands face to face with eternity. The vast silence, the immensity of it all, tend to produce a feeling that the Canyon has a personality—that it is something that might swallow you up as if you were a mere chip in a whirlwind.

In the dark of night beside some roaring fall, with the thunder crashing as if those towering walls were tumbling from their heights; with the lightning flashing and the rain descending in torrential floods that leap and gather from the confining precipices, one truly feels in the very heart of elemental nature, and marvels that man has survived the constant destroying onslaughts of storm and fire, and is able not merely to protect himself, but even to utilize the annihilating forces for his own comfort.

The Colorado River teaches much that is not geology.

FREDERICK S. DELLENBAUGH.

New York,
    May 30, 1926.

A CANYON VOYAGE

CHAPTER I

A River Entrapped—Acquaintance not Desired—Ives Explores the Lower Reaches —Powell the Conqueror—Reason for a Second Descent—Congressional Appropriation—Preparation—The Three Boats—The Mighty Wilderness— Ready for the Start.

THE upper continuation of the Colorado River of the West is Green River which heads in the Wind River Mountains at Frémont Peak. From this range southward to the Uinta Mountains, on the southern boundary of Wyoming, the river flows through an open country celebrated in the early days of Western exploration and fur trading as " Green River Valley," and at that period the meeting ground and "rendez-vous" of the various companies and organisations, and of free trappers. By the year 1840 the vast region west of the Missouri had been completely investigated by the trappers and fur-hunt-ers in the pursuit of trade, with the exception of the Green-and-Colorado River from the foot of Green River Valley to the termination of the now famous Grand Canyon of Arizona. The reason for this exception was that at the southern ex-tremity of Green River Valley the solid obstacle of the Uinta Range was thrown in an easterly and westerly trend directly across the course of the river, which, finding no alternative, had carved its way, in the course of a long geological epoch, through the foundations of the mountains in a series of gorges with extremely precipitous sides; continuous parallel cliffs be-tween whose forbidding precipices dashed the torrent towards the sea. Having thus entrapped itself, the turbulent stream, by the configuration of the succeeding region, was forced to continue its assault on the rocks, to reach the Gulf, and ground its fierce progress through canyon after canyon, with scarcely an intermission of open country, for a full thousand miles from the beginning of its entombment, the entrance of Flaming Gorge, at the foot of the historical Green River Valley. Some few attempts had been made to fathom the mystery of this long series of chasms, but with such small success that the exploration of the river was given up as too difficult and too dangerous. Ashley had gone through Red Canyon in 1825 and in one of the succeeding winters of that period a party had passed through Lodore on the ice. These trips proved that the canyons were not the haunt of beaver, that the navigation of them was vastly difficult, and that no man could tell what might befall in those gorges further down, that were deeper, longer, and still more remote from any touch with the outer world. Indeed it was even reported that there were places where the whole river disappeared underground. The Indians, as a rule, kept away from the canyons, for there was little to attract them. One bold Ute who attempted to shorten his trail by means of the river, shortened it to the Happy Hunting Grounds immediately, and there was nothing in his fate to inspire emulation.

The years then wore on and the Colorado remained unknown through its canyon division. Ives had come up to near the mouth of the Virgin from the Gulf of California in 1858, and the portion above Flaming Gorge, from the foot of Green River Valley, was fairly well known, with the Union Pacific Railway finally bridging it in Wyoming. One James White was picked up (1867) at a point below the mouth of the Virgin in an exhausted state, and it was assumed that he had made a large part of the terrible voyage on a raft, but this was not the case, and the Colorado River Canyons still waited for a conqueror. He came in 1869 in the person of John Wesley Powell, a late Major[1] in the Civil War, whose

[1] Powell had received an appointment as Colonel before he left the Volunteer Service, but he was always called Major.

The Toll.

Unidentified skeleton found April 1906 by C. C. Spaulding in the Grand Canyon 300 feet
above the river, some miles below Bright Angel trail.   There were daily papers
of the early spring of 1900 in the pocket of the clothes.
Photograph 1906 by KOLB BROS.

Red Canyon.
Photograph by E. O. BEAMAN, 1871.

scientific studies had led him to the then territory of Colorado where his mind became fired with the intention of exploring the canyons. The idea was carried out, and the river was descended from the Union Pacific Railway crossing to the mouth of the Virgin, and two of the men went on to the sea. Thus the great feat was accomplished — one of the greatest feats of exploration ever executed on this continent.[1]

Circumstances had rendered the data collected both insufficient and incomplete. A second expedition was projected to supply deficiencies and to extend the work; an expedition so well equipped and planned that time could be taken for the purely scientific side of the venture. This expedition was the first one under the government, the former expedition having been a more or less private enterprise. Congress made appropriations and the party were to start in 1870. This was found to be inexpedient for several reasons, among which was the necessity of exploring a route by which rations could be brought in to them at the mouth of what we called Dirty Devil River—a euphonious title applied by the men of the first expedition. This stream entered the Colorado at the foot of what is now known as Narrow Canyon, a little below the 38th parallel, —the Frémont River of the present geographies. Arrangements for supplies to be brought in to the second expedition at this place were made by the Major during a special visit to southern Utah for the purpose.

By great good fortune I became a member of the second expedition. Scores of men were turned away, disappointed. The party was a small one, and it was full. We were to begin our voyage through the chain of great canyons, at the same point where the first expedition started, the point where the recently completed Union Pacific Railway crossed Green River in Wyoming, and we arrived there from the East early on the morning of April 29, 1871. We were all ravenous after the long night on the train and breakfast was the first consideration, but when this had re-established our energy we went to look for the flat car with our boats which had been sent

[1] For the history of the Colorado River the reader is referred to *The Romance of the Colorado River*, by F. S. Dellenbaugh.

ahead from Chicago. The car was soon found on a siding and
with the help of some railroad employés we pushed it along to
the eastern end of the bridge over Green River and there, on
the down side, put the boats into the waters against whose
onslaughts they were to be our salvation. It was lucky perhaps that we did not pause to ponder on the importance of
these little craft ; on how much depended on their staunchness
and stability; and on our possible success in preventing their
destruction. The river was high from melting snows and the
current was swift though ordinarily it is not a large river at
this point. This season had been selected for the start because
of the high water, which would tide us over the rocks till
tributary streams should swell the normal volume; for our
boats were to be well loaded, there being no chance to get
supplies after leaving. We had some trouble in making a
landing where we wanted to, in a little cove on the east side
about half a mile down, which had been selected as a good
place for our preparatory operations. Here the three boats
were hauled out to receive the final touches. They were
named *Emma Dean*, *Nellie Powell*, and *Cañonita*. A space
was cleared in the thick willows for our general camp over
which Andy was to be master of ceremonies, at least so far as
the banqueting division was concerned, and here he became
initiated into the chemistry necessary to transform raw materials into comparatively edible food. But it was not so hard
a task, for our supplies were flour, beans, bacon, dried apples,
and dried peaches, tea and coffee, with, of course, plenty of
sugar. Canned goods at that time were not common, and
besides, would have been too heavy. Bread must be baked
three times a day in the Dutch oven, a sort of skillet of cast
iron, about three inches deep, ten or twelve inches in diameter,
with short legs, and a cast-iron cover with a turned-up rim that
would hold hot coals. We had no other bread than was made
in this oven, or in a frying-pan, with saleratus and cream of
tartar to raise it. It was Andy's first experience as a cook,
though he had been a soldier in the Civil War, as had almost
every member of the party except the youngest three, Clem,
Frank, and myself, I being the youngest of all.

For sleeping quarters we were disposed in two vacant
wooden shanties about two hundred yards apart and a somewhat greater distance from the cook-camp. These shanties
were mansions left over, like a group of roofless adobe ruins
near by, from the opulent days of a year or two back when this
place had been the terminus of the line during building operations. Little remained of its whilom grandeur; a section house,
a railway station, a number of canvas-roofed domiciles, Field's
"Outfitting Store," and the aforesaid shanties in which we
secured refuge, being about all there was of the place. The
region round about suggested the strangeness of the wild
country below, through the midst of which led our trail. Arid
and gravelly hills met the eye on all sides, accentuated by huge
buttes and cliffs of brilliant colours, which in their turn were intensified by a clear sky of deep azure. In the midst of our operations, we found time to note the passing of the single express
train each way daily. These trains seemed very friendly and
the passengers gazed wonderingly from the windows at us and
waved handkerchiefs. They perceived what we were about by
the sign which I painted on cloth and fastened across the front
of our house, which was near the track: "Powell's Colorado
River Exploring Expedition." Above this was flying our
general flag, the Stars and Stripes.

The white boats were thoroughly gone over with caulking-
iron and paint. Upon the decks of the cabins, canvas, painted
green, was stretched in such a way that it could be unbuttoned
at the edges on three sides and thrown back when we wanted
to take off the hatches. When in place this canvas kept the
water, perfectly, out of the hatch joints. Each boat had three
compartments, the middle one being about four feet long,
about one-fifth the length of the boat, which was twenty-two
feet over the top. Two places were left for the rowers, before and abaft the middle compartment, while the steersman
with his long oar thrust behind was to sit on the deck of the
after-cabin, all the decks being flush with the gunwale, except
that of the forward cabin the deck of which was carried back
in a straighter line than the sheer of the boat and thus formed
a nose to help throw off the waves. It was believed that when

the hatches were firmly in place and the canvases drawn taut over the decks, even if a boat turned over, as was expected sometimes might be the case, the contents of these cabins would remain intact and dry. As so much depended on keeping our goods dry, and as we knew from Powell's previous experience that the voyage would be a wet one, everything was carefully put in rubber sacks, each having a soft mouth inside a double lip with a row of eyelets in each lip through which ran a strong cord. When the soft mouth was rolled up and the bag squeezed, the air was forced out, and the lips could be drawn to a bunch by means of the cord. When in this condition the bag could be soaked a long time in water without wetting the contents. Each rubber bag was encased in a heavy cotton one to protect it; in short, we spared no effort to render our provisions proof against the destroying elements. At first we put the bacon into rubber, but it spoiled the rubber and then we saw that bacon can take care of itself, nothing can hurt it anyhow, and a gunny-sack was all that was necessary. Though the boats were five feet in the beam and about twenty-four inches in depth, their capacity was limited and the supplies we could take must correspond. Each man was restricted to one hundred pounds of baggage, including his blankets. He had one rubber bag for the latter and another for his clothing and personal effects. In the provision line we had twenty-two sacks of flour of fifty pounds each. There was no whiskey, so far as I ever knew, except a small flask containing about one gill which I had been given with a ditty-bag for the journey. This flask was never drawn upon and was intact till needed as medicine in October. Smoking was abandoned, though a case of smoking tobacco was taken for any Indians we might meet. Our photographic outfit was extremely bulky and heavy, for the dry plate had not been invented. We had to carry a large amount of glass and chemicals, as well as apparatus.

The numerous scientific instruments also were bulky, as they had to be fitted into wooden cases that were covered with canvas and then with rubber. Rations in quantity were not obtainable short of Salt Lake or Fort Bridger, and we had

Congressional authority to draw on the military posts for supplies. The Major and his colleague, Professor Thompson, went to Fort Bridger and to Salt Lake to secure what was necessary, and to make further arrangements for the supplies which were to be brought in to us at the three established points: the mouth of the Uinta, by way of the Uinta Indian Agency; the mouth of the Dirty Devil; and the place where Escalante had succeeded in crossing the Colorado in 1776, known as the Crossing of the Fathers, about on the line between Utah and Arizona.

Mrs. Thompson and Mrs. Powell, who had come out on the same train with us, had gone on to Salt Lake, where they were to wait for news from the expedition, when we should get in touch with the Uinta Agency at the mouth of the Uinta River, something over two hundred miles further down. At length all was provided for and the Major and Prof. returned to our camp from Salt Lake bringing a new member of the party, Jack Hillers, to take the place of Jack Sumner of the former party who was unable to get to us on account of the deep snows in the mountains which surrounded the retreat where he had spent the winter trapping. Prof. brought back also an American flag for each boat with the name of the boat embroidered in the field of blue on one side while the stars were on the other. We all admired these flags greatly, especially as they had been made by Mrs. Thompson's own hands.

We had with us a diary which Jack Sumner had kept on the former voyage, and the casual way in which he repeatedly referred to running through a "hell of foam" gave us an inkling, if nothing more, of what was coming. Our careful preparations gave us a feeling of security against disaster, or, at least, induced us to expect some degree of liberality from Fortune. We had done our best to insure success and could go forward in some confidence. A delay was caused by the non-arrival of some extra heavy oars ordered from Chicago, but at length they came, and it was well we waited, for the lighter ones were quickly found to be too frail. Our preparations had taken three weeks. Considering that we were obliged to provide against every contingency that might occur in descending this torrent so completely locked in from assistance and supplies, the time was not too long. Below Green River City, Wyoming, where we were to start, there was not a single settler, nor a settlement of any kind, on or near the river for a distance of more than a thousand miles. From the river out, a hundred miles in an air line westward, across a practically trackless region, would be required to measure the distance to the nearest Mormon settlements on the Sevier, while eastward it was more than twice as far to the few pioneers who had crossed the Backbone of the Continent. The Uinta Indian Agency was the nearest establishment to Green River. It was forty miles west of the mouth of the Uinta. In southern Utah the newly formed Mormon settlement of Kanab offered the next haven, but no one understood exactly its relationship to the topography of the Colorado, except from the vicinity of the Crossing of the Fathers. Thus the country through which we were to pass was then a real wilderness, while the river itself was walled in for almost the entire way by more or less unscalable cliffs of great height.

Finally all of our preparations were completed to the last detail. The cabins of the boats were packed as one packs a trunk. A wooden arm-chair was obtained from Field and fastened to the middle deck of our boat by straps, as a seat for the Major, and to the left side of it—he had no right arm—his rubber life-preserver was attached. Each man had a similar life-preserver in a convenient place, and he was to keep this always ready to put on when we reached particularly dangerous rapids. On the evening of the 21st of May nothing more remained to be done. The Second Powell Expedition was ready to start.

Andy,   Clem, Beaman   Prof., Steward,   Cap., Frank
                    Jones, Jack, the Major, Fred
      Cañonita   *Emma Dean*   *Nellie Powell*

The dark box open.   **Before the Start at Green River City, Wyoming.**

Photograph by E. O. Beaman, 1871.

CHAPTER II

Into the Wilderness—The Order of Sailing—Tobacco for the Indians Comes
Handy—A Lone Fisherman and Some Trappers—Jack Catches Strange
Fish—The Snow-clad Uintas in View—A Larder Full of Venison—En-
trance into Flaming Gorge.

THE 22d of May, 1871, gave us a brilliant sun and a sky of
sapphire with a sparkling atmosphere characteristic of
the Rocky Mountain Region. The great buttes near the station,
which Moran has since made famous, shone with a splendour
that was inspiring. To enable us to pick up the last ends more
easily and to make our departure in general more convenient,
we had breakfast that morning at Field's outfitting place, and
an excellent breakfast it was. It was further distinguished by
being the last meal that we should eat at a table for many a
month. We were followed to the cove, where our loaded
boats were moored, by a number of people; about the
whole population in fact, and that did not make a crowd.
None of the Chinamen came down, and there were no Indians
in town that day. The only unpleasant circumstance was the
persistent repetition by a deaf-mute of a pantomimic representa-
tion of the disaster that he believed was to overwhelm us.
"Dummy," as we called him, showed us that we would be upset, and, unable to scale the cliffs, would surely all be drowned.
This picture, as vividly presented as possible, seemed to give
him and his brother great satisfaction. We laughed at his
prophecy, but his efforts to talk were distressing. It may be
said in excuse for him, that in some paddling up the river from
that point, he had arrived at perhaps an honest conviction of
what would happen to any one going below; and also, that
other wise men of the town predicted that we would never see
"Brown's Hole," at the end of Red Canyon.

9

At ten o'clock we pushed out into the current.   There were " Good-bye and God-speed " from the shore with a cheer, and we responded with three and then we passed out of sight.   The settlement, the railway, the people, were gone ; the magnificent wilderness was ours.   We swept down with a four-mile current between rather low banks, using the oars mainly for guidance, and meeting no difficulty worse than a shoal, on which the boats all grounded for a few moments, and the breaking of his oar by Jones who steered our boat.   About noon having run three miles, a landing was made on a broad gravelly island, to enable Andy to concoct a dinner.   A heavy gale was tearing fiercely across the bleak spot.   The sand flew in stinging clouds, but we got a fire started and then it burned like a furnace.   Andy made another sample of his biscuits, this time liberally incorporated with sand, and he fried some bacon.   The sand mainly settled to the bottom of the frying pan, for this bacon was no fancy breakfast table variety but was clear fat three or four inches thick.   But how good it was! And the grease poured on bread !   And yet while at the railway I had scorned it ; in fact I had even declared that I would never touch it, whereat the others only smiled a grim and confident smile.   And now, at the first noon camp, I was ready to pronounce it one of the greatest delicacies I had ever tasted ! They jeered at me, but their jeers were kind, friendly jeers, and I recall them with pleasure.   In warm-hearted companionship no set of men that I have ever since been associated with has been superior to these fellow voyageurs, and the Major's big way of treating things has been a lesson all my life.   We had all become fast true friends at once.   With the exception of the Major, whom I had first met about two months before, and Frank whom I had known for a year or two, I had been acquainted with them only since we had met on the train on the way out.

In the scant shelter of some greasewood bushes we devoured the repast which the morning's exercise and the crisp air had made so welcome, and each drank several cups of tea dipped from the camp-kettle wherein Andy had boiled it.   We had no formal table.   When all was ready, the magic words,

"Well go fur it, boys," which Andy uttered stepping back from the fire were ceremony enough. Each man took a tin plate and a cup and served himself. Clem and Frank were sent back overland to the town for a box of thermometers forgotten and for an extra steering oar left behind, and the *Cañonita* waited for their return.

During the afternoon, as we glided on, the hills began to close in upon us, and occasionally the river would cut into one making a high precipitous wall, a forerunner of the character of the river banks below. The order of going was, our boat, the *Emma Dean,* first, with Major Powell on the deck of the middle cabin, or compartment, sitting in his arm-chair, which was securely fastened there, but was easily removable. S. V. Jones was at the steering oar, Jack Hillers pulled his pair of oars in the after standing-room, while I was at the bow oars. The second in line was the *Nellie Powell*, Professor A. H. Thompson steering, J. F. Steward rowing aft, Captain F. M. Bishop forward, and Frank Richardson sitting rather uncomfortably on the middle deck. The third and last boat was the *Cañonita,* which E. O. Beaman, the photographer steered, while Andrew Hattan, rowed aft, and Clement Powell, assistant photographer, forward. This order was preserved, with a few exceptions, throughout the first season's work. It was the duty of Prof. and Jones to make a traverse (or meander) of the river as we descended. They were to sight ahead at each bend with prismatic compasses and make estimates of the length of each sight, height of walls, width of stream, etc., and Cap was to put the results on paper. The Major on his first boat, kept a general lookout and gave commands according to circumstances. He remembered the general character of the river from his former descent, but he had to be on the *qui-vive* as to details. Besides every stage of water makes a change in the nature of the river at every point. In addition to this outlook, the Major kept an eye on the geology, as he was chief geologist; and Steward, being assistant geologist did the same. Richardson was assistant to Steward. Jack was general assistant and afterwards photographer. I was artist, and later, assistant topographer also. It was my duty to make any sketch that the geologists might want, and of course, as in the case of everybody, to help in the navigation or anything else that came along.   Each man had a rifle and some had also revolvers.   Most of the rifles were Winchesters.[1] We had plenty of ammunition, and the rifles were generally kept where we could get at them quickly.

In this order, and with these duties, we ran on down the Green, and so far at least as I was concerned, feeling as if we had suddenly stepped off into another world.   Late in the afternoon we were astonished to discover a solitary old man sitting on the right bank fishing.   Who he was we did not know but we gave him a cheer as we dashed by and were carried beyond his surprised vision.   As the sun began to reach the horizon a lookout was kept for a good place for camp.   I, for one, was deeply interested, as I had never yet slept in the open.   At length we reached a spot where the hills were some distance back on the right leaving quite a bottom where there were a number of cottonwood trees.   A deserted log cabin silently invited us to land and, as this was cordial for the wilderness, we responded in the affirmative.   The sky had a look of storm about it and I was glad of even this excuse for a roof, though the cabin was too small to shelter our whole party, except standing up, and the beds were all put down on the ground outside.   The night was very cold and the fire which we made for Andy's operations was most comforting. We had for supper another instalment of bacon, saleratus-bread, and tea, which tasted just as good as had that prepared at noon.   Sitting on rocks and stumps we ate this meal, and presently the raw air reminded some of the smokers that, while they had thrown their tobacco away there was, in the boats, the quite large supply designed for our Red friends, should we meet any. Of course we had more than was absolutely necessary for them, and in a few minutes the pipes which had been cast away at Green River appeared well filled and burning.   Per-haps we had pipes for the Indians too !   I had not thrown my pipe away for it was a beautifully carved meerschaum—a

---

[1] Two were of the original Henry pattern.

present. I knew just where it was and lighted it up, though I was not a great smoker. The Indians did not get as much of that tobacco as they might have wished.

To make our blankets go farther we bunked together two and two, and Jones and I were bed-fellows. It was some time before I could go to sleep. I kept studying the sky; watching the stars through the ragged breaks in the flying clouds. The night was silent after the gale. The river flowed on with little noise. The fire flickered and flickered, and the cotton-woods appeared dark and strange as I finally went to sleep. I had not been long in that happy state before I saw some men trying to steal our boats on which our lives depended and I immediately attacked them, pinning one to the ground. It was only Jones I was holding down, and his shouts and struggles to reach his pistol woke me, and startled the camp. He believed a real enemy was on him. There was a laugh at my expense, and then sleep ruled again till about daylight when I was roused by rain falling on my face. All were soon up. The rain changed to snow which fell so heavily that we were driven to the cabin where a glorious fire was made on the hearth, and by it Andy got the bread and bacon and coffee ready for breakfast, and also for dinner, for the snow was so thick we could not venture on the river till it stopped, and that was not till afternoon.

The country through which we now passed was more broken. Cliffs, buttes, mesas, were everywhere. Sometimes we were between high rocky banks, then we saw a valley several miles wide, always without a sign of occupation by white men, even though as yet we were not far from the railway in a direct course. Very late in the afternoon we saw something moving in the distance on the right. Our glasses made it out to be two or three men on horseback. A signal was made which they saw, and consequently stopped to await developments, and a bag of fossils, the Major had collected, was sent out to them with a request to take it to Green River Station, in which direction they were headed. They proved to be a party of prospectors who agreed to deliver the fossils, and we went on our way.

The mornings and evenings were very cold and frosty, but during the day the temperature was perfectly comfortable, and this was gratifying, for the river in places spread into several channels, so that no one of them was everywhere deep enough for the boats which drew, so heavily laden, sixteen or eighteen inches. The keels grated frequently on the bottom and we had to jump overboard to lighten the boats and pull them off into deep water. We found as we went on that we must be ready every moment, in all kinds of water, to get over into the river, and it was necessary to do so with our clothes on, including our shoes, for the reason that the rocky bottom would bruise and cut our feet without the shoes, rocks would do the same to our legs, and for the further reason that there was no time to remove garments. In the rapids further on we always shipped water and consequently we were wet from this cause most of the time anyhow. We had two suits of clothes, one for wear on the river in the day time, and the other for evening in camp, the latter being kept in a rubber bag, so that we always managed to be dry and warm at night. On making camp the day suit was spread out on rocks or on a branch of a tree if one were near, or on a bush to dry, and it was generally, though not always, comfortably so, in the morning when it was again put on for the river work. Sometimes, being still damp, the sensation for a few moments was not agreeable.

We snapped several of the lighter oars in the cross currents, as the boats were heavy and did not mind quickly, and to backwater suddenly on one of the slender oars broke it like a reed. Some of the longer, heavier oars were then cut down to eight feet and were found to be entirely serviceable. The steering oars were cut down from eighteen to sixteen feet. Extra oars were carried slung on each side of the boats just under the gunwales, for the Major on the former journey had been much hampered by being obliged to halt to search for timber suitable for oars and then to make them. There was one thing about the boats which we soon discovered was a mistake. This was the lack of iron on the keels. The iron had been left off for the purpose of reducing the weight when it should be nec-

essary to carry the boats around bad places, but the rocks and
gravel cut the keels down alarmingly, till there was danger of
wearing out the bottoms in the long voyage to come.[1]

Jack was a great fisherman, and it was not long before he
tried his luck in the waters of the Green. No one knew what
kind of fish might be taken—at least no one in our party—
and he began his fishing with some curiosity. It was rewarded
by a species of fish none of us had ever before seen, a fish
about ten to sixteen inches long, slim, with fine scales and large
fins. Their heads came down with a sudden curve to the mouth,
and their bodies tapered off to a very small circumference just
before the tail spread out. They were good to eat, and formed
a welcome addition to our larder. We were all eager for something fresh, and when we saw a couple of deer run across the
bluffs just before we reached our fourth camp, our hopes of
venison were roused to a high degree. Camp number four was
opposite the mouth of Black's Fork at an altitude above sea
level of 5940 feet, a descent of 135 feet from the railway
bridge. After this the channel was steadier and the water
deeper, Black's Fork being one of the largest tributaries of the
upper river. We now came in view of the snowy line of the
Uinta Range stretching east and west across our route and
adding a beautiful alpine note to the wide barren array of cliffs
and buttes. It was twenty or thirty miles off, but so clear was
the air that we seemed to be almost upon it.

As we were drifting along with a swift current in the afternoon, the day after passing Black's Fork, one of the party saw
a deer on an island. A rifle shot from our boat missed, and
the animal dashing into the river swam across and disappeared
in the wide valley. But another was seen. A landing was
made immediately, and while some of the men held the boats
ready to pick up a prize, the others beat the island. I was assigned to man our boat, and as we waited up against the bank
under the bushes, we could hear the rifles crack. Then all was
still. Suddenly I heard a crashing of bushes and a hundred
yards above us a superb black-tail sprang into the water

[1] For further description of these boats the reader is referred to *The Romance of the Colorado River*, page 236, by F. S. Dellenbaugh.

and swam for the east bank.   My sensation was divided between a desire to see the deer escape, and a desire to supplant
the bacon with venison for a time.   My cartridges were under
the hatches as it chanced, so I was unable to take action myself.   With deep interest I watched the animal swim and with
regret that our fresh meat was so fortunate, for it was two-
thirds of the way across, before a rifle cracked.   The deer's
efforts ceased instantly and she began to drift down with the
current.   We ran our boat out and hauled the carcass on
board.   At the same time as we were being carried down by
the swift current we got a view of the other side of the island
where Cap. up to his arms in the stream was trying to pull
another deer ashore by the horns.   It looked as if both deer
and Cap. would sail away and forever, till another boat went to
his rescue.   Presently the third boat came down bearing still
another deer.   The successful shots were from Prof., Andy, and
Steward.   Our prospects for a feast were bright, and we had it.
The deer were speedily dressed, Frank displaying exceptional
skill in this line.   Had we been able to stay in this region we
would never have been in want of fresh meat, but when we entered the canyons the conditions were so different and the task
of pursuing game so baffling and exhausting that we never had
such success again.   The whole of the next day we remained in a
favourable spot at the foot of a strangely tilted ledge, where
we jerked the venison by the aid of sun and fire to preserve
it.   Near this point as observations showed later we passed
from Wyoming into Utah.

About dusk we were surprised to discover a small craft with
a single individual aboard coming down the river.   Then we
saw it was a raft.   We watched its approach with deep interest
wondering who the stranger could be, but he turned out to
be Steward who had gone geologising and had taken this
easier means of coming back.   He tried it again farther down
and met with an experience which taught him to trust to the
land thereafter.

The next day our boat was held back for some special work
while the others proceeded toward a high spur of the Uintas,
directly in front of us.   We followed with a fierce and blinding

gale sweeping the river and filling our eyes with sharp sand. Nevertheless we could see high up before us some bright red rocks marking the first canyon of the wonderful series that separates this river from the common world. From these bright rocks glowing in the sunlight like a flame above the grey-green of the ridge, the Major had bestowed on this place the name of Flaming Gorge. As we passed down towards the mountain it seemed that the river surely must end there, but suddenly just below the mouth of Henry's Fork it doubled to the left and we found ourselves between two low cliffs, then in a moment we dashed to the right into the beautiful canyon, with the cliffs whose summit we had seen, rising about 1300 feet on the right, and a steep slope on the left at the base of which was a small bottom covered with tall cottonwood trees, whose green shone resplendent against the red rocks. The other boats were swinging at their lines and the smoke of Andy's fire whirling on the wind was a cheerful sight to the ever-hungry inner-man. Constant exercise in the open air produces a constant appetite. As long as we could protect our cargoes, and make our connections with our supplies as planned, we would surely not have to go hungry, but we had to consider that there was room for some variation or degree of success. There was at least one comforting feature about the river work and that was we never suffered for drinking water. It was only on side trips, away from the river that we met this difficulty, so common in the Rocky Mountain Region and all the South-west.

When the barometrical observations were worked out we found we had now descended 262 feet from our starting-point. That was four and a quarter feet for each mile of the sixty-two we had put behind. We always counted the miles put behind, for we knew they could not be retraced, but it was ever the miles and the rapids ahead that we kept most in our minds. We were now at the beginning of the real battle with the "Sunken River." Henceforth, high and forbidding cliffs with few breaks, would imprison the stream on both sides.

A loss of our provisions would mean a journey on foot, after climbing out of the canyon, to Green River (Wyoming) to Salt Lake City or to the Uinta Indian Agency. There was a trail from

2

Brown's Hole (now Brown's Park) back to the railway, but the difficulty would be to reach it if we should be wrecked in Red Canyon. We did not give these matters great concern at the time, but I emphasise them now to indicate some of the difficulties of the situation and the importance of preventing the wreck of even one boat.

CHAPTER III

The First Rapid—Horseshoe and Kingfisher Canyons—A Rough Entrance into Red Canyon—Capsize of the *Nell*—The Grave of a Bold Navigator—Discovery of a White Man's Camp—Good-bye to Frank—At the Gate of Lodore.

PROF. now took observations for time and latitude in order to fix with accuracy the geographical location of the camp in Flaming Gorge, and to check the estimates of the topographers as they sighted the various stretches of the river. It has been found that estimates of this kind are quite accurate and that the variation from exactness is generally the same in [1] the same individual. Hence one man may underestimate and another may overestimate, but each will always make the same error, and this error can be readily corrected by frequent observations to determine latitude and longitude. A series of barometrical observations was kept going whether we were on the move or not. That is, a mercurial barometer was read three times a day, regularly, at seven, at one, and at nine. We had aneroid barometers for work away from the river and these were constantly compared with and adjusted to the mercurials. The tubes of mercury sometimes got broken, and then a new one had to be boiled to replace it. I believe the boiling of tubes has since that time been abandoned, as there is not enough air in the tube to interfere with the action of the mercury, but at that time it was deemed necessary for accuracy, and it gave Prof. endless trouble. The wind was always blowing, and no tent we could contrive from blankets, and waggon sheets (we had no regular tents), sufficed to keep the

[1] Three points on Green River below the Union Pacific crossing had been determined by previous explorers, the mouth of Henry's Fork, the mouth of the Uinta, and Gunnison Crossing.

flame of the alcohol lamp from flickering. Nevertheless, Prof. whose patience and dexterity were unlimited, always succeeded. The mercurial barometers were of the kind with a buckskin pocket at the bottom of the cistern with a screw for adjusting the column of mercury to a fixed point.

Most of the men climbed out in various directions and for various objects. Prof. reached a high altitude whence he obtained a broad view of the country, a grand sight with the quiet river below and snow-capped mountains around, with rolling smoke and leaping flame, for there were great mountain fires not far off. The Major and Steward went geologising. Steward was rewarded by discovering a number of fossils, among them the bones of an immense animal of the world's early day, with a femur ten inches in diameter, and ribs two inches thick and six inches wide. These bones were much exposed and could have been dug out, but we had no means of transporting them.

Flaming Gorge is an easy place to get in and out of, even with a horse, and doubtless in the old beaver-hunting days it was a favourite resort of trappers. I am inclined to think that the double turn of the swirling river where it enters Flaming Gorge is the place known at that time as the Green River Suck. Our camp under the cottonwoods was delightful. We took advantage of the halt to write up notes, clean guns, mend clothes, do our washing, and all the other little things incident to a breathing spell on a voyage of this kind. It was Sunday too, and when possible we stopped on that account, though, of course, progress could not be deferred for that reason alone.

Monday morning we left the pleasant camp in the grove and went on with the tide. The river was rough from a heavy gale, but otherwise offered no obstacle. At a sudden bend we cut to the left deeper into the mountain till on both sides we were enclosed by almost perpendicular precipices of carboniferous formation, limestone, about 1600 feet high. The canyon was surprisingly beautiful and romantic. The river seemed to change its mood here, and began to flow with an impetus it had exhibited nowhere above. It swept on with a directness and a concentration of purpose that had about it something ominous. And just here, at the foot of the right hand wall

Flaming Gorge.
The Beginning of the Colorado River Canyons, N. E. Utah.
Photograph by E. O. BEAMAN, 1871.

Horseshoe Canyon.
Photograph by E. O. BEAMAN, 1871.

which was perpendicular for 800 feet, with the left more sloping, and clothed with cedar shrubs, we beheld our first real rapid, gleaming like a jewel from its setting in the sunlight which fell into the gorge, and it had as majestic a setting as could be desired.   For myself I can say that the place appeared the acme of the romantic and picturesque. The rapid was small and swift, a mere chute, and perhaps hardly worthy of mention had it not been the point where the character of the river current changes making it distinguished because of being the first of hundreds to come below. The river above had held a continual descent accelerating here and retarding there with an average current of two and a half miles an hour, but here began the quick drops for which the canyons are now famous.   There was one place where Prof. noted a small rapid but it was not like this one, and I did not count it at all.

The gorge we ran into so suddenly was short and by dinner-time we had emerged into a wider, more broken place, though we were still bound in by tremendous heights. We saw that we had described a complete horseshoe and this fact determined the canyon's name—number two of the series. When we landed for dinner, an examination was made of the locality from that base before we dropped down a little distance to the mouth of a fine clear creek coming in from the right. This was a fascinating place. The great slopes were clothed with verdure and trees, and the creek ran through luxuriant vegetation. A halt of a day was made for observation purposes. The air was full of kingfishers darting about and we immediately called the creek by their name.

I was sent with Steward on a geological expedition out over the right or western cliffs. We consumed two hours in getting out, having to climb up about 1000 feet over a difficult way. After a good deal of going up and down across rough ridges, we finally worked our way around to the head of Flaming Gorge. Here we reckoned up and found that eight steep ridges intervened between us and camp by the way we had come, and we concluded that we could get back easier through Flaming Gorge and thence by climbing over the tongue or base of the horseshoe which was lower than the end. Steward grew decidedly weary

and I felt my legs getting heavy too. Rain had fallen at intervals all day and we were wet as well as tired and famished.
We struck an old trail and followed it as long as it went our
way.   Then it became too dark to see which way it went and
we climbed on as best we could.   It was about half-past eight
when we reached our camp to find a splendid fire burning and
a good supper waiting for us.

The new canyon which closed in the next day had walls
about 1500 feet in height, that being the general height of the
spur of the Uintas through which we were travelling.   The
changes from one canyon to another were only changes in the
character of the bounding mountain walls, for there was no
break into open country.   The name of Kingfisher we gave
to the new gorge for the same reason we had called the creek
at our camp by that name, and so numerous were these birds
at one rounded promontory that there was no escape from
calling it Beehive Point, the resemblance to a gigantic hive
being perfect.   Kingfisher Canyon like its two predecessors
was short, all three making a distance by the river of only
about ten miles.   Flaming Gorge is the gateway, Horseshoe
the vestibule, and Kingfisher the ante-chamber to the whole
grand series.   At the foot of Kingfisher the rocks fell back
a little and steep slopes took their place.   Where the rocks
closed in again, we halted on the threshold of the next gorge,
in a fine grove of cottonwoods.   A significant roar came to us
out of the gate to Red Canyon, rolling up on the air with a
steady, unvarying monotony that had a sinister meaning.
It was plain that we were nearing something that was no
paltry gem like the rapid we had so much admired in Horseshoe Canyon.

The remainder of that day and all the next, which was June
1st, we stayed at this camp completing records, investigating
the surroundings, and preparing for rough work ahead.   On Friday morning the cabins were packed carefully, the life preservers
were inflated, and we pulled out into the current.   The cliffs
shot up around us and rough water began at once.   The descent was almost continuous for a considerable distance, but
we divided it into three rapids in our notes, before we reached

a sharp turn to the right, and then one just as sharp to the left, with vertical walls on both sides and a roaring torrent, broken by rocks, whirling between. Our boat shot down with fierce rapidity and would have gone through without a mishap had not the current dashed us so close to the right-hand wall that Jack's starboard row-lock was ripped off by a projection of the cliff as we were hurled along its rugged base. At the same moment we saw the *Nell* upsetting against some rocks on the left. Then we swept out of view and I was obliged to pull with all my strength, Jack's one oar being useless. We succeeded in gaining a little cove on the left, and jumped out as soon as shallow enough, the Major immediately climbing the cliffs to a high point where he could look down on the unfortunate second boat. Prof., it seems, had misunderstood the Major's signal and had done just what he did not think he ought to do. He thought it meant to land on the left and he had tried to reach a small strip of beach, but finding this was not possible he turned the boat again into the current to retrieve his former position, but this was not successful and the *Nell* was thrown on some rocks projecting from the left wall, in the midst of wild waters, striking hard enough to crush some upper planks of the port side. She immediately rolled over, and Frank slid under. Prof. clutched him and pulled him back while the men all sprang for the rocks and saved themselves and the boat from being washed away in this demoralised condition. With marvellous celerity Cap. took a turn with a rope around a small tree which he managed to reach, while Steward jumped to a position where he could prevent the boat from pounding. In a minute she was righted and they got her to the little beach where they had tried to land. Here they pulled her out and, partially unloading, repaired her temporarily as well as they could. This done they towed up to a point of vantage and made a fresh start and cleared the rapid with no further incident. Meanwhile the *Cañonita* had come in to where we were lying, and both boats were held ready to rescue the men of the other. After about three-quarters of an hour the unfortunate came down, her crew being rather elated over

the experience and the distinction of having the first capsize.

Setting out on the current again we passed two beautiful
creeks entering from the right, and they were immediately
named respectively, Compass and Kettle creeks, to commem-
orate the loss of these articles in the capsize. At the mouth
of Kettle Creek, about a mile and a half below the capsize
rapid, we stopped for dinner. Then running several small
drops, we arrived at a long descent that compelled careful
action. We always landed, where possible, to make an examination and learn the trend of the main current. Our not
being able to do this above was the cause of the *Nell's* trouble.
We now saw that we had here landed on the wrong side and
would have to make a somewhat hazardous crossing to the
opposite, or right bank. Our boat tried it first. In spite of
vigorous pulling we were carried faster down towards the rapid
than to the objective landing. When we reached water about
waist deep we all sprang overboard, and I got to shore with the
line as quickly as I could. We were able to turn and catch the
Nell as she came in, but the *Cañonita* following ran too far down.
We all dashed into the stream almost at the head of the rapid,
and there caught her in time. The load was taken out of our
boat and she was let down by lines over the worst part. Load-
ing again we lowered to another bad place where we went into
camp on the same spot where the Major had camped two
years before. We unloaded the other boats and got them
down before dark, but we ate supper by firelight. The river
averaged about 250 feet wide, with a current of not less than
six miles an hour and waves in the rapids over five feet in
vertical height. These waves broke up stream as waves do
in a swift current, and as the boats cut into them at a high
velocity we shipped quantities of water and were constantly
drenched, especially the bow-oarsmen. The cliffs on each side,
wonderfully picturesque, soon ran up to 1200 or 1500 feet, and
steadily increased their altitude. Owing to the dip of the
strata across the east and west trend of the canyon the walls
on the north were steeper than those on the south, but they
seldom rose vertically from the river. Masses of talus, and

Red Canyon.

Photograph by E. O. BEAMAN, 1871.

Red Canyon.

Ashley Falls from Below.
Photograph by E. O. BEAMAN, 1871.

often alluvial stretches with rocks and trees, were strung along their base, usually offering numerous excellent landings and camping places. We were able to stop about as we wished and had no trouble as to camps, though they were frequently not just what we would have preferred. There was always smooth sand to sleep on, and often plenty of willows to cut and lay in rows for a mattress. It must not be imagined that these great canyons are dark and gloomy in the day-time. They are no more so than an ordinary city street flanked with very high buildings. Some lateral canyons are narrow and so deep that the sun enters them but briefly, but even these are only shady, not dark.

We remained on the Major's old camp ground a day so that Jones and Cap. could climb to the top of the cliff to get the topography. The next morning though it was Sunday was not to be one of rest. We began by lowering the boats about forty rods farther and there pulled out into the stream and were dashed along by a fierce current with rapid following rapid closely. The descent was nearly continuous with greater de-clivities thrown in here and there. As usual we took in a good deal of water and were saturated. We were growing ac-customed to this, and the boats being built to float even when the open parts were full, we did not mind sitting with our legs in cold water till opportunity came to bail out with the camp kettle left in each open space for the purpose. One rapid where Theodore Hook, of Cheyenne, was drowned in 1869, while attempting to follow the first party, gave us no trouble. We sailed through it easily. Hook had declared that if Powell could descend the river he could too, and he headed a party to follow.[1] The motive I believe was prospect-ing. I do not know how far they expected to go but this was as far as they got. Their abandoned boats, flat-bottomed and inadequate, still lay half buried in sand on the left-hand bank, and not far off on a sandy knoll was the grave of the unfor-tunate leader marked by a pine board set up, with his name painted on it. Old sacks, ropes, oars, etc., emphasised the completeness of the disaster.

[1] I do not know the number of men composing this party.

Not far below this we made what we called a "line portage," that is, the boats were worked along the edge of the rapid, one at a time, in and out among the boulders with three or four men clinging to them to fend them off the rocks and several more holding on to the hundred-foot hawser, so that there was no possibility of one getting loose and smashing up, or leaving us altogether. It was then noon and a camp was made for the remainder of the day on the left bank in a very comfortable spot. We had accomplished three and a half miles, with four distinct rapids run and one "let-down." I went up from the camp along a sandy stretch and was surprised to discover what I took to be the fresh print of the bare foot of a man. Mentioning this when I returned, my companions laughed and warned me to be cautious and give this strange man a wide berth unless I had my rifle and plenty of ammunition. It was the track of a grizzly bear. I saw many tracks on this expedition and on others afterwards but I have never seen a bear yet, except in captivity. The grizzly seemed to shun me; but I believe they will not often attack a man unprovoked, and will lie perfectly still while one may pass within a few feet of their hiding-place.

Three or four deer were seen but with no opportunity to get a shot. All through these upper canyons there was then a great abundance of game of every description, and had our object been to kill for sport, we undoubtedly could have made a pile of carcasses. One or two deer would have been welcome but we had no time to pursue them. Steward came in towards night from his geologising with a splendid bouquet of wild flowers which was greatly admired. Prof. and the Major climbed west of camp to a height of 1200 feet where they obtained a wide outlook and secured valuable notes on the topography. The view was superb as it is anywhere from a high point in this region. When they came back, the Major entertained us by reading aloud *The Lay of the Last Minstrel*, thus delightfully closing a beautiful Sunday which every man had enjoyed.

In the morning soon after leaving this camp a dull roar ahead told of our approach to Ashley Falls, for which we were on the lookout. The left bank was immediately hugged as closely as possible and we dropped cautiously down to the head of the descent. An immense rock stuck up in the middle of the river and the water divided on this and shot down on each side in a sharp fall of about eight feet. Each was a clear chute and not dangerous to look at, but the effect of so sudden a plunge on one of our loaded boats was too much of a prob-lem for trial. A portage was decided on. The left bank where we were was a mass of enormous broken rocks where it seemed next to impossible to haul a boat. A foot trail was first built which led up some fifty feet above the river, and over, under and around huge boulders to a place down below where it was proposed to carry the boats on skids. The cargoes were first taken over on our backs and when this was done we were about tired out. Our united strength was re-quired to work the *Dean* down to the selected haven without injury. This was such extremely hard work that the Major and Prof. concluded to shoot the *Cañonita* through, light, with no men in her, but controlled by one of our hundred-foot hawsers attached to each end. She was started down and went through well enough, but filling with water and knocking on hidden rocks. Prudence condemned this method and we resorted to sliding and carrying the *Nell* over the rocks as we had done with the *Dean*, certain that sleep and food would wipe out our weariness, but not injury to the boats which must be avoided by all means in our power. By the time we had placed the *Nell* beside the other boats at the bottom it was sunset and too late to do anything but make a camp. Just above the head of the fall was a rather level place in a clump of pines at the very edge of the river forming as picturesque a camp-ground as I have ever seen. A brilliant moon hung over the canyon, lighting up the foam of the water in strong contrast to the red fire crackling its accom-paniment to the roar of the rapid. A lunar rainbow danced fairy-like in the mists rising from the turmoil of the river. The night air was calm and mild. Prof. read aloud from *Hiawatha* and it seemed to fit the time and place admirably. We had few books with us; poems of Longfellow, Whittier, Emerson, and Scott, are all I remember, except a Bible my mother had given me.　I suppose Cap. had a Bible also, as he was very religious.

The huge boulders which dammed the river had fallen from the cliffs on the left within a comparatively recent time, transforming an ordinary rapid into the fall ; actually damming the water till it is smooth for half a mile above.　The largest block of stone is the one in the middle.　It is about twenty five feet square.　The only white men on record to reach this place except the Major's other party, was General Ashley, the distinguished fur trader with a number of trappers.　In his search for fresh beaver grounds he led his party in rude buffalo-skin boats through this canyon in 1825.　They had a hard time and nearly starved to death as they depended for food on finding beaver and other game, in which they were disappointed.　On one of my trips over the rocks with cargo I made a slight detour on the return to see the boulder where the Major had discovered Ashley's name with a date.　The letters were in black, just under a slight projection and were surprisingly distinct considering the forty-six years of exposure.　The "2" was illegible and looked like a " 3."　None of our party seemed to know that it could have been only a "2" for by the year 1835 Ashley had sold out and had given up the fur business in the mountains.　Considering his ability, his prominence, his high character, and his identification with the early history of the West, there ought to be greater recognition of him than there has been.

Below Ashley Falls the declivity of the river was very great with a correspondingly swift current, in one rapid reaching a velocity of at least fifteen miles an hour, and with waves that tossed our heavy boats like feathers.　These were the most violent rapids we had yet met, not excepting the ones we had portaged.　The cliffs, about 2500 feet high, of red sandstone, were often almost perpendicular on both sides, or at least they impressed us so at the time.　There was much vegetation, pine, spruce, willow-leaved cottonwood, aspens, alder, etc., which added to the beauty and picturesqueness of the wild scenery.　Beaman stopped each day where possible and desirable to take photographs, and at these times the others investigated the surroundings and climbed up side canyons when they existed. Late in the afternoon we came out suddenly into a small valley or park formerly called Little Brown's Hole, a noted rendezvous for trappers, and which we rechristened Red Canyon Park. This was a beautiful place bounded by round mountains, into which our great cliffs had temporarily resolved themselves, particularly on the right, the left side remaining pretty steep. Our camp was pitched under two large pine trees and every one was prepared, in the intervals of other duties, to take advantage of this respite to patch up clothing, shoes, etc., as well as to do what laundering was necessary. The river ran so quietly that we felt oppressed after the constant roaring since we had entered Red Canyon. I remember climbing up at evening with one of my companions, to a high altitude where the silence was deathlike and overpowering. Prof. and some of the others climbed to greater heights for topographical purposes, easily reaching an altitude of about 4000 feet above the river in an air-line distance of about five miles. Here they obtained a magnificent panorama in all directions, limited on the west by the snowy chain of the Wasatch, and on the north by the Wind River Range like white clouds on the horizon 200 miles away, and they could trace the deep gorges of the river as they cleave the mountains from distance to distance.

Here we saw signs of abundant game, elk, deer, bear, etc., but we had no time to go hunting as a business and the game refused to come to us. Each man had his work to accomplish so that we could get on. It was impracticable to go wandering over the mountains for game, much as we would have enjoyed a change from our bacon and beans. One day, only, was spent here for all purposes, geologising, topographic climbing, and working out the notes from up the river, making repairs and all the other needful things that crowded upon us. Here it was that I did my first tailoring and performed a feat of which I have ever since been proud; namely, transferring some coat-tails, from where they were of no use, to the knees and seat of my trousers where they were invaluable.

On June 8th, we left this "Camp Number 13" regretfully and plunged in between the cliffs again for about eight miles, running five rapids, when we emerged into a large valley known as Brown's Hole, where our cliffs fell back for two or three miles on each side and became mountain ranges.   Pulling along for a couple of miles on a quiet river we were surprised to discover on the left a white man's camp.   Quickly landing we learned that it was some cattlemen's temporary headquarters (Harrell Brothers), and some of the men had been to Green River Station since our departure from that place, the distance by trail not being half that by river.   They were expecting us and had brought some mail which was a glad sight for our eyes. These men had wintered about 2000 head of Texas cattle in this valley, noted for the salubrity of its winter climate since the days of the fur-hunters, and were on their way to the Pacific coast.   We made a camp near by, with a cottonwood of a peculiar "Y" shape, more stump than tree, to give what shade-comfort it could, and enjoyed the relaxation which came with the feeling that we had put twenty-five miles of hard canyon behind, and were again in touch, though so briefly and at long range, with the outer world.   As some of these men were to go out to the railway the following Sunday and offered to carry mail for us, we began to write letters to let our friends know how we were faring on our peculiar voyage.   This "Brown's Hole" was the place selected by a man who pretended to have been with the former party, for the scene of that party's destruction which he reported to the newspapers. He thought as it was called a "hole" it must be one of the worst places on this raging river, not knowing that in the old trapper days when a man found a snug valley and dwelt there for a time it became known as his "hole" in the nomenclature of the mountains.   The Major did not think this a satisfactory name and he changed it to "Brown's Park" which it now bears.   I met an "old timer" on a western train several years afterward, who was greatly irritated because of this liberty which the Major took with the cherished designation of the early days.   Fort Davy Crockett of the fur-trading period was located somewhere in this valley.

The next morning after reaching Harrell's camp we were told that, as Frank did not seem able to stand the voyage he

In Red Canyon Park.

Photograph by E. O. BEAMAN, 1871.

was to leave us here, to go over the mountains back to the railway, whence he would go home. We were all sorry to hear this and doubly sorry when on Sunday the 11th he mounted a mule and regretfully rode away with Mr. Harrell. The latter was to telegraph to Salt Lake to Mrs. Powell, to send our mail back to Green River Station so that it could be brought out to us on Mr. Harrell's return. Meanwhile we dropped down the river, now tranquil as a pond, with low banks covered with cottonwood groves. There were two small canyons the first of which we called "Little" about one-half mile long, and the second "Swallow," about two miles long. The cliffs were red sandstone about three hundred feet high, often vertical on both sides. Thousands of swallows swarmed there, and we did not resist giving it an obvious name. Below this the water spread out more and was full of islands. The current was sluggish, two miles an hour perhaps, and we indulged in the novelty of rowing the boats, though we did not try to make speed, for we had to wait for Mr. Harrell's return anyhow. The boats had been lightened by trading to Harrell some of our flour, of which we had an over abundance when it came to portages, for fresh beef, of which we were very much in need. At a convenient place we landed where there was a fine cottonwood grove and remained while Prof. made a climb and to jerk the beef. It was cut into thin strips and hung on a willow framework in the sun with a slow fire beneath. As the thermometer now stood at ninety-nine in the shade the beef was fairly well cured by the 13th and we went on, seeing one of the cattlemen and a Mexican boy on the left bank. In this neighbourhood we passed from Utah into Colorado. The river was six hundred feet broad and about six feet deep. We had no trouble from shoals, and finally lashed the three boats side by side and let them drift along in the slow current. The Major sitting in his arm-chair on the middle boat read aloud selections from *The Lady of the Lake* which seemed to fit the scene well. Steward and Andy amused themselves by swimming along with the boats and occasionally diving under them.

From our noon camp in a grove of cottonwoods opposite the mouth of Vermilion River, we could plainly see the great portal a mile or two away, the Gate of Lodore, where all this tranquillity would end, for the river cuts straight into the heart of the mountains forming one of the finest canyons of the series where the water comes down as Southey described it at Lodore, and the Major gave it that name. Before night we were at the very entrance and made our camp there in a grove of box-elders. Every man was looking forward to this canyon with some dread and before losing ourselves within its depths we expected to enjoy the letters from home which Mr. Harrell was to bring back from the railway for us. Myriads of mosquitoes gave us something else to think of, for they were exceedingly ferocious and persistent, driving us to a high bluff where a smudge was built to fight them off. We were nearly devoured. I fared best, a friend having given me a net for my head, and this, with buckskin gloves on my hands enabled me to exist with some comfort. The mountains rose abruptly just beyond our camp, and the river cleaved the solid mass at one stroke, forming the extraordinary and magnificent portal we named the "Gate of Lodore," one of the most striking entrances of a river into mountains to be found in all the world. It is visible for miles. Prof. climbed the left side of the Gate and also took observations for time.

I was sent back to the valley to make some sketches and also to accompany Steward on a geological tramp. We had an uncomfortable experience because of the excessive heat and aridity. I learned several things about mountaineering that I never forgot, one of which was to always thoroughly note and mark a place where anything is left to be picked up on a return, for, leaving our haversack under a cedar it eluded all search till the next day, and meanwhile we were compelled to go to the river two or three miles away for water. We had a rubber poncho and a blanket. Using the rubber for a mattress and the blanket for a covering we passed the night, starting early for the mountains, where at last we found our food bag. After eating a biscuit we went back to the river and made tea and toasted some beef on the end of a ramrod, when we struck for the main camp, arriving at dinner-time.

The Gate of Lodore seemed naturally the beginning of a new

stage in our voyage to which we turned with some anxiety, for it was in the gorge now before us that on the first trip a boat had been irretrievably smashed. We were now 130 miles by river from the Union Pacific Railway crossing, and in this distance we had descended 700 feet in altitude, more than 400 feet of it in Red Canyon. Lodore was said to have an even greater declivity.

CHAPTER IV

Locked in the Chasm of Lodore—Rapids with Railway Speed—A Treacherous
Approach to Falls of Disaster—Numerous Loadings and Unloadings—Over
the Rocks with Cargoes—Library Increased by *Putnam's Magazine*—Triplet
Falls and Hell's Half Mile—Fire in Camp—Exit from Turmoil to Peace.

ON Saturday the 17th of June, the member of the Harrell
party who was to travel overland from Green River
Station with mail for us from Salt Lake arrived with only two
letters. The despatch had been too late to stop the packet
which already had been started for the Uinta Indian Agency,
whence it would reach us at the mouth of the Uinta River. It
would be another month, at least, before we could receive those
longed for words from home. There was nothing now to delay
us further, and after dinner the boats were prepared for canyon
work again. Through Brown's Park we had not been obliged to
pay much attention to "ship-shape" arrangements, but now the
story was to be different. The cabins were packed with unusual
care, the life-preservers were inflated and put where they could
be quickly seized on the approach to a bad descent, and at four
o'clock we were afloat. The wide horizon vanished. The cliffs,
red and majestic, rose at one bound to a height of about 2000
feet on each side, the most abrupt and magnificent gateway to
a canyon imaginable. We entered slowly, for the current in the
beginning is not swift, and we watched the mighty precipices
while they appeared to fold themselves together behind and shut
us more than ever away from the surrounding wilderness. For
a short time the stream was quite tame. Then the murmur of
distant troubled waters reached us and we prepared for work.
The first rapid was not a bad one; we ran it without halting
and ran three more in quick succession, one of which was
rather ugly.

The Head of the Canyon of Lodore.
Just inside the Gate.
Photograph by E. O. BEAMAN, 1871.

Canyon of Lodore.
Low water.
Photograph by J. K. Hillers, 1874.

This success caused some of us prematurely to conclude that perhaps "the way the water comes down at Lodore," was not so terrific as had been anticipated. The Major said nothing. He kept his eyes directed ahead. The river ran about 300 feet wide, with a current of 10 to 15 miles an hour in the rapids. At every bend new vistas of beauty were exhibited, and the cliffs impressed us more and more by their increasing height and sublimity. Landing places were numerous. Presently there came to our ears a roar with an undertone which spoke a language now familiar, and we kept as close to the right bank as possible, so that a stop could be instantly made at the proper moment. When this moment arrived a landing was effected for examination. and it revealed a furious descent, studded with large rocks, with a possibility of safely running through it if an exact course could be held, but the hour being now late a camp was made at the head and further investigation deferred till the next morning.

This morning was Sunday, and the sun shone into the canyon with dazzling brilliancy, all being tranquil except the foaming rapid. The locality was so fascinating that we lingered to explore, finding especial interest in a delightful grotto carved out of the red sandstone by the waters of a small brook. The entrance was narrow, barely 20 feet, a mere cleft in the beginning, but as one proceeded up it between walls 1500 feet high, the cleft widened, till at 15 rods it ended in an amphitheatre 100 feet in diameter, with a domed top. Clear, cold water trickled and dropped in thousands of diamond-like globules from everything. Mosses and ferns filled all the crevices adding a brilliant green to the picture, while far up overhead a little ribbon of blue sky could be seen; and, beyond the mouth, the yellow river. It was an exquisite scene. At the request of Steward, it's discoverer, it was named after his little daughter, "Winnie's Grotto." So charming was it here that we did not get off till ten o'clock, Beaman meanwhile taking several views.

It was decided to run the rapid, for there was a comparatively straight channel about ten feet wide, and it was only a question of steering right. As our boat was to take it first the other crews came to a point where they could watch us to advantage and profit by our experience. Sticks, as usual, had been thrown in to determine the trend of the main current which must always be considered in dealing with any rapid. If it dashes against a cliff below, means must be found to cut across before reaching that point. On the other hand, if the main current has a comparatively clear chute, running through is not a difficult matter as in the present case. We pulled up-stream a short distance before putting out into the middle. Then we took the rapid as squarely as possible. We saw that we would have to go sharply to the left to avoid one line of rocks, and then to the right to clear another, both of which actions were successfully accomplished. Then we waited below for the others. They had no trouble either, and the three boats sped on and on into the greater depths beyond where wilder waters were foaming.

All rapids have "tails" of waves tapering out below, that is the waves grow smaller as they increase the distance from the initial wave. These waves are the reverse of sea waves, the form remaining in practically one place while the water flies through. In many rapids there is an eddy on each side of this tail in which a current runs up-river with great force. If a boat is caught in this eddy it may be carried a second time through a part of the rapid. We soon arrived at another rapid in which this very thing happened to our boat. We were caught by the eddy and carried up-stream to be launched directly into the path of the *Nell*, which had started down. Prof. skilfully threw his boat to one side and succeeded in avoiding a collision. Nothing could be done with our boat but to let her go where she would for the moment. We then ran two other rapids, rough ones too, but there was no trouble in them for any of the boats. The velocity at this stage of water was astonishing, and the opportunities to land in quiet water between the rapids now were few.

About dinner-time as we emerged at high speed from one rapid we saw immediately below lying in ominous shadow, another. It had a forbidding look. In Red Canyon owing to the east-and-west trend the sun fell to the bottom for many more hours than in Lodore which has a north-and-south trend. Hence here even at high noon, one side or the other might be in deep shadow. In this particular case it was the left wall which came down very straight to the river, the outside of a

bend.   Opposite was a rocky, wooded point.   Between these
the rapid swept down.   There was no slack water separating
the end of the rapid we left from the beginning of this one so
obscurely situated.   Landing was no easy task at the speed
with which we were flying, but it would not do to try to run
the rapid without an examination.   The only possible place to
stop was on the right where there was a cove with a little
strip of beach, and we headed for it instantly, pulling with
every muscle.   Yet we continued going on down at railway
speed.   When at last we arrived within a few feet of the bank
the problem was how to stop.   The water appeared shallow,
though we could not see bottom on account of its murky
character, and there was only one course, which was to jump
out and make anchors of our legs.   As we did so we sank to
our waists and were pulled along for a moment but our feet,
braced against the large rocks on the bottom, served the
purpose and the momentum was overcome.   Once the velocity
was gone it was easy to get the boat to the beach, and she
was tied there just in time to allow us to rush to the help of
the *Nell*.[1]   Scarcely had the *Nell* been tied up than the
Cañonita came darting for the same spot like a locomotive.
With the force on hand she was easily controlled, and the
fact that she carried the cook outfit as well as the cook added
to our joy at having her so speedily on the beach.   Andy went
to work immediately to build a fire and prepare dinner while
the rest overhauled the boats, took observations, plotted notes,
or did other necessary things, and the Major and Prof. went
down to take a close look at the rapid which had caused us such
sudden and violent exertion.   They reported a clear channel
in the middle, and when we continued after dinner, we went
through easily and safely, as of course we could have done in
the first place if the Major had been willing to take an unknown risk.   But in the shadow the fall might have been
almost anything and it would have been foolhardy to run it
without examination, even though we found it so hard to
stop.   Below the rapid that had halted us so abruptly there

[1] Professor Thompson's diary says he landed first after a hard pull, "and then
caught the other boats below, they not succeeding in getting in."

was nothing for about a mile but easy running, when we stopped in a cove to examine another rapid. Prof. here started up eleven mountain sheep, but by the time he had come back to the boats for a gun they were beyond reach. Though this rapid could be easily run, there was just below it only a short distance the fall where the *No-Name* was wrecked on the first trip, and we would have to be cautious, for the approach to that fall we knew was treacherous.

The river comes at this point from the east, bends south, then west, and it is just at the western bend that the steep rush of the big fall begins and continues for three-quarters of a mile. On the right the waters beat fiercely against the foot of the perpendicular wall, while on the left they are confined by a rocky point, the end of which is composed of enormous blocks. The space for the stream between this point and the opposite cliff is narrow, while the river above it spreads rather wide with a deep bay on the left where there is quiet water. This bay is protected a quarter of a mile up by a jutting point, and is merely back water. Just off the point the whole river suddenly becomes saucer-like, and quite smooth, with all the currents drawing strongly in from every direction and pouring toward and over the falls. An object once within the grip of this "sag," as we called it, is obliged to pass over the falls. The situation is peculiar and it occurs nowhere else on the whole river. Not being understood on the first voyage one of the boats, the *No-Name*, was trapped, driven over the falls, and broken to fragments, though the men were rescued below. The disaster was the cause of some unpleasantness on that voyage, the men blaming the Major for not signalling properly and he blaming them for not landing quickly when he signalled.

We were on the lookout for it and the Major having the wreck to emphasise the peculiarities of the "sag" desired to have every boat turn the point at the correct moment. Ours ran through the preliminary rapid easily and we dropped cautiously down upon our great enemy, hugging the left bank as closely as we could to reach the jutting point around which the boat must pass to arrive in the safe waters of the bay. We turned the point with no difficulty, and proceeded a distance across the bay where we landed on a beach to watch for the other boats, the steersmen having been informed as to the precariousness of the locality. Nevertheless it was so deceptive that when the *Nell* came in sight she was not close enough to the left shore for safety. The Major signalled vigorously with his hat, and Prof. took the warning instantly and turned in, but when the *Cañonita* appeared we saw at once that she was altogether too far out and for some seconds we stood almost petrified while the Major again signalled with all his might. It seemed an even chance; then she gained on the current and finally reached good water whence she came to our position. Beaman had been a pilot on the Great Lakes and was expert with a steering-oar, and probably for that reason he was somewhat careless. There was hardly an excuse in this instance for a boat not to take the proper course for the experience of the *No-Name* told the whole story, yet the place is so peculiar and unusual that one even forewarned may fail. Across the bay pulling was safe and we ran to a beach very close to the head of the falls where we made our camp, the sun now being low and the huge cliffs casting a profound and sombre shadow into the bottom. It was a wild, a fierce, an impressive situation. The unending heavy roar of the tumbling river, the difficulty if not impossibility of turning back even if such a thing had been desired, the equal difficulty if not impossibility of scaling the walls that stood more than 2000 feet above us, and the general sublimity of the entire surroundings, rendered our position to my mind intensely dramatic. Two years before, on this identical spot the Major had camped with the loss of one of his boats bearing heavily on his mind, though his magnificent will, his cheerful self-reliance, and his unconquerable determination to dominate any situation gave him power and allied him to the river itself. The place practically chose its own name, Disaster Falls, and it was so recorded by the topographers.

A hard portage was ahead of us and all turned in early to prepare by a good sleep for the long work of the next day. No tent as a rule was erected unless there was rain, and then a large canvas from each boat was put up on oars or other sticks, the ends being left open. In a driving storm a blanket would answer to fill in. As there was now no indication of a storm our beds were placed on the sand as usual with the sides of the canyon for chamber walls and the multitudinous stars for roof.

A short distance below the great rapid near which we were camped was a second equally bad, the two together making up the three-quarter mile descent of Disaster Falls. Between them the river became level for a brief space and wider, and a deposit of boulders and gravel appeared there in the middle above the surface at the present stage of water. It was this island which had saved the occupants of the *No-Name*, and from which they were rescued.

We were up very early in the morning, and began to carry the cargoes by a trail we made over and around the huge boulders to a place below the bad water of the first fall. The temperature was in the 90's and it was hot work climbing with a fifty-pound sack on one's back, but at last after many trips back and forth every article was below. Then the empty boats were taken one at a time, and by pulling, lifting, and sliding on skids of driftwood, and by floating wherever practicable in the quieter edges of the water, we got them successfully past the first fall. Here the loads were replaced, and with our good long and strong lines an inch thick, the boats were sent down several hundred yards in the rather level water referred to intervening between the foot of the upper fall and the head of the lower, to the beginning of the second descent. This all occupied much time, for nothing could be done rapidly, and noon came, in the midst of our work. Anticipating this event Andy had gone ahead with his cook outfit and had baked the dinner bread in his Dutch oven. With the usual fried bacon and coffee the inner man was speedily fortified for another wrestle with the difficult and laborious situation. The dinner bread was baked from flour taken out of a hundred-pound sack that was found lying on top of an immense boulder far above the river. This was flour that had been rescued by the former party from the wreckage of the *No-Name*, but as they could not add it to their remaining heavily laden boats, the Major had been compelled to leave it lying here. They needed it badly enough towards the end. It was still sweet and good, but we could not take it either. We were so much better provisioned than the former party that it was, besides, not necessary for us, and we also left it where it was. Our supplies were not likely to fail us at the mouth of the Uinta, and beyond that there was not yet need to worry. Although there were only two points below Gunnison Crossing in a distance of nearly 600 miles where it was known that the river could be reached, the Crossing of the Fathers and the mouth of the Paria not far below it, we felt sure that those who had been charged with the bringing of supplies to the mouth of the " Dirty Devil " would be able to get there, and as we were to stop for the season at the Paria, we would have time to plan for beyond. In any case our boats were carrying now all they could, and without a regret we turned our backs on the outcast flour. It was an ordinary sack of bolted wheat flour, first in a cotton bag then in a gunny bag and had been lying unbroken for two years. The outside for half an inch was hard, but inside of that the flour was in excellent condition. Two oars were also found. They were doubtless from the *No-Name.*

After dinner we once more unloaded the boats and carried everything on our backs up and across a long rocky hill, or point, down to a spot, about a third of a mile altogether, where the goods were piled on a smooth little beach at the margin of a quiet bay. It took many trips, and it was exhausting work, but in addition to bringing the cargoes down, we also by half past five got one of the boats there, by working it over the rocks and along the edge. Here we camped and had supper as soon as Andy could get it ready. It may be asked by some not familiar with scientific work, how we always knew the time, but as we had the necessary instruments for taking time astronomically, there was nothing difficult about it. We also carried fine chronometers, and had a number of watches.

In the sand near the camp, which place at highest water might have formed an eddy behind some huge rocks, a few old knives, forks, a rusty bake oven, and other articles were found, the wreckage from some party prior to that of the Major's first.

He said they had not left anything of that sort, and he had noticed the same things on the former trip.

The total fall of the river here is about fifty feet, and no boat could get through without smashing.

The morning of June 20th found us early at work bringing down the two boats we had left, and as soon as this was accomplished the cargoes were put on once more, and we lowered the three one at a time, along the left bank by means of our hundred-foot hawsers, with everything in them, about a quarter of a mile to another bad place which we called Lower Disaster Falls. Here we unloaded and made a short portage while Andy was getting dinner. When we had disposed of this and reloaded, we pulled into the river, which averaged about 350 feet wide, with a current in places of 15 miles or more, and quickly arrived at three bad rapids in succession, all of which we ran triumphantly, though the former party made portages around them In the third our boat took in so much water that we made a landing in order to bail out. Continuing immediately we reached another heavy rapid, but ran it without even stopping to reconnoitre, as the way seemed perfectly clear. We took the next rapid with equal success, though our boat got caught in an eddy and was turned completely round, while the others ran past us. They landed to wait, and there we all took a little breathing spell before attempting to run another rapid just below which we made camp in a grove of cedars, at the beginning of a descent that looked so ugly it was decided to make a "let-down" on the following day. Everybody was wet to the skin and glad to get on some dry clothes, as soon as we could pull out our bags. The cliffs had now reached an altitude of at least 2500 feet, and they appeared to be nearly perpendicular, but generally not from the water's edge where there was usually a bank of some kind or the foot of a steep talus. There were box-elder and cottonwood trees here and there, and cedars up the cliffs wherever they could find a footing. On the heights tall pine trees could be seen. The cliff just opposite camp was almost vertical from the rapid at its foot to the brink 2500 feet above, and flame red.

After supper as we all sat in admiration and peering with

F. S. Dellenbaugh
The Heart of Lodore.
Photograph by E. O. Beaman, 1871.

Canyon of Lodore—Dunn's Cliff.
2800 Feet above River.
Photograph by E. O. BEAMAN, 1871.

some awe at the narrow belt of sky, narrower than we had before
seen it, the stars slowly came out, and presently on the exact
edge of the magnificent precipice, set there like a diadem,
appeared the Constellation of the Harp. It was an impressive
sight, and immediately the name was bestowed " The Cliff of
the Harp." [1]

Prof. read *Marmion* aloud, and Jack gave us a song or two,
before we went to sleep feeling well satisfied with our progress
into the heart of Lodore.

This portion of the river has a very great declivity, the
greatest as we afterwards determined on the entire Green and
Colorado with the exception of a section of Cataract and a part
of the First Granite Gorge of the Grand Canyon, where the declivity is much the same, with Cataract Canyon in the lead.
A quarter-mile above our camp a fine little stream, Cascade
Creek, came in on the right. Beaman made some photographs
in the morning, and we began to work the boats down along the
edge of the rapid beside which we had camped. This took us
till noon, and we had dinner before venturing on. When we set
forth we had good luck, and soon put four rapids behind, running the first, letting down past two and running the fourth
which was a pretty bad one. Three-quarters of a mile of smooth
water then gave us a respite much appreciated, when we arrived
at a wild descent about as bad as Disaster Falls, though more
safely approached. This was called Triplet Falls by the first
party. We went into camp at the head of it on the left bank.
This day we found a number of fragments of the *No-Name* here
and there, besides an axe and a vise abandoned by the first
party, and a welcome addition to our library in a copy of
Putnam's Magazine. This was the first magazine ever to penetrate to these extreme wilds. The river was from 300 to 400
feet wide, and the walls ran along with little change, about 2500
feet high. Opposite camp was Dunn's Cliff, the end of the
Sierra Escalante, about 2800 feet high, named for one of the
first party who was killed by the Indians down in Arizona. We

---

[1] In his report the Major ascribes the naming of this cliff to an evening on the
first voyage. The incident could hardly have occurred twice even had the camps
been in the same place.

remained a day here to let the topographers climb out if they could. They had little trouble in doing this, and after a pleas-ant climb reached the top through a gulch at an altitude above the river of 3200 feet. The view was extensive and their efforts were rewarded by obtaining much topographical information. Late in the day the sky grew dark, the thunder rolled, and just before supper we had a good shower.

On the 23d progress was continued and every one felt well after the cessation for a day of the knocking about amidst the foam and boulders. It took us, with hard work, till two o'clock to get past Triplet Falls by means of a double portage. About half a mile below this we were confronted by one of the worst looking places we had yet seen, and at the suggestion of Steward it received the significant name of "Hell's Half Mile." The entire river for more than half a mile was one sheet of white foam. There was not a quiet spot in the whole distance, and the water plunged and pounded in its fierce descent and sent up a deafening roar. The only way one could be heard was to yell with full lung power. Landing at the head of it easily we there unloaded the *Dean* and let her down by line for some distance. In the worst place she capsized but was not damaged. Then the water, near the shore we were on, though turbulent in the extreme became so shallow on account of the great width of the rapid here that when we had again loaded the *Dean* there were places where we were forced to walk alongside and lift her over rocks, but several men at the same time always had a strong hold on the shore end of the line. In this way we got her down as far as was practicable by that method. At this point the river changed. The water became more concen-trated and consequently deeper. It was necessary to unload the boat again and work her on down with a couple of men in her and the rest holding the line on shore as we had done above. When the roughest part was past in this manner, we made her fast and proceeded to carry her cargo down to this spot which took some time. It was there put on board again and the hatches firmly secured. The boat was held firmly behind a huge sheltering rock and when all was ready her crew took their places. With the Major clinging to the middle cabin, as his chair had been left above and would be carried down later, we shoved out into the swift current, here free from rocks, and literally bounded over the waves that formed the end of the descent, to clear water where we landed on a snug little beach and made the boat secure for the night. Picking our way along shore back to the head of the rapid, camp was made there as the darkness was falling and nothing more could be done that night.

It was next to impossible to converse, but every one being very tired it was not long after supper before we took to the blankets and not a man was kept awake by the noise. It seemed only a few moments before it was time to go at it again. All hands were up early and the other two boats were taken laboriously down in the same manner as the *Dean* had been engineered, but though we toiled steadily it was one o'clock by the time we succeeded in placing them alongside that boat. Anticipating this, Andy's utensils were taken down on the *Nell*, and while we were working with the *Cañonita*, our good chef prepared the dinner and we stopped long enough to fortify ourselves with it. Having to build a trail in some places in order to carry the goods across ridges and boulders, it was not alone the work on lowering the boats which delayed us. While we were absorbed in these operations the camp-fire of the morning in some way spread unperceived into the thick sage-brush and cedars which covered the point, and we vacated the place none too soon, for the flames were leaping high, and by the time we had finished our dinner at the foot of the rapid, the point we had so recently left was a horrible furnace. The fire was jumping and playing amidst dense smoke which rolled a mighty column, a thousand feet it seemed to me above the top of the canyon ; that is over 3000 feet into the tranquil air.

At two o'clock all three boats were again charging down on a stiff current with rather bad conditions, though we ran two sharp rapids without much trouble. In one the *Nell* got on a smooth rock and came near capsizing. The current at the spot happened to be not so swift and she escaped with no damage. Then we were brought up by another rapid, a very bad one. Evening was drawing on and every man was feeling somewhat used up by the severe exertions of the day. Camp was therefore ordered at the head of this rapid in the midst of scenery that has probably as great beauty, picturesqueness, and grandeur as any to be found in the whole West. I hardly know how to describe it. All day long the surroundings had been supremely beautiful, majestic, but at this camp everything was on a superlative scale and words seem colourless and futile. The precipices on both sides, about 2200 feet high, conveyed the impression of being almost vertical. Our camp was several hundred yards from the rapid and we could talk with some comfort. After supper I wandered alone down beside the furiously plunging waters and came upon a brood of young magpies airing themselves on the sand. The roar of the fall prevented their hearing and I walked among them, picked one up and took it to camp to show their comicality, when I let it go back to the rendezvous. I was censured especially by the Major, for cruelty to animals.

The next day was Sunday and it came with a radiance that further enhanced the remarkable grandeur around us. Near by was a side canyon of the most picturesque type, down which a clear little brook danced from ledge to ledge and from pool to pool, twenty to thirty feet at a time. We named it Leaping Brook. The rocks were mossy, and fir trees, pines, cedars, and cottonwoods added the charm of foliage to the brilliant colours of the rocks and the sheen of falling water, here and there lost in the most profound shadows. Beaman made a number of views while the rest of the men climbed for various purposes. Steward, Clem, and I by a circuitous route arrived at a point high up on Leaping Brook where the scene was beyond description. To save trouble on the return we descended the brook as it was easy to slide down places that could not be climbed. In this manner we succeeded in getting to the last descent near camp, to discover that it was higher than we thought and almost vertical with rough rocks at the bottom. As we could not go back and had no desire to break a leg, we were in trouble. Then we spied Jack in the camp a short distance away and called to him to put a tree up for us. Good-natured Jack, always ready to help, assumed a gruff tone and pretended he would never help us, but we knew better, and presently he threw up a long dead pine which we could reach by a short slide, and thus got to the river level. It was now noon, and as soon as dinner was over the boats were lowered by lines past the rapid beside camp and once below this we shot on our way with a fine current, soon arriving at two moderate rapids close together, which we ran. This brought us to a third with an ugly look, but on examination Prof. and the Major decided to run it. Getting a good entrance all the boats went through without the slightest mishap. A mile below this place we landed at the mouth of a pretty little stream entering through a picturesque and narrow canyon on the left. We called it Alcove Brook.

Beaman took some negatives here. This was not the easy matter that the dry-plate afterwards made it, for the dark tent had to be set up, the glass plate flowed with collodion, then placed in the silver bath, and exposed wet in the camera, to be immediately developed and washed and placed in a special box for carriage.

This would have been an ideal place for a hunter. Numerous fresh tracks of grizzlies were noticed all around, but we did not have the good luck to see any of the animals themselves. Happy grounds these canyons were at that time for the bears, and they may still be enjoying the seclusion the depths afford The spot had an additional interest for us because it was here that on the first trip the brush caught fire soon after the party had landed, and they were forced to take to the boats so unceremoniously that they lost part of their mess-kit and some clothing.

On leaving Alcove Brook we ran a rapid and then another a little farther on, but they were easy and the river was much calmer though the current was still very swift. At the same time the walls to our satisfaction began to give indications of breaking. They became less high, less compact, and we ventured to hope that our battle with the waters of Lodore was about over. The Major said that, as nearly as he could remember, the end of the great gorge was not very far below. Though the sky was beginning to show the evening tints we kept on and ever on, swiftly but smoothly, looking up at the sky and at the splendid walls. The sun went down. The chasm grew hazy with the soft light of evening and the mystery of the bends deepened. There was no obstruction and in about three miles from Alcove Brook we rather abruptly emerged into a beautiful small opening, where the immediate walls were no more than six hundred feet high. A river of considerable size flowed in on the left, through a deep and narrow canyon. This was the Yampa, sometimes then called Bear River. By seven o'clock we had moored the boats a few yards up its mouth and we made a comfortable camp in a box-elder grove. We had won the fight without disaster and we slept that night in peace.

Lodore is wholly within the State of Colorado. It is 20¾ miles long with a descent of 420 feet,[1] mostly concentrated between Disaster Falls and Hell's Half-Mile, a distance of about 12 miles. The total descent from the Union Pacific crossing was 975 feet in a distance, as the river runs, of about 153 miles.

[1] In my *Romance of the Colorado River* these figures were changed to 275 because of barometrical data supplied me which was supposed to be accurate. I have concluded that it was not.

Jones   Hillers F. S. Dellenbaugh
Canyon of Lodore.
Photograph by E. O. BEAMAN, 1871.

Echo Park.
Mouth of Yampa River in Foreground, Green River on Right.
Photograph by E. O. BEAMAN, 1871.

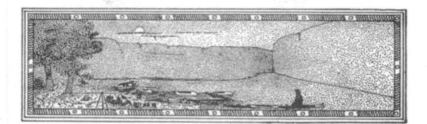

CHAPTER V

A Remarkable Echo—Up the Canyon of the Yampa—Steward and Clem Try a
Moonlight Swim—Whirlpool Canyon and Mountain Sheep—A Grand Fourth-
of-July Dinner—A Rainbow-Coloured Valley—The Major Proceeds in Advance
—A Split Mountain with Rapids a Plenty—Enter a Big Valley at Last.

THE little opening between canyons we named Echo Park,
first because after the close quarters of Lodore it seemed
very park-like, and second because from the smooth bare cliff
directly opposite our landing a distinct echo of ten words was
returned to the speaker. I had never before, and have never
since, heard so clear and perfect an echo with so many words
repeated. We were camped on the right bank of the Yampa
as the left was a bottom land covered with cedars and we preferred higher ground. This bottom was an alluvial deposit
triangular in shape about a mile long and a quarter of a mile
wide with the Yampa and Green on two sides and a vertical
sandstone wall on the third. Behind our camp the rocks broke
back in a rough, steep slope for perhaps a quarter of a mile, and
this with the bottom-land and the lack of height in the walls
near the river conveyed an impression of wide expanse when
compared with the narrow limits in which we had for eight days
been confined. The Green was here about 400 feet wide and
was held in on the western side of the park by the Echo Cliff
which was a vertical wall some 600 feet high composed of homogeneous sandstone, and consequently almost without a crack
from top to bottom where its smooth expanse dropped below
the surface of the water. It extended down river about three-
fourths of a mile, the river doubling around its southern end.

The next day after arriving here most of us did not feel
like doing any climbing and remained around camp, mending
clothes and other articles, adjusting things that had become

deranged by our rough work in the last canyon, recording notes, and making entries in diaries. Prof. took observations for latitude and longitude to establish the position of the Yampa so that it could be properly placed on the map. The Major during an exploring trip from the eastward in 1868 had reached the Yampa Canyon, but he could not cross it. He now decided to go up with a boat as far as possible in three days to supplement his former observations as well as to study the canyon in general. He had estimated its length at thirty miles, and this has proved to be correct. The *Dean* was unloaded, and with three days' rations the Major started with her in the morning manned by Jack, Beaman, Jones, and Andy. Of course they were all still tired from the strain of Lodore, and they were not enthusiastic about seeing the Yampa. In such work as was common through Lodore, it is as much the tension on the nerves, even though this is not realised at the time, as it is the strain on the muscles in transporting the cargoes and the boats, which makes one tired. I was entirely satisfied not to go with the Yampa party and I believe all the others left behind felt much the same.

Steward with Clem, when the Yampa expedition had gone, started back over the cliffs for Alcove Brook to geologise, leaving Prof. busy with observation, Cap. plotting the topographical notes and making his map thereby, and me with no special duty at the time. Every man who wants to be efficient in the field must learn to cook. This was my opportunity as Andy was absent and the others had their special work on hand, so I turned my attention to the culinary realm. A few directions and an example from Cap. who was a veteran gave me the method and I succeeded as my first offering, in placing before my comrades some biscuits hot from the Dutch oven, which compared favourably with those of Andy himself. With the constant practice Andy by this time had become an expert. The day wore away and at evening I got supper with more biscuits of which I was proud, but Steward and Clem failed to come to partake of them as we expected. Darkness fell and still there was dead silence outside of our camp. Much concerned we then ate supper momentarily expecting to hear their

voices, but they did not come.   Something had happened, but
we could not follow their trail till morning to find out what it
was.   At ten o'clock we gave them up for the night deeply
troubled about them.   I had been sitting alone by the fire
keeping the coffee hot and listening, when suddenly I heard a
crackling of the bushes between me and the river and in a second or two Clem, laughing as over a joke, came to the fire with
the water running off him in streams.   While I was trying to
get an explanation Steward also appeared in the same condition.
At first they would not tell what had occurred but finally they
confessed on condition that I would keep the matter a secret.
They had made a long hard climb and late in the afternoon had
come to a place where Steward found it necessary to descend
to the river in examining the strata.   They intended to climb
back, but when the work was done the sun had set and it was
too late to venture up as they could not climb in the dark.
Rather than stay there all night they made a raft of two little
dead cedars and tying their shoes upon it, they waited for the
moon to rise.   This was very soon and they slipped into the
current relying on the raft merely to keep their heads above
water.   They knew there were no rapids between them and
camp but they did not properly estimate the velocity of the
river and the eddies and whirlpools.   They kept near the left
wall so as not to be carried past camp and in this they made a
great mistake for they were caught in a whirlpool caused by a
projection, and the raft was wrenched from them while they
were violently thrown around.   Steward being a powerful
swimmer succeeded after nearly going under for good in re-
gaining the raft which Clem meanwhile had been losing and
recovering quickly several times.   He was not a good swimmer.
After this whirlpool was passed they reached the locality of our
camp with no further adventure.   They were very desirous that
the story be kept from the rest of the party but they had hardly
finished telling me when Prof. came and insisted on knowing
what had occurred.   Their punishment for this indiscretion was
the hard climb back again to where they had left a rifle and
other things that must be recovered.
A delightful episode of this camp was a row which several

of us made up the Yampa in the moonlight. As far as we went the current was not swift and we were able to pull gently along under the great cliffs in shadows made luminous by the brilliancy of the moon. A song the Major was fond of singing, *Softly and Sweetly it Comes from Afar*, almost involuntarily, sprang from us all, though our great songster, Jack, was not with us. Jack had an extensive repertory, an excellent voice, and a hearty, exuberant spirit. He would sing *Write Me a Letter from Home, The Colleen Bawn, The Lone Starry Hours, Beautiful Isle of the Sea*, and many others in a way that brought tranquillity to our souls. We missed him on this evening but nevertheless our song sounded well, echoing from wall to wall, and we liked it. Somehow or other that night remains one of the fairest pictures I have ever seen.

Another day I went with Steward down across the triangular bottom to the lower end of the park where we climbed out through the canyon of a little brook to a sandy and desolate plateau. Currant bushes laden with fruit abounded and there were tracks of grizzlies to be seen. Possibly some may have been lying in the dense underbrush, but if so they kept their lairs as these bears generally do unless directly disturbed.

On the 30th of June Prof., Steward, and Cap. went for a climb. They proceeded to the lower end of the park by boat and through the little canyon that came in there, got out to the plateau where Steward and I had before been, but there they went farther. After a very hard climb they succeeded in reaching the crest where they had a broad view and could see nearly all of the next canyon with its rapids which we would have to pass through; the canyon the Major had called Whirlpool on his first trip. They could also see the Yampa River for twenty miles and discovered the *Dean* coming back down that stream, their attention being attracted by a gunshot in that direction, which they knew could be only from our own men. In camp during the day I again experimented in the culinary department, and produced two dried-apple pies, one of which Clem and I ate with an indescribable zest, and the other we kept to astonish the absentees with when they should reach camp. I have since learned that my method of pie-making was original

I soaked the dried apples till they were soft then made a crust which had plenty of bacon grease in it for shortening and put the apples with sugar between, baking the production in the Dutch oven.

About five o'clock the Yampa explorers came. They were ragged, tired, and hungry having had nothing to eat all day, and not enough any day, as the Major had not taken sufficient supplies in his desire to make the boat light. They were all rather cross, the only time on the whole expedition that such a state existed, but when they had eaten and rested their genial spirits came back, they even liked my pie, and they told us about their struggle up the canyon.

We were all rather sorry to pull away from this comfortable camp at the mouth of the Yampa on July 3d, but the rapids of Whirlpool were challenging and we had to go and meet them. At the foot of Echo Park the Green doubles directly back on itself for a mile as it turns Echo Rock, the narrow peninsula of sandstone 600 feet high. The canyon became suddenly very close and assumed a formidable appearance. We listened for the roar of a rapid but for some time nothing was heard. The splendour of the walls impressed us deeply rising 2000 feet, many coloured, carved, and terraced elaborately. Our admiration was interrupted by a suggestive roar approaching and suddenly a violent rapid appeared. There was ample room and we got below it by a let-down, that is by lowering the boats one at a time with their cargoes on board, along the margin, working in and out of the side currents. Then we had dinner while waiting for the *Cañonita* which had remained behind for pictures.

A part of my work was to make a continuous outline sketch of the left wall for the use of the geologists and this I was able to do as we went along. I had a pocket on the bulkhead in front of my seat in which I kept a sole leather portfolio, which I could use quickly and replace in the waterproof pocket.

The walls of the canyon became more flaring as soon as the rapid was passed at noon, but they lost none of their majesty. We now expected very bad river and whirlpools from the experience of the first party, but the river is never twice alike.

Not only does its bottom shift, but every variation in stage of water brings new problems or does away with them entirely. It was an agreeable surprise to be able to run three rapids with ease by four o'clock, when we saw on some rocks two hundred feet above the stream a flock of mountain sheep. An immediate landing was made with fresh mutton in prospect. Unluckily our guns in anticipation of severe work had all been securely packed away, and it was some moments before they could be brought out. By that time the sheep had nimbly gone around a corner of the wall where a large side canyon was now discovered bringing in a fine creek. It was useless to follow the sheep though one or two made a brief trial, and camp was made in a cottonwood grove at the mouth of the creek. Cottonwoods fringed the stream as far as it could be seen from our position. Brush Creek we called it believing it to be the mouth of a stream in the back country known by that name. The next day, two or three miles up, a branch was found to come from the south, and as this was thought to be Brush Creek, the larger one was named after Cap., and "Bishop's Creek" was put on our map. Doubtless there are plenty of trout in this creek and in others we had passed, but we had no proper tackle for trout and besides seldom had time for fishing when at these places. Jack, when not too tired, fished in the Green and generally had good success. Our present locality would have been a rare place for a month or two's sojourn had we been sportsmen with time on our hands. Sheep, deer, and bear existed in abundance as well as smaller game, but we had to forget it though none of us cared about shooting for fun. Our minds were on other things. Often we went out leaving rifles behind as they were heavy in a climb.

Scarcely had we settled ourselves in this beautiful camp when we discovered that we ourselves were the hunted, and by an enemy that we could not vanquish—ants. There was no place in the neighbourhood that was out of their range. The best I could do was to make my bed two feet from the nearest hill and let them have their way. Morning was hailed with unusual delight for this reason and also because it was the "glorious Fourth," a day that every American remembers wherever he may be. We fired several rounds as a salute, and the Major concluded to keep this camp till the next morning. To enable Andy to have a day off and a climb out with a party to the open, I agreed to run the cook outfit, and felt highly complimented that they were willing to trust me after the pie episode. I immediately resolved to try my skill again in that quarter and expected to astonish the camp. I succeeded. The bill of fare which I evolved was ham, dried-apple pie, dried apples stewed, canned peaches, sugar syrup, bread, coffee, and some candy from Gunther's in Chicago. The candy had been presented to me at Green River Station by some passing friends, and I had hidden it in my bag waiting for this grand occasion. Ham was quite as much of a luxury as candy, for we had started with but three or four, and only used them on special days. As for the canned peaches, they were the only ones we had. The supper was a memorable one; not a grumble was heard from anybody, indeed they all praised it, and the only drawback, from my point of view, was that the scouting party did not return early enough to taste it in its prime. The Major threatened to expel the member who had smuggled in the candy as all the men declared they would go no farther unless they could have a plate of it for desert at every meal!

The next morning we were on the river early, glad to get away from the army of ants. The canyon walls ran along at about the same height as on the previous day, about 2400 feet, and while the river was swift and full of rapids everything seemed to favour us. Before halting for dinner we had run five rapids, three rather ugly, as well as letting down past one with lines. From where a stop was made for Andy's noonday operations, a flock of sheep was seen on the opposite side, and several went after them with no result but disappointment. When we started again we ran a rapid at once, then let down past the next, and followed that by running two more, the last the worst. The boats bumped occasionally on hidden rocks, but no harm was done them. The whole canyon was exceedingly beautiful, nevertheless we did not mourn when late in the afternoon, just after running the last rapid, the magnificent cliffs fell back and we saw more sky than at any time since leaving Brown's Park. On the right the rocks melted away into beautiful rainbow-coloured hills while on the left they remained steep, though retreating a mile or so from the water. The stretch of sky seemed enormous. Breathing appeared to be easier. The eye grows weary with the short range views, and yearns for space in which to roam.

The valley we were now in was not long; about four miles in a straight line, with a width of two. In this space the river meanders nine miles, one detour being very long. It spreads also amongst a number of islands, and the numerous channels became shallow till our keels grated here and there. Then they concentrated once more and we floated along on waters deep and black and slow. The marvellous colouring in the surrounding landscape impressed us, and the Major was for a time uncertain whether to call this "Rainbow" or "Island" Park, the decision finally being given to the latter. Shortly before sunset our meanderings terminated at the foot of the valley where the river once more entered the rocks, in a gateway as abrupt, though not as imposing as that of Lodore. A fine grove of box-elders on the right just above this gate, offered an attractive camping place, and there we stopped.

We were now in Utah again, having crossed the boundary somewhere in Whirlpool Canyon. The altitude was 4940 feet, showing a descent in Whirlpool Canyon of 140 feet in a distance of 14¼ miles. The next day I went with Beaman and Clem with a boat back to the foot of Whirlpool Canyon, in order that Beaman might get some views. It was a hard pull, and we discovered that what appears sluggish going down, is often the reverse to a boat going up. We could make headway only by keeping very close to the bank. It was supper-time when we again reached camp. The Major now announced that he intended to take the *Dean* and go on ahead, without stopping anywhere, to the mouth of the Uinta River, leaving us to follow as we could in doing the work. Cap. was to be taken in my place because of his previous experience in the army and in the West. That evening all was made ready. By break of day the camp was astir, breakfast was disposed of as quickly as possible, the *Dean* was manned, the Major went to his place on the middle cabin, they

Whirlpool Canyon.
Mouth of Bishop Creek—Fourth of July Camp.
Photograph by E. O. BEAMAN, 1871.

Split Mountain Canyon.
Photograph by E. O. BEAMAN, 1871

cast off and disappeared in the canyon gate. We then called this "Craggy Canyon," but later it was changed to Split Mountain.

All of the others crossed the river to climb to the top of the cliffs for observations and for photographs. I was left alone to watch camp. I longed to experiment further in the cooking line, and discovering a bag of ground coffee leaning against the foot of a tree, I said to myself, "coffee cake." I had heard of it, I had eaten it, I would again surprise the boys. I had no eggs, no butter, no milk (condensed milk was unknown at that time), but I had flour, water, cream of tartar, saleratus, sugar, salt, and ground coffee. I thought these quite enough, and went at my task. The mixture I made I put in a small tin and baked in the Dutch oven. I was so much occupied with this interesting experiment that I forgot all about time and about having something substantial ready for the return of the hungry climbers, so when they did come about noon, as famished as coyotes and dead tired, all I could offer was *the* cake, ever after famous on that trip, a brown, sugary solid, some six inches in diameter, two inches thick, and betraying its flavour everywhere by the coffee-grounds scattered lavishly through it. Andy gave it one brief sad look, and then went to work to get dinner. But they were such a rare lot of good fellows that they actually praised that cake and not only that, they ate it. The cake led to the discovery that the Major's party had left behind all their coffee, which was what I had used for flavouring, and they would have to content themselves with tea. From the heights our men had reached they could see, with a glass, the *Dean* working rapidly down the river. Next day another party went up to the same place, and I went along. The photographic outfit had been left there because rain the day before had spoiled the view, and we were to bring it down when more views had been taken. After a strong, steep climb we found ourselves on a peak or pinnacle about 3000 feet above the river, and therefore 7940 above sea-level.

The view from this point was extraordinary. Far below gleamed the river cleaving the rocks at our feet, and visible for several miles in the canyon churning its way down, the rapids indicated by bars of white. One hardly knew which way to

look. Crags about us projected into the canyon, and I was in-
spired to creep out upon a long finger of sandstone where I
could sit astride as on a horse and comfortably peer down into
the abyss. It was an absolutely safe place, but Beaman and
Clem feared the crag might break off with me, and they compelled me to come back to relieve their minds. Seldom does
one have such a chance to see below as well as I could there.
The long, narrow mountain stretched off to the west, seeming
not more than a half-mile wide, and split open for its whole
length by the river, which has washed its canyon longitudinally
through it. In all directions were mountains, canyons, and
crags in bewildering profusion.

When Beaman had ended his labours we started down the
cliffs with his apparatus. This was the terror of the party.
The camera in its strong box was a heavy load to carry up the
rocks, but it was nothing to the chemical and plate-holder box,
which in turn was a featherweight compared to the imitation
hand-organ which served for a dark room. This dark box was
the special sorrow of the expedition, as it had to be dragged
up the heights from 500 to 3000 feet. With this machinery we
reached camp pretty tired and glad to rest the remainder of
the day, especially as Prof. said we would enter the new canyon the next morning. This was Sunday. A few minutes
after starting we passed between perpendicular strata rising out
of the water, and gradually bending above over to the horizontal, then breaking into crags. I never saw anything more like
an artificial wall, so evenly were the rocky beds laid one against
another. As we passed into the more broken portion a
flock of sheep came into view high up on the crags on the
right standing motionless evidently puzzled by the sound of
our oars. We fired from the moving boats, but without result.
Recovering from their surprise the sheep bounded lightly
away. Our attention was required the next moment by a
rapid which we ran—it was a small one—to find it followed by
many thickly set with rocks. At the first we let down by line
for half a mile, when we had dinner. Then we let down by
line another half-mile, and ran half a mile more in easy water
to the head of a very bad place, one of the worst we had seen,

where we made another let-down. There was never any
difficulty about landing when we desired, which made the work
comparatively easy. The *Cañonita* got some hard knocks and
had to be repaired at one place before we could go on. The
total distance made was only about three miles, but we could
have gone farther had we not stopped for investigations, and
to mend the boat.

Wet and weary we welcomed the order to camp, about five
o'clock, and made ourselves comfortable with dry clothes from
our rubber bags, the wet ones being spread, as was our custom,
on rocks to dry. At high water many of these rapids would be
rendered much easier. A quarter of a mile below camp was a
small cave thirty or forty feet deep, very picturesque, with the
river dashing into it, and in the water in front a rock twenty
feet high, which had dropped down from somewhere above.
Beaman got a very good picture here.

The river was falling fast and as the water lowered rocks
more and more showed themselves in the rapids. Low water
increases the labour but it increases the safety as well, for the
velocity is less and the boats are more easily controlled.

The next day, July 10th, we did not start on down the
river till one o'clock. Then we lowered the boats past two
rapids and ran six, of which four were very bad on account of
numerous rocks. Occasionally a boat would strike but none
was injured seriously. The sun was directly in our faces blinding us, and a high wind was blowing which added to the difficulties. The walls were often vertical for a thousand feet or
more, and the river was wide and shallow. There was a scorch-
ing hot sun, the temperature being near 100 in the shade.
The rocks and even the sand became so hot that they were
uncomfortable to the touch, but there was one advantage in
this dry heat—our clothes were soon dry. During this day we
landed on the wrong side to examine one rapid and had to run
it from there. Both boats got through with only slight raps
and we went on a short distance to camp at the head of a bad
descent which was not runable at this stage of water. In the
morning a line-portage was easily accomplished and we ran
down a short distance farther when we stopped for dinner on a

sandy beach.   The sand scorched my feet for I had been without shoes for several days.   All our shoes were giving out and
mine were the first to go completely.   Fortunately Beaman
had an extra pair of army brogans which he lent me till we
should reach Uinta.   I had ordered, by advice in Chicago, two
pairs of fine shoes at thirteen dollars a pair, but I now discovered
that I ought to have bought shoes at two dollars instead for
such work as this.   We hoped to be able to get some new shoes
from Salt Lake when we reached the Uinta River and again
would be in touch, even though a very long touch, with the
outside world.   Our soap was all gone too, and supplies of
every kind were getting low.

In the afternoon three more rapids were run and at a fourth
we were compelled to make a line-portage.   Then we saw the
strata begin to curve over and down and finally drop into
the river just as they had come out of it at the beginning.   The
crevices were filled with ferns and in places clear water was
dripping from these little green cliff gardens.   As we ran along
the foot of the left wall we saw a peculiar and beautiful spring
which had carved out a dainty basin where a multitude of ferns
and kindred plants were thriving, a silvery rill dropping down
from them.   We emerged from the canyon as abruptly as we
had entered it, and saw a broad valley stretching before us.
Running a quarter of a mile on a smooth river camp was made
on the right on a level floor carpeted with grass and surrounded
by thickets of oak.   We were in the beginning of what is now
called Wonsits (Antelope) Valley, about eighty-seven miles long,
the only large valley on the river above the end of Black Canyon.
Split-Mountain Canyon eight miles long has one of the greatest
declivities on the river, coming next to Lodore, though it differs
from the latter in that the descent is more continuous and not
broken into short, violent stretches.   There would be plain
sailing now to the head of the Canyon of Desolation.

CHAPTER VI

A Lookout for Redskins—The River a Sluggard—A Gunshot!—Someone Comes!
—The Tale of a Mysterious Light—How, How! from Douglas Boy—At the
Mouth of the Uinta—A Tramp to Goblin City and a Trip down White River
on a Raft—A Waggon-load of Supplies from Salt Lake by Way of Uinta
Agency—The Major Goes Out to Find a Way In.

OUR thoughts now were mainly directed to pushing on to
the mouth of the Uinta River and picking up our advance
party, which by this time must have gotten in touch with the
Uinta Agency. We felt gratified that another of the long line
of canyons was a thing of the past and that for a brief time we
would have easy water, so far as rapids were concerned. We
were reminded that this was Indian country by discovering on
a smooth face of rock wall not far from camp a lot of drawings
pecked into the stone. They represented figures of natives,
bison, elk, deer, mountain sheep, grizzly tracks, etc., and as they
were the first pictographs I had ever seen I was particularly
interested. The bison pictures indicated the former presence
here in this valley of that fine animal. Numbers indeed once
ranged these hills and valleys, but they had all disappeared
many years before our voyage. We were on the lookout for
Indians. As long as we were encompassed by the mighty
walls of the canyons there was little probability of our meeting
with any of the original people of this soil, but the valley now
opening wide before us was their favourite haunt. Two divisions of Utes roamed the surrounding region. On the west it
was the Uinta Utes who, we knew, were peaceable, and on the
east it was the White River Utes, whose status as to peace and
war was at that period somewhat vague and uncertain. We
expected no trouble with any of them, yet the possibility of

running at any moment on a band gave added interest and colour to the voyage. This was intensified by the feeling that we had suddenly been thrown out of doors, unprotected, as the huge, dominating precipices broke so suddenly back on both sides, leaving us hardly a rock with which, in case of necessity, to emulate the example of Roderick Dhu. Probably if we had travelled here on horseback in the open there would not have been this sense of having left our fortification behind.

July 12th the boats proceeded down a river so sluggish that the term "down" seemed a misnomer, and we actually had to row; had to work at the oars to make the boats go; these same boats which so recently had behaved like wild horses. This was not to our taste at all, the weather being extremely hot. But there was no help for it. The boats fairly went to sleep and we tugged away at their dull, heavy weight, putting the miles behind and recalling the express-train manner of their recent action. On each side of us there were occasional groves of cottonwoods and wide bottoms bounded by low hills. After about ten miles of steady pulling we discovered that we were only 2½ miles from our starting place in a straight line. Here there was a superb cottonwood grove, massive trees with huge trunks like oaks, on the left. We found the remains of a camp-fire and decided that our advance party had come this far from Island Park the first day. They had accomplished a phenomenal run, but it showed what might be done with light boats and a full crew. As Steward desired to make some geological examinations at this point, Prof. announced that we would stay till morning. Another cause for stopping was a gale which blew with great force, making rowing exceedingly hard work, and it was hard enough anyhow with no good current to help.

Steward wished to go across the river, and I went with him. We tramped with our Winchesters on our shoulders for several hours, examining rocks and fossils. On our return we found that Andy was occupied in boiling a goose which Prof.'s sure aim had bestowed on the larder, and we had the bird for supper. If it was not one of the fossils it certainly was one of the "oldest inhabitants," which are found in every locality, and though a steady diet of bacon enthused us with an ambition to masticate this noble morsel, it had to be relegated to the impossibilities. We had a good deal of entertainment out of it, and while so engaged every ear caught the sound of a faint, distant gunshot. This was proof that we were no longer alone, and the question was, "How many Indians are there?" We simply waited developments. Night came on and the fierce wind died away completely as the sun went down. We gave no more thought to the shot, but all went to bed without even leaving a watch, so confident was Prof. that there was no enemy, and no danger of a surprise. He was always "level-headed" and never went off on a tangent doing wild or unwarranted things. He was a man of unusually sound judgment.

In the absence of Cap. the duty of reading barometer had fallen to me, and sometimes, when waiting for the hour to arrive, I had to sit alone for a time when the others already had turned in. It was that way on this night, and I waited with some impatience for nine o'clock to come. For the purpose of reading the scale we used a small bull's-eye lantern belonging to a transit instrument, and it threw out a long beam of light. I entertained myself by flashing this beam of light in various directions to the distress of one member lying near not asleep, who was somewhat nervous as to the character of the Indians responsible for the shot.

"Confound it," he growled, "you'll have the whole Ute tribe down on us! You know they are not far off!"

Of course I desisted in my "signalling," but Prof., not yet asleep, spoke up saying he did not believe any Indians would bother us. Finishing the observations I put out the lantern, and settled in my blankets. At that instant there was the flash of a light through the trees and then it glowed steadily for a moment and went out. My nervous neighbour saw it too. "There," he cried, "an answer to your confounded signal!" Several saw it. "The evening star setting beyond the hill," they declared, derisively, but we two maintained that it was nothing less than a light near by. Then sleep ruled the camp. In the middle of the night there was a sudden terrific cracking, rending, and crashing, starting all to their feet except Clem, who was not wakened by it. What had happened? We perceived in a second. One of the enormous limbs, weakened by the wind, had broken off and dropped to the ground in the middle of the camp. Luckily no one was under it and no harm was done, but for a moment, in connection with the light episode and the gunshot, it gave us a shock. Every one laughed, and soon the camp was still again. The sun was well up before we awoke. Immediately the discussion of the strange light came up, and it formed a lively and amusing topic, not only then, but ever after for months. Breakfast became a stirring debating scene, when plump into the midst of our hilarity, as if to emphasise the declarations of the nervous member, there came a sharp call from beyond a line of bushes. Almost on the instant appeared an Indian mounted on a dark bay horse trotting towards us exclaiming, "How, how!" and holding out his hand in token of friendship. His long black hair hung behind in two tails braided with red and black cotton cloth. The scalp at the part was painted vermilion, and around each eye was a ring of the same bright colour. His shirt was of the kind called hickory, and his leggins were of red woollen stuff. Altogether he was a good looking specimen of his race, and about twenty-five years old. How many more might be behind we could not tell.

He dismounted and Clem grasped him warmly by the hand, exclaiming with his most cordial smile, "Well, how are all the folks at home?" to which the visitor of course made no answer. Not one of our party understood Ute, and I had never seen a "wild" Indian at such close quarters before. The man motioned for something to eat, so Andy gave him a plate of breakfast, but there was a twinkle in Andy's blue eye, for the breakfast consisted largely of the rejected goose. When the red man's vision rested on the goose he gave a grunt of disgust and made no effort to even taste it, though he relished the other things and a cup of hot coffee. I have noticed that all Indians are very fond of coffee. We gleaned that he was alone with his squaw, and had a wickiup down the river a short distance. Doubtless he had examined our camp the previous night. The barometer hanging to a tree-branch caught his eye, and I tried by signs to explain it to him with no success except to convulse the whole crew. At length with the exclamation " Squaw," he rode away and came back with his fair partner riding behind. By this time we were packed up and we pushed off, the pair watching us with deep interest. About a mile and a half below by the river, we came on them again at their camp, they having easily beaten us by a short cut. Here was his wickiup made of a few cottonwood boughs, and in front of it the ashes of a fire. Our side immediately claimed this was the light we had seen, and the discussion of this point continued until another night put an end to it. In the bough shelter sat the blooming bride of " Douglas Boy," as he called himself, Douglas being the chief of the White River Utes. She was dressed well in a neat suit of navy-blue flannel and was lavishly adorned with ornaments. Her dress was bound at the waist by a heavy belt of leather, four inches wide, profusely decorated with brass discs and fastened by a brass buckle. She was young and quite pretty, and they were a handsome couple. He intimated that he would be grateful to be ferried across the river, here almost half a mile wide, so his blankets, saddles, and whole paraphernalia were piled on the boats, while the two horses were driven into the water and pelted with stones till they made up their minds that the farther shore offered greater hospitality, and swam for it. Then the squaw and the brave were taken on separate boats. She hesitated long before finally trusting herself, and was exceedingly coy about it. She had probably never seen a boat before. At last, overcoming her fear she stepped tremblingly on board and in a few minutes we had them landed on the other side, where we said farewell and went on.

In the afternoon we discovered a number of natives on the right bank and landed to see what they were. Nothing more terrible than several badly frightened squaws and children occupied the place, the men being away. We thought this call on the ladies would suffice, and presenting them with a quantity of tobacco for their absent lords, we pulled away, leaving them still almost paralysed with fright and astonishment at our sudden and unexpected appearance and disappearance.

The valley was now very wide, and the river spread to a great width also, giving conditions totally different from any we had found above. Rowing was real labour here, but Prof. was eager to arrive at the mouth of the Uinta the next day so it was row, row, with a strong, steady, monotonous stroke, hour after hour till we had put twenty miles behind when we stopped for the night. Next morning the same programme was continued from seven o'clock on, with a brief halt for dinner. About four a storm came up, compelling us to wait an hour, when on we pulled, with a temperature something like 100° F., in the shade, till sunset, when about forty miles from our starting point, we arrived at the mouth of a river on the right, which we thought must be the Uinta. But finally as there was no sign of our advance party we concluded there must be a mistake. There was so little current in the tributary we thought it might be something besides a river, the mouth of a lake perhaps, and that the Uinta was farther on. About a mile down in the dim light there appeared to be a river mouth, but on reaching the place there was nothing of the kind. Several signal shots were fired. They fell dead on the dull stillness of the night which was dropping fast upon us. We took to the oars once more and pulled down nearly another mile till the dark grew so thick it was not prudent to proceed, and Prof. ordered a landing on the left where we made a hasty cup of coffee to refresh the inner man, and turned in, much puzzled and troubled by the absence of any kind of a signal from the advance party. Some one suggested that they had all been killed, but Prof. met this with scornful ridicule and went to sleep. When daylight came a river was discovered less than half a mile below our camp coming in from the east. Prof. knew this to be White River from the map, the mouths of White and Uinta rivers having long been quite accurately established. The mouth of the Uinta must therefore be where we had been the night before, and Prof. walked back till he came opposite to it. We then got the boats back by rowing and towing, and landed on the right or west bank about a quarter of a mile above the mouth of the Uinta, where the old time crossing had been, and which we had passed unnoticed in the evening light. Here were the ashes of a camp-fire, and after much searching a tin can was found with a note in it from the Major, saying they had all gone out to the Agency, and that we were to wait here.

A large cottonwood tree stood on the low bank where travellers before had camped, not in going up and down the river, but on their way across country. It was a very old tree and its bark presented many marks, names, and dates, and I regret now that I did not copy them for reference. This was one of the known crossings for a long period, in fact, it was through this valley that Escalante, the first white man to cross Green River, travelled in 1776, and it is possible that he may have camped under this very tree.[1] We settled there to wait, harassed by multitudes of voracious mosquitoes. All day we remained, expecting the absentees, but the sun went down and still there was no word. About seven o'clock while we were eating supper, some shots and yells from the west took us to the top of the bank, and we saw two horsemen galloping towards our position. We soon made them out to be Cap. and Jones. They brought a large mail, a portion of it the same we had tried to stop at Salt Lake, and have returned to us at the Gate of Lodore, and they reported that the Major had gone out to Salt Lake. We built up a good fire, and by its light everyone was quickly lost in letters from home.

The next morning we got the *Dean* out of the bushes where she had been well hidden, and moved across the river with the whole outfit, to a place in front of a half-finished log cabin called Fort Robideau, after the trapper of that name, who years before had roamed this country. A road crossing here from Golden to Provo, 413 miles long, was laid out in 1861 by Berthoud and Bridger for the Overland Stage Company, but the Civil War and the building of the Union Pacific had prevented

[1] Two days after crossing the San Clemente, as he called White River, Escalante crossed the Rio San Buenaventura (Green River) somewhere above the mouth of White River. Here were six large "black poplars," on one of which they left an inscription. After resting two days they went south-west along the Buenaventura, ten leagues, and from a hill saw the junction of the San Clemente. He evidently went very near the mouth of the Uinta, and then struck westward. The Uinta he called Rio de San Cosme.

its realisation.[1]　The cabin had no windows or doors, but for summer that was not a defect.　The mud roof was intact, and we used the cabin for headquarters, though we preferred to sleep out on the ground.　Back of the building a wide level plain spread away and deer and antelope ranged there in large numbers.　Any short walk would start up antelope, but we had other matters on our mind, and made no special effort to shoot any.　It would have been easy for a trained hunter to get all he wanted, or even for one of us to do it had we dropped other things and given our minds to the work.

The following Monday, July 17th, Prof. and Beaman left for the Agency, and on Friday of the same week Jack returned accompanied by a man named Basor, driving a large four-horse waggon loaded with supplies for us.　We were in need of them. We had been completely out of soap for two weeks or more, and a box of that essential article was broken open the first thing.　Jack also brought from the Agency garden some lettuce, new potatoes, and turnips.　Not having tasted any vegetables for two months, these were a great treat.　The same afternoon Basor went away taking letters from us with him to be sent to Salt Lake.　One of the special things he had brought was three long, narrow pieces of flat iron made by the Agency blacksmith from old wagon tires, for the keels of the boats, which were badly worn by scraping on shoals and rocks in our portaging and letting-down operations.

On the next Monday, Cap., Steward, and I with five days' rations on our backs as well as blankets enough for the warm nights, and our rifles, started on a journey up White River to a place called Goblin City by one of the earlier explorers who had crossed the valley.　As we were going through some heavy willows about noon, I discovered standing still before me and not a hundred feet away the finest stag I have ever seen.　He stood like a Landseer picture, head erect and alert with huge branching antlers poised in the air.　He was listening to my companions who were a little distance from me.　My gun being tied to my pack for easy travelling I could not quickly

[1] A regiment of California volunteers marched this way from Salt Lake on the way to Denver during the Civil War.

extricate it and before I could bring it to bear he dashed through the willows and a sensible shot was impossible.   I admired him so much that I was rather glad I could not shoot. We came across a great deal of game, antelope, mountain sheep, and deer but we never seemed to have the opportunity to stalk it properly. When we finally came in sight of the Goblin City it was six o'clock of the second day and we had travelled steadily.   At the farther end of a level little valley surrounded by cliffs were numerous small buttes and square rocks, almost in rows and about the size of small buildings, so that there was a striking suggestion of a town. We slept near the river and spent the next morning in examining the locality. When we had completed the observations I got dinner while Steward and Cap. with our gun-straps and some buckskin strings made a raft from small cottonwood logs we found on the bank. Upon this weaving affair we all three embarked to descend the river in order to meander the course as well as to save our legs. Steward and Cap. stood at either end with long poles while I sat in the middle and took the compass sights as we passed along. There were some sharp little rapids full of rocks, and sometimes it was all we could do to stick on, for the raft being flexible naturally would straddle a big rock and take the form of a very steep house roof. The banks were thick with currant bushes loaded with ripe fruit and we kept a supply of branches on the raft to pick off the currants as we went along. Everywhere there were many fresh tracks of bears for they are fond of this fruit, but if they saw us we failed to see them, though some of the tracks appeared to have been made not more than a few minutes before. As we drifted between high banks there was a violent crashing of bushes and a beautiful fawn, evidently pursued by bear or wolf, plunged through and dropped into the stream.   Cap. took a shot at it from the wobbling raft but of course failed. The fawn landed at the bottom of a mud wall ten feet high and for a moment seemed dazed, but by some herculean effort it gained the plain and sped away to freedom and we were not at all sorry to see it go. All the next day we kept on down White River on the raft and at seven o'clock were still five miles from camp in a direct course and no

food left.   As the stream meandered a great deal we parted
from it and went to headquarters on foot.

We now expected hourly the return of Prof. and the Major,
but another day passed without them or any message.   The
next day was Saturday and it faded away also without any
event.   Just after supper there was a hail from the west bank
and on going over with a boat we found there Prof., Beaman, and
an Indian.   The Major had not come because Captain Dodds,
commanding the party which was charged with the taking of
rations for us to the mouth of the Dirty Devil River, our next
supply station, had sent word that he could not find a way
through the unknown region.   The Major concluded that he
would have to go and try it himself.   His plan was for us to
go on and he would join us again August 25th at Gunnison
Crossing, at the end of the Canyon of Desolation, the next
canyon of the series. Gunnison Crossing was an established
point with a trail leading there from east and west.   We were
to wait for him till September 3d in that neighbourhood, and if
he failed to arrive we were to go on and get through as best we
could on the rations remaining.   Our present intercourse with
the world was now terminated by our sending the Indian who
had come with Prof. back to the Agency with our mail.   Prof.
had brought in some fresh beef which was a great treat but
there was little of it and after a couple of meals we were on
bacon and beans again.   Had an Indian from the Agency been
hired for the purpose of hunting, we might have had plenty of
venison during our stop here.   Sunday our old acquaintance
Douglas Boy came to camp and was employed to make moccasins to save our shoes.   Some new shoes had been sent in to
us, but for climbing and walking the rawhide-soled moccasins
were excellent and would save our shoes for river work.   The
Indian had a beaded cap pouch which I secured from him for
some vermilion and he was ready to trade, but the next day
Jack caught him trying to steal our buckskin by hiding it in
his blankets which rudely sundered our business relations.
Jack himself acquired the art of moccasin-making and he made
each of us an excellent pair in his spare time.   Steward and I
went back up White River to finish our work but the raft

timbers were gone and we could find no others, so we had to do what we could on foot. When we returned I discovered some ginger among the supplies and thinking it time for variety in our bill of fare, and it being Cap.'s birthday, I made a large ginger-cake which was voted prime. We ate half of it at one sitting with an accompaniment of lime-juice "lemonade."

At the Agency Prof. found out that Douglas Boy had eloped from the White River country with his squaw, who was betrothed to another, and when we first met him he was engaged in eluding pursuit. According to Ute law if he could avoid capture for a certain time he would be free to return without molestation to his village. Beaman photographed him and a number of the Uintas under the direction of the Major, who wished to secure all the information possible about the natives, their language, customs, and costumes. We now spent several days arranging our new supplies in the rubber sacks, putting the iron strips on the boat-keels, and doing what final repairing was necessary. The topographers plotted the map work, and all finished up their necessary notes and data. By the afternoon of Friday, August 4th, all was in readiness for continuing the voyage. We had now descended 1450 feet from our starting point towards sea-level and we knew that the next canyon would add considerably to these figures.

CHAPTER VII

On to Battle—A Concert Repertory—Good-bye to Douglas Boy—The Busy, Busy Beaver—In the Embrace of the Rocks Once More—A Relic of the Cliff-Dwellers—Low Water and Hard Work—A Canyon of Desolation—Log-cabin Cliff—Rapids and Rapids and Rapids—A Horse, Whose Horse? —Through Gray Canyon to the Rendezvous.

WE were up early on the morning of August 5th prepared to leave Camp 32. Prof. took a lunar observation, and at eight we entered the boats and turned our backs on " Fort " Robideau, the only house on or near the whole river at that time from the mouth of the Virgin, to our Camp No. 1 where we had the snow-storm, a distance of about one thousand miles. We had vanquished many rapids and now we pushed on ready for our next battle with the river in the Canyon of Desolation, just before us. The order of going was slightly changed in the absence of the Major, for Prof., being now in sole command, went ahead with his boat, the *Nellie Powell*, while ours, the *Emma Dean*, for the time being took second place. The river for a brief distance ran smoothly with only enough current, about two miles an hour, to help us along without hard rowing. I missed the Major while we were on the water, probably more than any one else in the party, for as we were facing each other the whole time and were not separated enough to interfere with conversation we had frequent talks. He sometimes described incidents which happened on the first voyage, or told me something about the men of that famous and unrivalled journey. Besides this he was very apt to sing, especially where the river was not turbulent and the outlook was tranquil, some favourite song, and these songs greatly interested me. While he had no

fine voice he sang from his heart, and the songs were those he
had learned at home singing with his brothers and sisters. One
of these was an old-fashioned hymn, *The Home of the Soul*, or
rather the first two verses of it. These verses were among his
special favourites.[1]

> " I will sing you a song of that beautiful land,
>   The far away home of the soul,
>   Where no storms ever beat on the glittering strand,
>   While the years of eternity roll,
>   While the years of eternity roll ;
>   Where no storms ever beat on the glittering strand
>   While the years of eternity roll.

> " Oh ! that home of the soul in my visions and dreams,
>   Its bright jasper walls I can see ;
>   Till I fancy but thinly the veil intervenes
>   Between the fair city and me
>   Till I fancy, etc."

Another was a pretty four-part song, *The Laugh of a Child*, of
which he sang the air. The words ran :

> " I love it, I love it, the laugh of a child.
>   Now rippling, now gentle, now merry and wild.
>   It rings through the air with an innocent gush,
>   Like the trill of a bird at the twilight's soft hush,
>   It floats on the breeze like the tones of a bell,
>   Or music that dwells in the heart of a shell.
>   Oh, the laugh of a child is so wild and so free
>   'T is the merriest sound in the world to me."

Still another of which he sang the English words often was the
well-known air from *Figaro*. I give a few bars :

[1] Many, many years after the canyon voyage as Major Powell with his sister,
Mrs. Thompson, and Professor Thompson were approaching Fort Wingate in New
Mexico, the sun was setting, and sky and rocks combined to produce a glorious
picture. Suddenly he asked his companions to halt and sitting on their horses
looking into the wonderful sky he sang with them the above two stanzas.

NON PIÙ ANDRAI—PLAY NO MORE. Air. Figaro.

At times he imitated a certain pathetic yet comical old woman he had heard singing at some camp-meeting, "The dear blessed Bible, the Fam-i-ly Bible," etc. He told me one day that this fondness for singing, especially amid extremely unpromising or gloomy circumstances, had on more than one occasion led the men of the first expedition to suspect his sanity. When he was singing, I could see that frequently he was really not thinking about his song at all, but of something quite foreign to it, and the singing was a mere accompaniment. Our party as a whole commanded an extensive repertory of song for an exploring expedition and while most of the voices were somewhat below concert requirement, there was no one to object, and one of us, Jack, did have an excellent voice. A song often heard was, *Shells of Ocean* and also that one most appropriate, *What Are the Wild Waves Saying?* Then there was *If I Had but a Thousand a Year, Gaffer Green,* and of course, *Annie Laurie.* Never was there an American or an English expedition to anywhere that did not have that song, as well as *Way Down upon the Suwanee River.* In addition to all these and the ones previously mentioned of which

> "Oh, the lone starry hours give me Love
> When still is the beautiful night,"

was a special favourite, Jack's individual repertory contained an exhaustless number, both sad and gay. There were *Carry me Back to Old Tennessee, The Sailor's Grave, Aura Lee,* with her golden hair, who brought sunshine and swallows indiscriminately to each locality which she graced with the said golden hair, and *Come where my Love Lies Dreaming, Seeing Nellie Home*, and scores or at least dozens that I fail to recall.

But while we had a great store of songs we were deficient to the last degree in musical instruments, the one solitary example being an humble mouth-organ which in a moment of weakness I had thrown in with my outfit. We just escaped having a flute. Frank, who left us on the 10th of June, possessed one, and when he was preparing to go Steward negotiated for this instrument. He gave Cap. his revolver to trade for it, considering the flute more desirable property for the expedition. Cap., being an old soldier, concluded to fire at a mark before letting the revolver pass forever from our possession. Presently there was an explosion which demolished the pistol and all our prospects of acquiring the musical treasure at one and the same moment. Possibly Fortune was kinder to us than we dreamed. The mouth-organ then remained the sole music machine in all that immense area. I did not feel equal to the position of organist but Steward boldly took up the study, and practised so faithfully that he became a real virtuoso.

As a boy in New York Jack, though not a Hibernian himself, had associated closely with descendants of the Shamrock Isle, and he could speak with a fine emerald brogue. A refrain of one of his songs in this line was: " And if the rocks, they don't sthop us, We will cross to Killiloo, whacky-whay!" This sounded our situation exactly, and it became a regular accompaniment to the roaring of the rapids. Jack had many times followed in the wake of the Thirteen Eagles fire company, one of the bright jewels with a green setting, of the old volunteer service. The foreman, fitting the rest of the company, was Irish too, and his stentorian shout through the trumpet " Tirtaan Aigles, dis wai!" never failed to rise above the din, and when the joyful cry smote the ears of the gallant " Tirtaan," the rocks nor the ruts nor the crowds nor anything could stop them ; through thick and through thin they went to the front, for there was rivalry in those days and when the Aigles time after time got first water on, they won triumphs which we of this mercenary epoch cannot understand. The Aigles were in for glory, nothing else. So when we heard the roar of a rapid and sniffed the mist in the air, " Tirtaan Aigles dis wai," was our slogan.

Where the river now ran smoothly, as it did for a considerable distance below the Robideau crossing we could drift with the slow current and enjoy the study of the surroundings, the boats requiring no attention. Passing the mouths of the Uinta and the White, both rivers entering very quietly through a level valley, we pulled gently along watching the banks for something new. When we had thus gone a couple of miles we discovered our first acquaintance of this valley, Douglas Boy, encamped on the right with his runaway bride. They had a snug and secluded hiding-place protected by the river and some low cliffs. We landed to pay our parting call. Both had their faces completely smeared with the bright vermilion obtained by trade from us, and they presented in our eyes a ludicrous appearance. They had recently killed a fat deer and seemed very happy. Prof. exchanged some sugar for enough venison for our dinner and we said farewell to them, the first as well as the last human beings we had met with in this valley. Clem, as usual, gave them various messages for the " folks at home " and assured them with gracious smiles, that they " would ever be the subject of his most distinguished consideration." They smiled after us and we were soon beyond their vision. Presently low cliffs, 100 to 150 feet began to show themselves, on one side or the other, and the wide valley vanished. The great canyon below was reaching out for us. There were numerous islands covered with immense accumulations of driftwood or with growing cottonwoods where high enough. Hundreds of beaver swam about. Occasionally a shot from the boats would kill or wound one, but it was next to impossible to secure any as they seemed to sink immediately to the bottom and we gave up trying as long as they were in deep water. The stream being so tranquil reading poetry was more to our taste than hunting the beaver, and Prof. read aloud from Emerson as we slowly advanced upon the enemy.

After about nine miles of this sort of thing we stopped for dinner in a pretty cottonwood grove at the foot of a cliff on the right with beaver swimming around as if they did not know what a human being was. When our venison had been disposed of the boats were shoved out into the river again and we continued our approach to the canyon. The surrounding region became a desolate waste; a broken desert plateau elevated above us about two hundred feet. Some deer seen on an island caused us to land and try to get a good shot at one, but we failed to get near enough for success and they quickly disappeared. The ground was too difficult for pursuit. After some seventeen miles, camp for the night was made in another grove of rather small cottonwoods at 5.30. We were on a large island with the surrounding waters thick with beaver busy every moment though their great work is done at night. Many trees felled, some of them of a considerable diameter, attested the skill and energy of these animals as woodchoppers. Cap. tried to get one so that we could eat it, but though he killed several he failed to reach them before they sank, and gave it up.

As we looked around we saw that almost imperceptibly we had entered the new canyon and at this camp (33) we were fairly within the embrace of its rugged cliffs which, devoid of all vegetation, rose up four hundred feet, sombre in colour, but picturesque from a tendency to columnar weathering that imparted to them a Gothic character suggestive of cathedrals, castles, and turrets. The next day was Sunday and as Beaman felt sick and we were not in a hurry, no advance was made but instead Prof. accompanied by Steward, Cap., and Jones climbed out for notes and observations. They easily reached the top by means of a small gulch. They got back early, reporting an increasing desolation in the country on both sides as far as they could see. They also saw two graves of great age, covered by stones. In the afternoon Prof. entertained us by reading aloud from Scott and so the day passed and night fell. Then the beavers became more active and worked and splashed around camp incessantly. They kept it up all through the dark hours as is their habit, but only Steward was disturbed by it. This would have been an excellent opportunity to learn something about their ways, but for my part I did not then even think of it.

By 7.30 in the morning of August 7th we were again on our way towards the depths ahead, between walls of rapidly increasing altitude showing that we were cutting into some great rock structure. Here and there we came to shoals that compelled us to get overboard and wade alongside lifting the boats at times. As these shoals had the peculiarity of beginning gradually and ending very abruptly we got some unexpected plunge baths during this kind of progression. But the air was hot, the thermometer being about 90° F., and being soaked through was not uncomfortable. At one place Prof. succeeded in shooting a beaver which was near the bank and it was secured before it could get to its hole, being badly wounded. Steward caught it around the middle from behind and threw it into the boat—he had jumped into the water—and there it was finished with an oar. It measured three feet from tip to tip. We had heard a good deal about beaver as food and would now have a chance to try it. About eleven o'clock, we stopped for examinations and for dinner on the right but, of course, could not yet cook the beaver. Prof., Steward, and Cap. climbed to the top of a butte 1050 feet above the river upon which they found a small monument left there by the Major on the former trip. Though this butte was so high the average of the walls was only about five hundred feet. We made seventeen miles this day.

That night our camp (No. 35) was again on an island. There Cap. skinned and dressed the beaver and turned over the edible portions to Andy who cooked some steak for breakfast the next morning. It tasted something like beef, but we were not enthusiastic for I fear this beaver belonged to the same geological epoch as the goose we had cooked at the upper end of the valley. Fortified by the beaver steak we pushed off and ran about a mile on a smooth river when a stop was made for pictures and geologising. This consumed the whole morning, a fact Andy took advantage of to make some beaver soup for dinner. This concoction was voted not a success and we turned to bacon and beans as preferable thereafter. Opposite this dinner place was a rough lateral canyon full of turrets and minarets which had the remarkable property of twice distinctly repeating a shout as loud as the original, and multiplying a rifle shot to peals of thunder. There had been people here before any white men, for Steward found an artificial wall across an indentation of the cliff, the first work of the ancient builders we had encountered. It was mysterious at the time, the South-western ruins having then not been discovered with one or two exceptions. We ascribed this wall, however, to the ancestors of the Moki (Hopi).

In the afternoon as we pulled along we came to a small rapid and the walls by this time being closer together and growing constantly higher, we knew that we were now fairly within the Canyon of Desolation and for about one hundred miles would have a rough river. Not more than two miles below our dinner camp we reached a locality where the stream doubled back on itself forming a vast and beautiful amphitheatre. We could not pass this by without taking a picture of it and Beaman was soon at work with his apparatus while I got out my pencils. The photograph did not turn out well, and Prof. determined to remain till the next day. Our camp was on the left in a thick grove of cottonwoods, and box-elders or ash-leaved maples, at the end of the point. As the sun sank away bats flew about and an insect orchestra began a demoniacal concert that shrilled through the night and made us feel like slaughtering the myriads if we could. The noises ceased with the day, or most of them, though some seemed to intensify with the light. We helped Beaman get his dark box and other paraphernalia up to the summit of the ridge back of camp, which was easy so far as climbing was concerned, the rocks rising by a series of shelves or steps. I made several pencil sketches there, which I have never seen since the close of the expedition. The crest of the promontory was about forty yards wide at its maximum and three yards at the minimum, with a length of three-fourths of a mile. From the middle ridge one could look down into the river on both sides, and it seemed as if a stone could almost be thrown into each from one standpoint. The opposite amphitheatre was perhaps one thousand feet high, beautifully carved by the rains and winds. It was named Sumner's Amphitheatre after Jack Sumner of the first expedition.

Several of our men climbed in different directions, but all did not succeed in getting out. The day turned out very cloudy with sprinkles of rain and Prof. decided to wait still longer to see if Beaman could get a good photograph, and we had another night of insect opera. The next day by noon the photographer had caught the scene and we continued our descending way. The river was perfectly smooth, except a small rapid late in the day, with walls on both sides steadily increasing their altitude. Desolation in its beginning is exactly the reverse of Lodore and Split Mountain. In the latter the entrance could hardly be more sudden, whereas the Canyon of Desolation pushes its rock walls around one so diplomatically that it is some little time before the traveller realises that he is caught. The walls were ragged, barren, and dreary, yet majestic. We missed the numerous trees which in the upper canyons had been so ornamental wherever they could find a footing on the rocks. Here there were only low shrubs as a rule and these mainly along the immediate edge of the water, though high up on north slopes pines began to appear. Altitude, latitude, and aridity combine to modify vegetation so that in an arid region one notices extraordinary changes often in a single locality. The walls still had the tendency to break into turrets and towers, and opposite our next camp a pinnacle stood detached from the wall on a shelf high above the water suggesting a beacon and it was named Lighthouse Rock. Prof. with Steward and Cap. in the morning, August 11th, climbed out to study the contiguous region which was found to be not a mountain range but a bleak and desolate plateau through which we were cutting along Green River toward a still higher portion. This was afterwards named the Tavaputs Plateau, East and West divisions, the river being the line of separation.

The walls now began to take on a vertical character rising above the water 1200 to 1800 feet, and at that height they were about a quarter of a mile apart. From their edges they broke back irregularly to a separation as nearly as could be determined of from three to five miles, the extreme summit being 2500 feet above the river.

While waiting for Prof. to come down from the cliffs, Bea-

Steward.

Canyon of Desolation.

Photograph by E. O. BEAMAN, 1871.

man made some photographs and then two boats dropped down a quarter of a mile where he made some more and Andy got dinner. I remained with the *Nell* and about eleven o'clock the climbers came. We went down on the boat to the noon camp, and as soon as we had refreshed the inner man we proceeded thinking it about time for rapids to appear. We had not gone far before we distinguished a familiar roar just preceding the turn of a bend which disclosed three lying within half a mile. They were not bad but the river was wide and shallow, making the descent more difficult than it would ordinarily have been. The river was now approaching its lowest stage, and we saw an uncomfortable looking lot of rocks. High water makes easy going but increases the risk of disaster; low water makes hard work, batters the boats, and delays progress, but as a rule it is less risky. All the boats cleared the first rapid without any difficulty, but in the second the *Nell* struck a sunken rock, though lightly, while our boat landed squarely on the top of a large boulder partially submerged, where we hung fast with the water boiling furiously around and almost coming over the sides. I tried to get out over the port bow but the current drew me under the boat and I had to get back. Jack concluded we were only fast by the extreme end of the keel and Jones coming forward Jack slid cautiously out over the stern and felt around with his feet till he touched the rock and put his weight on it. Thus relieved, the boat lifted slightly and shot away like an arrow but not before Jack leaped on again. As soon as we could we made land and watched the *Cañonita* which fared still worse. She struck so hard that two of the after ribs and some planks were stove in. They then extricated her and pulling her up on the rocky shore we went to work to repair with cleats made from a broken oar. This delayed us an hour and a half. Then saws and hammers were stowed away and the third rapid was run without a mishap. It was only the low stage of water that caused the trouble. A little farther on a fourth rapid was vanquished and we went into camp on the left bank in a cottonwood grove at the head of another. "If the rocks, they don't sthop us," sang Jack, "We will cross to Killiloo, whacky-whay!" And there were

6

plenty of rocks in the midst of foaming waters, but one great advantage of low water is the decreased velocity, and velocity on a river like this with so heavy and constant a fall is one of the chief factors to reckon with in navigation.

The high cliffs, two thousand feet, red and towering in the bright sun, became sombre and mysterious as the night shadows crept over them, the summits remaining bright from the last western rays when the river level was dim and uncertain. There was plenty of driftwood, and our fires were always cheery and comfortable. The nights were now quite cold, or at least chilly, while the days were hot as soon as the sun came over the edge of the cliffs. Through some of the narrow promontories at this particular camp there were peculiar perforations suggesting immense windows looking into some fairer land. I would have been glad to examine some of these closely, but as it was not necessary they were passed by. It would also have been difficult to reach them as they were very high up.

The rapid at our camp was a starter the next day on a line of them following one after the other till we had run without accident nine before halting for dinner; and nine in $6\frac{3}{4}$ miles was not a bad record. We landed for noon on the same spot where the first party had stopped and our last night's camp was also coincident with theirs, according to their map which we had for consultation. Prof. decided to remain here for the rest of the day and also the next one which was Sunday. Up in a high gulch some pine trees were visible, and Jack and I climbed up to them and collected several pounds of gum for repairing the boats. Sunday morning Prof., Jones, and Steward struck for the summit up the cliffs to get observations. An hour and a half of steady hard work put them 2576 feet above the river, but they were still three hundred feet below the general level of the great plateau which we were bisecting. Prof. thought he would like to make better time down the river, which we could easily have done up to this point, but if we arrived at the end of the canyon too soon we would have to wait there and it was better to distribute the wait as we went along. It was now August 14th and we were not due below till September 3d.

On Monday morning we pushed and pulled and lifted the boats through a shallow rapid half a mile long. It was hard work. Then came one which we ran, but the following drop was deemed too risky to trust our boats in, and they were lowered by lines. Then in a short distance this same process was repeated with hard work in a very bad place, and when we had finished that we were tired, hungry, wet, and cold, so under a cottonwood tree on the right we stopped for needed refreshment, and while it was preparing most of us hung our clothes on the branches of a fallen tree to dry. The rapid foaming and fuming presented so vigorous an appearance and made so much noise we thought it ought to be named, and it was called Fretwater Falls. At three o'clock we took up our oars again and were whirled along at runaway speed through a continuous descent for half a mile. After another half-mile a small rapid appeared, which we dashed through without a second thought, and then came our final effort of the day, a line-portage over a particularly bad spot. It was a difficult job, requiring great exertion in lifting and pushing and fending off, so when Prof. gave the word to camp on the left, we were all glad enough to do so. We had made only $5\frac{1}{4}$ miles and seven rapids. The let-downs had been hard ones, with a couple of men on board to fend off and two or three on the hawser holding back.

The next morning, August 15th, we made another let-down around a bad piece of river, and ran two or three small rapids before dinner. At the let-down the water dropped at least ten feet in two hundred yards, and Prof. estimated thirty in half a mile. The river was also narrow, not more than sixty or seventy feet in one place. Many rocks studded the rapids, and great caution had to be exercised both in let-downs and in runs, lest the boats should be seriously injured. With two or three more feet of water we could have run some that were now impossible. Fortunately there was always plenty of room on both banks, the cliffs being well back from the water. A series of small rapids gave us no special trouble, and having put them behind, we ran in at the head of a rough-looking one, had dinner, and then made a let-down. Starting on, we soon came to a very sharp rapid, which we ran, and found it was only an introduc-

tion to one following that demanded careful treatment Another let-down was the necessary course, and when it was
accomplished we stopped for the night where we were on the
sand, every man tired, wet, and hungry. We had made only
four miles. A significant note of warning was found here in
the shape of fragments of the unfortunate *No-Name* mixed up
with the driftwood, fully two hundred miles below the falls
where the wreck occurred.

The precipices surrounding us had now reached truly magnificent proportions, one section near our camp springing almost
vertically to a height of 2800 or 3000 feet. On the dizzy summit we could discern what had the appearance of an old-
fashioned log-cabin, and from this we called it " Log-cabin
Cliff." The cabin was in reality a butte of shale, as we could
see by means of our glasses, and of course of far greater size
than a real cabin, but from below the illusion was complete.
At this camp, No. 40, we remained the next day, Prof. wishing
to make some investigations. He and Jones crossed to the
other side and went down on foot two or three miles; then
returning he went up some distance, while the rest of us
mended our clothes, worked up notes, and did a score of little
duties that had been neglected in the river work. Jack and I
climbed up the cliffs and got more pine gum, with which we
caulked up the seams in our boat. Cap. kindly turned barber
and redeemed me from the danger of being classed as orang-
outang. The air was too hazy for photographing or for getting
observations from the summit, and Prof. concluded to stay till
next day at this place and then go to the top of the world; in
other words, to the summit. Very early in the morning,
August 17th, Steward and Cap. started with Prof. for the
climb. Keeping up the main canyon for a mile they came
to a side gorge where Prof. had been the day before, which
they followed for half a mile and then boldly mounted the
cliffs, reaching an altitude of 3100 feet above the river. While
they were gone, Jack and I climbed after more pine gum, and
succeeded in getting five or six pounds for future use. As I
was descending along a terrace, Jack being some distance behind
and above, a fine, large mountain sheep, sleek and clean, with

beautiful strong horns, sprang along four or five hundred feet from me, and stopped in full view listening to Jack's footsteps. I had no gun, and could only admire him till he bounded lightly away.

About one o'clock the climbing party came back. Steward had shot a mountain sheep with a revolver, only to find that a deep canyon intervened between him and his prize and there was no way of getting it.

About half past two we shoved out into the river again, running a small rapid immediately. The water was so shallow that our keel struck a number of times but no damage was done. We had hardly cleared this when we arrived at a drop of about six feet in a few yards with the whole river filled with bad rocks. At this place, according to the map made by the first party, their *Emma Dean* was capsised. We made a let-down and a quarter of a mile farther on repeated the operation, Following this were some swift shoals which brought us to another ugly descent where the *Nell* stove a hole in her side and came near upsetting. Prof. was knocked half out of the boat but got in again. The other boats we lowered by lines and they passed through uninjured. Near this point a fine clear little stream about a rod wide entered from the west. After running two more rapids Prof. decided to camp which we did on the right, Camp 41. Our run footed up 3¾ miles. Our camp was in some cottonwoods and we had to cross a wide rocky bar to get to it but it was preferable to camping on the sand. In this canyon there was generally a valley about one-quarter mile wide on one side or the other, and with the abundant supply of driftwood for fires and a whole river for drink we fared well. The great canyon now appeared deeper than at any point above, about three thousand feet we estimated. the walls being extremely precipitous. One cliff not far from camp appeared to be nearly perpendicular.

Steward got up very early the next morning in order to mend his shoes, and he succeeded so well as cobbler, we declared he had missed his calling, but we did not start till ten o'clock, waiting for Beaman to take views. The first thing we then did was to run a very shallow rapid, followed by another, long, difficult, narrow, and rocky. Then there was a short, easy one, with the next below compelling a very hard let-down. There was nothing but rocks, large rocks, so close together that it was all we could do to manœuvre the boats between them. There was no channel anywhere. For the greater part of the way we had to pull them empty over the rocks on drift-wood skids which taxed our muscles considerably and of course saturated our clothing for half the time we were in the water, as was always the case at let-downs. This over we had our noon ration of bread, bacon, and coffee and took a fresh start by running a nice, clear rapid and then another a half-mile below, and we thought we were getting on well when we saw ahead a fall of some ten feet in fourteen rods, turbulent and fierce. The only prudent thing for this rapid was a let-down and we went at it at once. It was the usual pulling, hauling, fending, and pushing, but we got through with it after a while and naming it at the suggestion of some one, Melvin Falls, we went on to the eighth and last rapid for the day. This was half a mile long and very rocky, but it was thought we could run it and all went through safely except the *Nell* which caught her keel on a rock and hung for a moment, then cleared and finished with no damage. We made Camp 42 on a sand-hill. These hills were a feature of the wide banks, being blown up by the winds, sometimes to a height of fifteen or twenty feet. Our run for the day was less than five miles, yet as we had passed eight rapids one way and another, we were all pretty tired and of course wet and hungry. A good big camp-fire was quickly started, our dry garments from the rubber bags donned in place of the flapping wet ones, and we were entirely comfortable, with the bread baking in the Dutch oven, the coffee or tea steaming away, and the inspiring fragrance of frying bacon wafted on the evening air. When we stopped long enough Andy would give us boiled beans or stewed dried apples as a treat. If we desired to enliven the conversation all that was necessary was to start the subject of the "light" back at the camp where we first met Douglas Boy. Every one would soon be involved except Prof. who only laughed and inserted from time to time a well-chosen remark to keep up the interest. Jack would always give us a half-dozen songs and to this Steward would add a solo on the mouth-organ. The evenings were growing longer, and we sat closer to the fire. Sometimes Cap. and Clem would play a game of euchre, but no one else seemed to care anything about cards. Our beds, when possible, were made by first putting down willows or cedar twigs in regular order, on which the blankets would be spread making a luxurious bed on which sleep instantly overtook us, with the sound of falling water generally the last thing and the first in our ears.

At 7.30 the next morning, August 19th, we were speeding on our way and ran the rapid which had sent its lullaby to our camp. Another came right after it, shallow and bad, and then one more where the channel was beset with innumerable boulders hidden under the surface. Happily the boats were not seriously damaged, they needed no repairs, and we kept on to the next barrier which proved to be not runable with any prospect of getting through whole so we made a portage. Then there was a rapid we ran easily, but as if to revenge itself for making one gentle for us, the river obliged us to work a laborious passage at the next two. We had good hard work, lowering by lines, wading alongside where necessary to ease the boats, or clinging to their sides where the water was deep, while the men on shore at the hawser's end lowered away to a shallow place. We were glad to halt at 11.30 for dinner, and a short rest.

There was a heavy rapid beside us as we ate, and Steward named it Chandler Falls. It had a descent of about twelve feet in twenty rods. On the opposite side of the river a clear little creek came in, and this was named Chandler Creek, Chandler being the maiden name of Steward's wife. Beaman and Clem selected a position with their photographic outfit and made some photographs of us as we were working the boats through. A mile below we halted on the right for Beaman to get more views. None of his photographs of the rapids came out well as the plates were too slow. Up a gulch on the right we could see a remarkable topographic feature, nothing less than a gigantic aperture, or natural arch, in the cliff. It had a span of at least 300 feet with a height of about half as much. It was 1500 or 1800 feet above the river. Hundreds of cedar trees grew around the arch on the ledges of the huge wall through which it was cut by the action of the elements.

The cliffs everywhere were now becoming more broken, and there was an entrance somewhere from the back country, or it may have been up the canyon, for we discovered remains of tipis and camps with metates or grinding stones, the first evidences of human beings we had seen since the "Moki" wall. This and the breaking of the cliffs caused us to believe that we were nearing the end of the canyon. Prof. with Jones and Steward went down-stream on foot for a distance to see what was coming next and found a stretch of very bad water. On the return a rattlesnake struck at Steward but luckily failed to hit him. Steward killed it. We concluded to stop for the night where we were with the day's record—four rapids run, three let-downs, and 4⅝ miles in distance. This camp was not satisfactory and we got out of it early the next morning. While Beaman was making some views across the river we lowered the other two boats through one rapid and then ran them through a second in three-quarters of a mile to a better camping place, from which we went back and helped the third boat, the *Cañonita*, do the same. Prof. wanted to climb out, but the morning being half gone he planned to start after dinner and meanwhile he read Emerson aloud to us till Andy shouted his "Go fur it boys!" Accompanied by Steward and Clem, in the afternoon he climbed up 1200 or 1500 feet to a point where he could see down the river two or three miles. They counted seven rapids, and confirmed the belief that the walls were breaking. The surrounding country was made up of huge ridges that ran in toward the river from five miles back.

Our Camp 44 was in a little valley about a quarter of a mile wide, the bottom covered with cedars and greasewood. The scenery was still on a magnificent scale but barren and desolate. The next morning, August 21st, we were under way at 7.30 and plunged almost immediately into the rapids which had been sighted from the cliffs above. In a little over four

miles we let down six times. A seventh rapid we ran and then
stopped for noon on the left, every man, as usual, soaking wet.
A little rain fell but not enough to consider. After dinner
four more rapids were put behind; we ran all but one at which
we made a let-down. Our record for this day was eleven
rapids in a trifle less than seven miles, and we were camped at
the head of another rapid which was to form our eye-opener
in the morning. The walls receded from the river three-
fourths of a mile and now, though still very high, had more the
appearance of isolated cliffs.

We had not a single unpleasant incident till Beaman on this
day ran one rapid contrary to Prof.'s orders. He was sharply
reprimanded, and for the time being his tendency to insubor-
dination and recklessness was checked. He probably did not
mean to be either, but his confidence in his ability to steer
through anything led him astray. In the evening by the
camp-fire light Prof. read aloud from *Miles Standish.* Although a heavy wind blew sand all over us, no one seemed to
complain.

The next morning, August 22d, the first thing we did was
to run the rapid beside our camp, a beautiful chute, swift,
long, and free from rocks. Immediately below this was one
half a mile long in the form of a crescent, the river making
a sharp bend with a bad current, but we ran it. This was, in
fact, a part of the other rapid, or it might be so classed, as was
frequently the case where the descent was nearly continuous
from one rapid to another. The river was very narrow at this
place, not more than seventy-five feet wide. We had not gone
far before we reached a rapid where it was prudent to lower
the boats, and not more than a few hundred yards below this
there was another of a similar character but necessitating
harder work. Then we were brought face to face with one
more that could not be run with safety on the present stage of
water, though we ran a part of it and made a let-down past the
remainder. When this was finally accomplished with everything in good order, we found ourselves in front of still another that refused to grant us clear passage, and we worked
the boats down with lines as in the previous rapids without

removing the cargoes. The method was the usual one for the let-downs, three or four men on the line and a couple on board the boat to manœuvre and protect her. Having by this time advanced three and one-eighth miles from last night's camp we stopped for dinner. On taking up the oars again the first rapid was a fine, clear descent with extremely large waves, through which all three boats dashed with exhilarating speed, leaping part of their length out of the water as their velocity carried them zipping over the crests. Our boat happened to strike near the finish on a submerged rock to the right of the main channel and near shore and there she hung for some moments. The first boat had landed below and some of the men quickly came up to where I could throw them our line, and this pulled us off without any damage worth mentioning. A little below this we ran another successfully and had not gone far before we were astonished at the sight of a horse grazing unconcernedly on some low bluffs on the right. Prof. had discovered this horse with his field glass while we stopped above to examine one of the rapids. He thought it might indicate the presence of the Major, or of Indians, but he did not mention the matter to any of us. When we were at a good point, and just as all hands had discovered the animal, he ordered a sharp landing on the same side. We ran in quickly. Prof. went up the bank and gave several shouts while we held ourselves ready for action. There was no response. He then went to the horse and found it very lame which, coupled with the absence of any indication of visitors within recent months, caused us to conclude that the horse had been abandoned by Indians who had been encamped here a good while before. We left the place and running another rapid, a little one, we came to a fine spot for a camp on the right at the beginning of a heavy rapid, and there we stayed for the night.

There was now a marked change in the geology, and fossiliferous beds, which for a long time had been absent, appeared. The canyon walls also broke away considerably. The next morning it was decided that we should remain at this camp till after dinner for observation work. I went out with Steward to help him gather fossils, and Beaman took some views, while the others occupied themselves with various duties. The afternoon began by letting the boats by line past the rapid at camp which Beaman called Sharp Mountain Falls, from a pointed peak overhead. There was a drop of about fifteen feet in thirty rods. Beaman wanted to photograph us in the midst of our work, and got ready for it, but a rain-storm came on and we had to wait till it cleared for him to get the picture We then went ahead dashing through a pretty rapid with a swift current, and next had a long stretch of rapid, though not difficult river, making in all 2¾ miles, and camping at five o'clock on the left. The only trouble we had was that in choosing one of four channels our boat got where she was inevitably drawn into the top of a sunken dead tree lodged in the rocks and my starboard row lock was broken off. On shore Steward killed another rattlesnake, of which there seemed to be a good many along the river.

We were now actually out of the Canyon of Desolation and in the beginning of what the Major at first called Coal Canyon, then Lignite, and finally Gray, the name it bears to-day, because of the colour of the walls. The division between the two canyons was the break down where we had seen the horse. Casting up we found that the Canyon of Desolation is ninety-seven miles long. Early the next morning, August 24th, we pulled away from Camp 47 soon running two small rapids of no consequence, and in three miles came to a descent of some ten feet in a very short space, where we made a let-down. Three fair rapids were next run easily when we halted to examine a hard-looking place where we let down again. An encounter with three more, two of them each a quarter of a mile long, took us till noon, though we ran them and we came to a stop for dinner. Now the walls had narrowed, the canyon being about half a mile wide at the top—sometimes not more than a quarter. The colour was buff, and there were seams of coal and lignite in places. On one or the other side the cliffs were nearly vertical for about three hundred feet then breaking back to jagged heights reaching about two thousand feet. After dinner having run two more rapids without trouble we arrived at a very difficult locality where the first cliffs, six hundred feet high, came down vertically on both sides quite close to the water. We saw how we could navigate it, but at flood time it would be a most serious proposition, as there would be no footing on either side, unless, perhaps on the huge masses of fallen rock. At the present stage we were able to let the boats down by lines. Then we had two easy rapids, followed by another not more difficult but less safe. A little farther on we ran two more which completed the record for the day, and we were glad to camp with a total run of 12⅜ miles, and many rapids with three let-downs. A feature of the cliffs this day was numerous alcoves and grottoes worn into the sandstone some of them like great caverns with extremely narrow canyons leading into them.

In the morning Prof. with Jones, Cap., and Steward climbed out. The country was elevated above the river about two thousand feet, a wild labyrinth of ragged gulches, gullies, and sharp peaks devoid of vegetation except a few piñons on some slopes, the whole presenting a picture of complete desolation. At a quarter past twelve we were again gliding down on a stiff current. We ran seven easy rapids and let-down by lines twice, before arriving about three o'clock at the mouth of a stream-bed sixty feet wide, which Prof. said was Little White, or Price River. The mouth was so devoid of water that we camped on the smooth sand, it being the only ground free from brush. A sudden rise or cloud-burst would have made it an active place for us but we decided to take the risk for one night. Prof. and Jones tried to get out by following up this river bed but they were not successful. Game was abundant and they thought there might be an Indian trail but they saw none. In the evening Steward gave us a mouth-organ recital and Jack sang a lot of his songs in fine style. The air was soft and tranquil, and knowing we had now conquered the Canyon of Desolation without a serious mishap we all felt well satisfied.

In the morning, August 25th, breakfast was disposed of early, the boats were put in trim and away we went again on a good current running many rapids and making one let-down in a distance of eight miles. I counted fourteen rapids, Steward ten or eleven, Prof. only eight, showing that it is not always easy to separate the rapids where they come so close together. In one the river was no more than thirty feet wide with big waves that made the boats jump and ship water. We reached a bend and saw the end of the canyon only a mile or two away, but we had to make the let-down mentioned before we got there. Our camp, Number 50, was made about noon, just inside the mouth of the canyon on the left, opposite a high, beautiful pinnacle we called Cathedral Butte afterwards changing the name to Gunnison. Here we would wait till the time appointed for the Major to join us according to the plan. Gray Canyon was now also behind us with its thirty-six miles and numerous rapids. Adding to it the ninety-seven miles of Desolation made the total canyon from Wonsits Valley 133 miles with a descent of about 550 feet distributed through a hundred rapids, some small, some heavy. The entire fall from our starting point was now some two thousand feet. Prof. and Jones went down the valley two miles with the hope of seeing signs of the Major but not a human being was to be found anywhere.

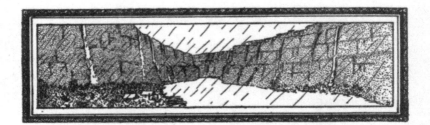

CHAPTER VIII

Return of the Major—Some Mormon Friends—No Rations at the Elusive Dirty Devil — Captain Gunnison's Crossing — An All-night Vigil for Cap. and Clem—The Land of a Thousand Cascades—A Bend Like a Bow-knot and a Canyon Labyrinthian—Cleaving an Unknown World—Signs of the Oldest Inhabitant—Through the Canyon of Stillwater to the Jaws of the Colorado.

THERE was little energy in our camp the day after our arrival at the end of the long struggle with Desolation and Gray canyons, and, also, it being Sunday, we lounged around in a state of relaxation, joyful that we did not have to roll up our blankets and stow them and everything else in the rubber bags and pack the cabins to go on. The boats had been unloaded and hauled on the beach, which was smooth sand, to dry out preparatory to our caulking and repairing them with the pine gum collected in Desolation. During the morning Prof. sent Jack and me down the river a short distance to put up a signal, a small American flag, on the lower end of an island, where it could easily be seen by any one looking for us. All hands kept an ear open for signal shots, which we hoped to hear soon, and have the Major once more in our company. After dinner Prof. and Steward took another walk down the open valley about five miles to reconnoitre, but though they came upon remains of a great many Indian camps, all were old, and the valley appeared as silent and deserted as it was desolate and barren. Along the river there were a few groves of cottonwood, the only vegetation of any consequence to be seen.

Through this valley passed the famous trail from Santa Fé to Los Angeles, laid out in 1830 by that splendid pioneer, William Wolfskill. The reason he came so far north was because there was no place to cross the canyons below that was known.[1] This path was occasionally travelled for years, and became celebrated as the "Old Spanish Trail." Here it was that Captain Gunnison of our army in his notable explorations crossed in 1853 on his westward journey, which a few days later proved fatal to him, as he was killed by the Gosi-Utes. Before leaving he established the latitude and longitude of this crossing, which ever after bore his name.[2] Together with the mouth of the Uinta, the mouth of Henry's Fork, and the mouth of Diamond Creek, this made four points astronomically fixed before the Major came between the Union Pacific crossing and the end of the Grand Canyon. Diamond Creek mouth was determined accurately by Ives in 1858. The trappers and fur hunters between 1824 and 1840, men like Jim Bridger and Kit Carson, had roamed more or less over the region we had come through, and occasionally they had tried to see the river in the canyons. The aridity of the country generally held them back. Ashley, as already noted, had made the passage of Red Canyon, and the trapper Meek with several companions had gone through Lodore and Whirlpool one winter on the ice. Frémont, Simpson, Berthoud, Selden, and some other scientific explorers had passed here and there reconnoitring, and Macomb in 1859 had made a reconnaissance to the south and south-west of Gunnison Crossing, so that a general idea of the character of the region had been obtained and a kind of approximate topography had been tentatively thrown in, yet it was mainly an unknown wilderness so far as record went, particularly contiguous to the river. But south from the San Rafael to the Paria and west to the High Plateaus forming the southward continuation of the Wasatch Range, an area of at least 10,000 square miles, there was still a completely unknown country. Indeed, even from the Paria on down to

[1] In fact there was only one practicable place, El Vado de los Padres, and that was difficult. The alternative would have been to cross Arizona south of the Colorado. By this Gunnison Crossing route there were better wood, water, and grass to compensate for distance.

[2] It is here that the Denver and Rio Grande railway crossed, bridging the river in 1883. From here also the Brown Expedition started in May, 1889, and the Best Expedition in 1891.

the Grand Wash the region on the right was hardly better understood, though there were several Mormon settlements on the headwaters of the Virgin, and recently the settlement of Kanab had been made farther east. On the south of the Grand Canyon Ives had reconnoitred to some extent, reaching the river at the mouth of Diamond Creek, but at no other point above that did he come to the river nor get anywhere near its canyon above the tributary Habasu (Cataract).

In the entire stretch from Gunnison Crossing to the end of the Grand Canyon, a distance of 587½ miles, but two points were known where the river could be crossed, the Crossing of the Fathers (El Vado de los Padres), about latitude 37, and the mouth of the Paria, only thirty-five miles lower down. This latter place had been discovered by Jacob Hamblin, or "Old Jacob," as he was familiarly called, and he was the first white man to cross there, which he did in October, 1869. He was a well-known Mormon scout and pioneer of those days. He forded at El Vado his first time in 1858, possibly the first white man after Escalante, though the ford was known to at least Richard Campbell, the trapper, in 1840 or earlier. In 1862 Jacob circumtoured the Grand and Marble canyons, going from St. George by way of the Grand Wash to the Moki Towns and returning by way of El Vado. Thus the region below us to the left or east had been reconnoitred in a general way by Macomb, while that to the right or west had not had even bird's-eye exploration. Until the Major's unrivalled first descent in 1869 the river was equally unknown. Even above Gunnison Crossing, despite the spasmodic efforts at exploration referred to, the river had remained a geographical enigma, and to the Major belongs the sole credit for solving this great problem throughout its length from the Union Pacific crossing in Wyoming to the mouth of the Virgin River—the last problem of this kind within the United States. Hampered as the first party was by loss of provisions and instruments, they nevertheless made a plat of the immediate course of the stream, portions of which were lost with the men who were killed by the Shewits on leaving the party near the end of the Grand Canyon. So far we had not been bothered in the least by lack of provisions, instruments, time, health, or strength, and we had been able to make an accurate meander of the river, note the topography and geology as we went along, climb out frequently to examine the surrounding country, and in every way carry forward the scientific work as planned. It was now a question whether or not we would get our supplies at the next appointed station, the mouth of the Dirty Devil River, or whether we would be obliged to weigh out what we had, and by limiting ourselves to strict rations put the work through anyhow. By September 5th we would probably have information on this point, that being the limit set for our waiting. Should the Major not arrive by that time, it would mean that we were to go on as best we could with the supplies on hand.

Monday was devoted to overhauling the boats, while Prof. took observations. During a rest he also read aloud to us from Tennyson,

> " A land of streams! some, like a downward smoke,
>   Slow dropping veils of thinnest lawn, did go;
>   And some thro' wavering lights and shadows broke,
>   Rolling a slumbrous sheet of foam below.
>   They saw the gleaming river seaward flow
>   From the inner land; far off three mountain-tops,
>   Three silent pinnacles of aged snow,
>   Stood sunset-flushed; and, dew'd with showery drops,
>   Up-clomb the shadowy pine above the copse."

He was an excellent reader and we enjoyed his various selections. They gave variety and new drift to our thought which was refreshing and beneficial. When the boats were completed they were returned to the river, but for the time being the rations and other things forming their cargoes were permitted to remain on shore covered by the paulins. The boats swung gracefully at their lines and Jack was tempted to get out his fishing tackle in the early evening and seat himself on one of the cabins to wait patiently for a bite. Softly the river rippled by with an innocent murmur as if it had never been guilty of anything but the calmest and best-behaved motion such as now reflected the great pinnacle across the way standing 1200 feet clear cut against the glowing sky. The air was balmy, no wind blew, and a universal quiet prevailed when suddenly Jack uttered several exclamations not entirely in harmony with the moment. He thought his precious hook was caught on a snag. Pulling gently in order not to break his line the snag lifted with it and presently he was astounded to see, not the branch of a tree or a water-logged stick, but the head of an enormous fish appear above the surface. Had there been some splashing he would have been prepared for the extraordinary sight but the monster came with barely a wriggle as if he did not know what it was to be caught. He was successfully landed in the middle cabin of the boat, which was empty except for some water, and lay there unhurt as if it were the natural place for him. Casting again another of the same kind came forth and then a third. The longest appeared to be the length of the cabin, as he floated in the water, and that was four feet. He was at least thirty or thirty-six inches with a circumference of fifteen inches. The others were considerably shorter but nevertheless very large fish. The big one was killed for food and Steward noted that the heart after removal kept up pulsations of twenty beats to the minute for half an hour. These fish are now called Colorado River salmon. The flesh was white and they seemed to us good eating.

On Tuesday, August 29th, the third day of our waiting, as we were about to return to various occupations after dinner three rapid shots broke suddenly on the quiet air from down the valley. It was our signal. "The Major" cried all in a breath, and a reply signal was instantly fired. Clem and I were sent immediately to the end of the island, carrying our rifles, of course, for while we had little doubt as to who it was, there might be a surprise. We hurried down while the others watched the bank beyond. As soon as we cleared the bushes and could see the western shore we distinguished the Major and a stranger by his side, with horses. We shouted to them directions for reaching our camp and they rode up till they came opposite to it whence they were ferried over while Jones took the horses down to their camp about four miles below.

The Major reported an absolute failure in the attempt to find a way to the mouth of the Dirty Devil River, and he had not himself been able to do anything about it. The first trial was eastward from Glencove, a Mormon settlement on the Sevier. It failed because the Indian guides refused to proceed beyond fifty miles and it was not practicable to go on without them. A second party was then sent in a little later under Old Jacob north-eastward from Kanab. They reached a river flowing to the Colorado at about the right place and for many miles followed it with extreme difficulty and hazard even at the low stage of water prevailing, down through a deep, narrow canyon. Sometimes they were compelled to swim their horses where the rapid stream filled the chasm from wall to wall, and continual crossing and re-crossing were necessary from one footing to another. This perilous effort was also abandoned. The Major had gone to Salt Lake and from there, being informed of these results, down to a village called Manti whence he made his way across country to our present position, with several pack animals bringing three hundred pounds of flour, a quantity of jerked beef, and twenty pounds of sugar. This was not exactly adequate to the circumstances but he probably thought it was all he could get through with to the meeting place appointed in the time alloted. While he and Fred Hamblin, the man accompanying him, were eating their dinner, we packed the boats, and when all was ready took them on board, the Major in his old place in the armchair on our boat, and Hamblin on the middle deck of another. In the run down to the camp Hamblin was very uncomfortable for he was not accustomed to boats, especially to boats that ran so fast. There were two little rapids, some swift chutes, and in several places the river shoaled and we grated slightly on the gravel.

Stretching away westward from Gunnison Butte we saw an exquisitely modelled line of cliffs, some portions being a clear azure blue. At first it was proposed to name them Henry Cliffs, but they were finally called from their colour, Azure. Presently we arrived at the camp where we found another man, Lyman Hamblin, a son of Jacob and nephew of Fred. They were both Mormons from Kanab near the Arizona

line in southern Utah.   They had a large amount of mail for
us and every one fell to reading letters and papers. August
30th and 31st were spent here getting our work in shape, making sketches and observations, as well as writing letters and
helping the Hamblins prepare for their trip back through the
wild country.   They had met with no Indians on the way in
and they hoped to be equally fortunate going back having no
desire to see any.   In this, as they told me afterwards, they
were not successful.   They mounted their horses, Friday, September 1st, about four in the afternoon when the west was
taking on a rich evening glow and turning in that direction
vanished, with a wave of the hand and a good-bye, into the
mystery of colour, bearing our letters, the geographic data,
the geologic notes, and all the other material which we had
collected since leaving the mouth of the Uinta, and which it
was thought advisable to send out both for safety and to relieve
our crowded cabins.   They said that the next evening before
they realised it they found themselves so near a large encamp-
ment of Indians that there was no getting away, and they did
the only thing they could sensibly do, rode boldly on straight
into the midst of the strangers with the hope that the band
belonged where they were on the west side of the river, in
which case they were surely peaceful.   Both men spoke Ute well
and they had had long experience.   The Indians proved to be
entirely friendly, and the Hamblins camped with them for the
night; not because they wanted to but because they thought it
inexpedient to do otherwise.   When they left us we felt that
they were old friends for they were fine men and most agreeable.
Besides, with the exception of Basor who had driven the team
down from Salt Lake to the Uinta with our rations, they were
the only white men which those of us who had not visited the
Uinta Agency had seen since the Harrells in Brown's Park, nearly
three months before.   An hour after their departure we pushed
off and ran down about half a mile, passing one little rapid, to
the old crossing where we stopped on the left for the night.
Beaman and I were commissioned to go back to our Camp Gunnison to get a saw which had been forgotten there; we could
not afford to lose so valuable an implement.   A well-beaten

Indian trail leading up the river gave us easy going and we
made good time. The effects of light and colour all around us
playing over the mountains and valley gave the surroundings
a weird interest. The day was ending. Long shadows stole
across the strange topography while the lights on the variegated
buttes became kaleidoscopic. As for us, we appeared ridicu-
lously inadequate. We ought to have been at least twenty feet
high to fit the hour and the scene. Gradually the lights faded,
the shadows faded, then both began to merge till a soft grey-
blue dropped over all blending into the sky everywhere except
west where the burnish of sunset remained. Before dark the
old camp was reached; we found the saw by the last dying rays
and then picked our backward path by starlight following
the trail as we had come. Silence and the night were one as
in the countless years that had carved the dim buttes from the
rocks of the world primeval when man was not. Beautiful is
the wilderness at all times, at all times lovely, but under the
spell of the twilight it seems to enfold one in a tender embrace,
pushing back the sordid, the commonplace, and obliterating
those magnified nothings that form the weary burden of civil-
ised man. With keen appreciation we tramped steadily on
till at last we perceived through the night gloom the cheerful
flicker of our camp-fire, a sight always welcome, for the
camp-fire to the explorer is home.

At eight the next morning our business was resumed with
the Major happy in his accustomed place. We made a nice
run of eighteen miles on a smooth, shallow river, with broken,
picturesque low cliffs and isolated buttes everywhere. The
valley was wide and filled with these rocky hills. For a quarter
of a mile on each side of the river there were cottonwood
groves offering fine spots for camping, before and after crossing.
There seemed to be several places where crossing was accomplished. At one of these we discovered where some Indians
had been in camp a few hours before. The placidity of the
river permitted the lashing together of the boats once more for
a time and while we drifted this way down with the easy current the Major and Prof. took turns at reading aloud from
Whittier. *Mogg Megone* was one selection that was quite in

harmony with the surroundings while other poems offered a delightful contrast. There were songs, too, and I specially identify with this particular locality that old college favourite, *Dear Evelina, Sweet Evelina* which everybody sang, and which the Major often sang alone as he peered ahead into the vista unfolding.

Before night the valley narrowed, the banks looked more like low canyon walls, and the current stiffened. A clump of small cottonwoods suggested a camp as the sun ran down and there we halted. Nor did we go on the next day as the Major desired to go out to a ridge lying to the west, which he had seen from his horse on his way to us across country. Jones went with him and they came back with a fine collection of Cretaceous fossils. Steward and Cap. also went collecting and were successful. Our surroundings were now even more peculiar than heretofore. In many places the region was absolutely barren of all vegetation; thousands of acres at a time had upon them hardly a living plant of any description, being simply bare and barren rock, as devoid of soil as the deck of a ship. Prof. took observations for latitude and longitude and the rest of us were busy at our usual affairs. We had very little time to spare when the various necessary duties had been regularly attended to.

As we went on the next morning the desolation of the surroundings increased, if that were possible, and it was easy to read in this one cause of the tardiness of its exploration. The acreage of bare rock grew wider and broader. The buttes now often turned to walls about 150 feet high, all much broken, but indicating the approach to another closing in of the rocks upon us. Many of these buttes were beautiful in their castellated form as well as because of a picturesque banded character, and opposite our dinner-camp, which was on a ledge of rock, was one surprisingly symmetrical, resembling an artificial structure. I thought it looked like an art gallery, and the Major said it ought to be named after the artist, so he called it " Dellenbaugh's Butte " then and there. Another singular feature of this day was a number of alkaline springs discovered bubbling up from the bottom of a sort of bayou

Colorado River White Salmon.
Photograph by the Denver, Colorado Canyon, and Pacific Railway Survey under
ROBERT BREWSTER STANTON, 1889.

Dellenbaugh Butte.
Near Mouth of San Rafael.
Photograph by E. O. BEAMAN, 1871.

or branch of the river. There were at least seventy-five of them, one throwing a column six or eight inches above the surface of the water here about two feet deep. We thought the place worth a name, and called it Undine Springs. Three or four miles below the butte named after me we arrived at the mouth of a river, twenty-five feet wide and eight or ten inches deep, coming in from the right. This was the San Rafael. Our camp was made near some cottonwoods between its left bank and the Green. As soon as we landed we perceived that the ground was strewn with flaked chips of chalcedony, jasper, and similar stones. It was plain that here was a favourite workshop of the native arrowhead maker, an artisan now vanished forever. Numerous well-finished beautiful arrowheads of stone were found, all being placed in the general collection for the Smithsonian Institution. Our Camp 54 was elevated considerably above the river, and the surroundings being open, we had views in all directions. Towards the east we could see the Sierra La Sal, two clusters of rounded peaks, forty or fifty miles away, forming a majestic picture. The place was easy of access, and had been a favourite resort for natives, several acres of camp remains being found. In the morning Prof. began a series of observations to fix the position of the mouth of the San Rafael, while the Major and Jones, with rations, blankets, etc., on their backs for a two days' trip, started early up the tributary stream to see what kind of a country it flowed through. Steward feeling somewhat under the weather did not attempt to do anything, while the photographer and the others busied themselves in their respective lines. The following day the Major and Jones returned as planned, having traced the San Rafael for twenty-five miles. Before they arrived Cap. and Clem went across the Green to travel eastward to some high red buttes, one of which they intended to climb for topographical purposes. These buttes loomed up in a striking way, and appeared to be no more than six miles off even to Cap.'s experienced eye. The Major described the drainage basin of the San Rafael as wofully barren and desolate, like the rest of our surroundings. They had seen mountains lying beyond the Dirty Devil River, which were the range we then called the Unknown Mountains, there being no record of any one ever having seen them before the Major on his first trip.

Steward, recovering his poise, walked back alone on the east bank of the Green four miles to Dellenbaugh's Butte to examine it and the intervening geology. He found the butte to be about four hundred feet high and composed of stratified gypsum, thinly bedded and of fine quality.

As evening approached we looked for the return of Cap. and Clem, especially when the supper hour arrived, but twilight came, then darkness, and still their footfall was not heard. The Major was greatly disturbed over their failure to come, fearing they had gotten out of water, missed their way, and might now be suffering or demoralised in the arid wastes to eastward. He ordered a large fire to be built on a high spot near camp, where it would be visible for miles in the direction the missing men had gone. We divided into watches of two hours each to keep the fire going, in order that the men should have a guide if they were trying to reach the river in the night. I was called for my turn at two in the morning, and read Whittier while feeding the flames. The sky was mottled with clouds driving impetuously across the zenith, the bright moon gleaming through the interstices as they rapidly passed along. My attention was divided between the Quaker poet, the blazing fire, the mysterious environment into which I peered from time to time, and the flying scud playing hide-and-seek with the moon. At three I called Andy, who had breakfast ready before five, and all hands were up prepared to start on a search. By the time we had eaten there was light enough for operations to begin, and the Major, accompanied by Jack, carrying between them two days' rations and as much water as possible, were put across the Green to strike out directly eastward. A couple of hours later Prof. took a boat, with Steward and me to man it and another supply of food and water, and ran down the river a mile, where we headed back into the dry region to intersect at a distance the route the Major was following. We had not gone far before signal shots came to our ears, and through a glass turned in that direction we rejoiced to see that the Major and Jack had met the lost ones and all was well.

Prof. directed me to go back on foot to our camp with instructions for the other boats to come down, while he, in response to further signals, dropped his boat to a point nearer to the position of the rescue party and easier for them to reach. Cap. had underestimated the distance to the butte, which was twice as far as he thought. They walked eight hours to get there only to discover that scaling it was out of the question. A mile and a half beyond they found one they could climb, but by the time they had completed their observations on top of this evening overtook them and they were at least fifteen miles from camp. Having consumed their lunch at noon and drank all their water they were in something of a predicament, but luckily found some water-pockets in the barren rock, recently filled by the rains, so they did not suffer for thirst, and going hungry is not dangerous. Over the wide surfaces of bare rock they travelled toward camp till night forced them to wait for daylight, when they kept on till they met the Major and Jack with water and food.

No sooner had I arrived at the camp than the sky which was leaden and low began to drop its burden upon us. Packing up could not be done till the rain slackened, and we sheltered ourselves as well as we could. As we waited a deep roaring sound from not far off presently fell on our ears and we were puzzled to explain it till an examination showed a recently dry gulch filled with a muddy torrent which leaped the low cliff into the river, a sullen cascade. The San Rafael, too, was a booming flood. We packed the boats as soon as we could and ran down about two miles and a half to where the first boat was. Cliffs bordered the river again, 50 to 100 feet high, then 200 or 300, and we saw we were in the beginning of the next canyon called from its winding course, Labyrinth. Over these straight walls hundreds of beautiful cascades born of the rain were plunging into the river. They were of all sizes, all heights, and almost all colours, chocolate, amber, and red predominating. The rocky walls, mainly of a low purplish-red tint, were cut into by the river till the outside curves of the bends were perpendicular and sometimes slightly more than perpendicular, so that some of the cascades fell clear without a break. The acres of bare rock composing the surface of the land on both sides collected the rain as does the roof of a house, and the rills and rivulets rapidly uniting soon formed veritable floods of considerable proportions seeking the bosom of the river. This seemed the most fantastic region we had yet encountered. Buttes, pinnacles, turrets, spires, castles, gulches, alcoves, canyons and canyons, all hewn, "as the years of eternity roll" out of the verdureless labyrinth of solid rock, made us feel more than ever a sense of intruding into a forbidden realm, and having permanently parted from the world we formerly knew.

About noon we caught up to the other boat and all had dinner together, happy that nothing serious had befallen Cap. and Clem. During the whole afternoon rain steadily fell upon the top of this rock-roofed world till the river rose several inches while its colour turned to a dull yellow, then to a red, showing how heavy the rainfall had been in the back country. We had our rubber ponchos on but we were more or less damp and we began to notice that summer had passed for the air was chilly. The river was perfectly smooth making navigation easy and we were able to pull steadily along with no interruption from rapids. The walls ever increased their height while over the edges the numberless astonishing rain cascades continued to play, varying their volume according to the downpour from the sky. Before long the cliffs were from 800 to 1000 feet high, often perpendicular, giving the waterfalls grand plunges. These graceful tributaries were now occasionally perfectly clear and they sometimes fell so far without a break that they vanished in feathery white spray. A projecting ledge at times might gather this spray again to form a second cascade before the river level was reached. The scene was quite magical and considering the general aridity for a large part of the year, it appeared almost like a phantasm.

> "A land of streams! some, like a downward smoke,
>   Slow dropping veils of thinnest lawn, did go."

The river twisted this way and that with the tongues of the bends filled with alluvial deposit bearing dense clumps of scrub-oak, and grass. Each new bend presented a fresh picture withthe changing waterfalls leaping over by the dozen till we might have thought ourselves in some Norwegian fiord, and we gave far more attention to admiring the scenery than to navigating the boats. Late in the day we landed at the left on the point of a bend and chopped a path through the thick oak brush to a grassy glade, where we soon had the paulins stretched across oars supported by other oars forming comfortable shelters in front of which huge fires of dead oak and driftwood were kept going to dry things out. Andy set his pots to boiling and supper was soon prepared.

All night the rain fell but our shelters kept us dry and every one had a good rest. When the morning of September 8th dawned clear and bracing we met it with good spirits, though the spirits of our party seldom varied no matter what the circumstances, and every man took as much personal interest in the success of the expedition as if he were entirely responsible for it.

In order that Beaman might take some pictures and the topographers get notes, no move was made. Prof. climbed out obtaining a wide view in all directions and securing valuable data. I also went up on the cliffs and made a pencil sketch, and in the afternoon we explored a peculiar three-mouthed side canyon across the river. Three canyons came together at their mouths and we called the place Trin Alcove. Prof. and the Major walked up it some distance and then sent for Beaman to come to photograph. At nightfall rain began once more, and the shelters were again erected over the oars. Another morning came fair and we went on leaving Beaman to finish up views and the *Nell* crew for other work. As we proceeded we would occasionally halt to wait but it was noon before they overtook us. Rain had begun before this and continued at intervals during the dinner stop. As soon as we started we ran into a heavy downpour and while pulling along in the midst of this our boat ran on a sand-bar and got so far and fast aground that it required all ten men to get her off, the other crews walking in the water to where we were, as the shoal was very wide. While thus engaged a beautiful colour effect developed softly before us through an opalescent, vaporous shroud. The sun came forth with brilliant power upon the retreating mists creating a clear, luminous, prismatic bow ahead of us arching in perfect symmetry from foot to foot of the glistening walls, while high above it resting each end on the first terraces a second one equally distinct bridged the chasm; and, exactly where these gorgeous rainbows touched the rocks, roaring rain cascades leaped down to add their charm to the enchanting picture.

We were now at the beginning of a very long loop of the river, which we named Bow-knot Bend. Just at the start of this great turn we camped with a record for the whole day of 15⅛ miles. Steward found some fragments of pottery. The next morning we remained here till ten for views, and then we left Beaman on the summit of the low dividing ridge, where one could look into the river on either side and see a point which we rowed more than five miles to reach.[1] On the right bank we stopped for dinner, and when it was about ready several of us crossed, and, helping Beaman down with his heavy boxes, ferried him to our side. The opposite bank was no more than one thousand feet in a straight line from our starting-place of the morning. Instead of now going on, a halt was made, because Steward, prowling around after his custom, had found some fossils that were important and he wanted more. The Major, with Jack, crossed the river for further geological investigations, while Prof. and Jones started to climb out, though the prospect was not encouraging. They ascended over rock, strangely eroded by water into caverns and holes, then along a ledge till Jones, being a taller man than Prof., got up and pulled Prof. after him with his revolver belt. They obtained a remarkable view. Buttes, ridges, mountains stood all round, with the river so completely lost in the abruptness

[1] Many years afterward on a rock face half-way round this bend the inscription, D. Julien 1836 3 Mai, was found. The same inscription was also found in two other places just below the mouth of Grand River and near the end of Cataract Canyon.

of its chasm that a mile from the brink the whole region was apparently solid, and the existence of the gorge with a river at bottom would not even be suspected. They could trace the line of Grand River by tower-like buttes and long ridges, and just at the gap formed by the junction with the Green a blue mountain arose. The Sierra La Sal, too, could be seen lying on the horizon like blue clouds. "Weird and wild, barren and ghost-like, it seemed like an unknown world," said Prof. The country was a vast plateau similar to the one through which the Canyon of Desolation is carved, that is tilting northward and increasing in altitude towards the south, so that as the river runs on its canyon becomes deeper from this cause as well as its cutting. These great terraces sloping to the north were not before understood. They terminate on the south in vertical cliffs through which the river emerges abruptly. From such features as these the Major named this the Plateau Province. The cliffs terminating each plateau form intricate escarpments, meandering for many miles, and they might be likened to a series of irregular and complicated steps. Occasional high buttes and mountain masses break the surface, but in general the whole area forming the major part of the basin of the Colorado may be described as a plateau country—a land of mesas, cliffs, and canyons.

The next day, September 11th, we were on the river at 7.30, and ran about seven miles on smooth water before we stopped for a mid-day rest and dinner on the right bank, as well as to enable Beaman to take some views he desired. Another three miles and we halted again for geologising and for photographs, while Prof., taking Andy in his boat, went ahead to establish a camp somewhere below for the night, in order that we would not be so late getting supper. The days were now growing short, and supper by firelight was a common thing. Rain soon began again and put a stop to the work, driving us forward between the scores of cascades which soon began to leap anew from every height to the river. At one place a waterfall shot out from behind an arch set against the wall, making a singular but beautiful effect, and revealing to us one method by which some of the arches are formed. The place Prof. had selected for camp was reached almost the same time that he got there. It was on the left among the grease-wood bushes, and there we put up our paulins for shelter on oars as before. We had made about fifteen miles. The walls receded from the river, forming what the Major named the Orange Cliffs, and were much broken, while the back country could be seen in places from our boats. Scores, hundreds, multitudes of buttes of bare rock of all shapes and sizes were in sight, and one was called the Butte of the Cross, because it suggested a cross lying down from one position, though from another it was seen to be in reality two distinct masses. Here ended Labyrinth Canyon according to the Major's decision. We credited it with a length of 62½ miles. Although winding through an extremely arid country, it had for us been a place of rain and waterfalls, and even though rapids were absent we had been nevertheless kept rather wet.

There was not much change in structure between Labyrinth Canyon and the following one of the series, Stillwater. The interval was one of lowered, much broken walls, well back from the river, leaving wide bottom lands on the sides. We went ahead in the morning on quiet water for seven or eight miles, and stopped on a high bank for dinner and for examinations. Prof., Cap., Steward, and the Major climbed out. Steward got separated from the others by trying to reach a rather distant butte, and when he tried to rejoin us he had considerable difficulty in doing so. For half an hour he searched for a place to get down, and we looked for one also from the bottom, and finally he was compelled to go down half a mile farther, where he made the descent only to find himself in a dense jungle of rose-bushes, willows, and other plants. We had to cut a way in to relieve him. The luxuriant growth of these plants seemed to indicate that the barrenness of the plateau was due not so much to aridity as to the peculiar rock formation, which, dis-integrating easily under the frosts and rains, prevented the accumulation of soil. The soil was washed away by every rain and carried by thousands of cataracts into the river. Only when the country reaches the " base level of erosion," as the Major called it, would vegetation succeed in holding its place;

Labyrinth Canyon—Bowknot Bend.
The Great Loop Is behind the Spectator.
Photograph by E. O. BEAMAN, 1871.

Stillwater Canyon.
Photograph by E. O. BEAMAN, 1871.

that is when the declivity of the surrounding region became reduced till the rain torrents should lack the velocity necessary to transport any great load of detritus, and the disintegrated material would accumulate, give a footing to plants, and thus further protect itself and the rocks.

The Major and Prof. now decided to use up all the photographic material between this point and the Dirty Devil, and leave one boat at the latter place till the next season, when a party would come in for it and take it down to the Paria. We would be obliged to examine the Dirty Devil region then in any event. Three miles below our dinner camp we arrived at a remarkably picturesque bend, and on the outer circumference we made our sixtieth camp, but so late that supper was eaten by firelight. The bend was named by Beaman "Bonito," and in the morning he made a number of views. The bottom lands along the river had evidently been utilised by the aboriginal inhabitants for farming, as fragments of pottery occasionally found indicated their presence here in former days. It was afternoon when we pushed off and left Bonito Bend behind. After a few miles the Major and Prof. tried to climb out, but they failed. A buff sandstone, resting on red shale, was vertical for about 140 feet everywhere and could not be surmounted. Above this stood another vertical wall of five hundred feet, an orange coloured sandstone, in which no break was apparent. These walls closed in on the river, leaving barely a margin in many places. There were few landings, the current, rather swift and smooth, swirling along the foot of the rocks, which rose vertically for 250 feet and were about four hundred feet apart. As the evening came on we could find no place to stop that offered room enough for a camp, and we drifted on and on till almost dark, when we discovered a patch of soil on the right that would give us sufficient space. The 13th of September happened to be my birthday, and Andy had promised to stew a mess of dried apples in celebration. This does not sound like a tremendous treat, but circumstances give the test. Our supply of rations being limited and now running low, Andy for some time had been curbing our appetites. Stewed dried apples were granted about once a week, and

boiled beans were an equal luxury. It was consequently a disappointment not to get the promised extra allowance of apples
on this occasion. Not only was the hour late, but there was
little wood to be had, though diligent raking around produced
enough driftwood to cook our supper of bacon, coffee, and
bread. Our camp was beneath an overhanging cliff about six
hundred feet high, and the walls near us were so heavily coated
with salt that it could be broken off in chunks anywhere. The
quarters were not roomy, but we got a good sleep. In the
morning before he was fairly awake Steward discovered fossils
in the rocks over his head, and we remained till one o'clock in
order that an investigation could be made. He collected about
a peck of fine specimens. When we started again the canyon
was so interesting, particularly to the geologists, that we stopped
several times in a run of five miles between vertical walls not
over six hundred feet apart. Camp was finally made on the
right in a sort of alcove, with a level fertile bottom of several
acres, where the ancients had grown corn. Evidences of their
former life here were numerous. Steward, climbing on the
cliffs, suddenly gave a loud shout, announcing a discovery.
He had found two small huts built into the rocks. Several of us
went up to look at them. They were of great age and so
small that they could have been only storage places. Withered
and hardened corncobs were found within them.

On returning to camp we learned that the Major had found
some larger house ruins on a terrace some distance up the
river. Around the camp-fire that evening he told us something about the Shinumos, as he called them, who long ago
had inhabited this region, and in imagination we now beheld
them again climbing the cliffs or toiling at their agriculture in
the small bottom land.

At daylight Steward, Clem, and I went up to the ruins, which
stood on a terrace projecting in such a way that a clear view
could be had up and down the river. There were two houses
built of stone slabs, each about 13 x 15 feet, and about six feet
of wall were still standing. Thirty feet or more below ran the
river, and there were remains of an old stairway leading down
through a crevice to the river, but too much disintegrated for

us to descend. These were the first ruins of the kind I had ever seen, and I was as much interested in them as I afterwards was in the Colosseum.

Prof., being desirous of arriving as speedily as possible at the junction of the Grand with the Green, which was now not far off, for the purpose of getting an observation for time, left us at seven o'clock and proceeded in advance, while the remainder of the party turned their attention to the locality where we were. We could see traces of an old trail up the cliffs, and the Major, Jack, Andy, and Jones started to follow this out. With the aid of ropes taken along and stones piled up, as well as a cottonwood pole that had been placed as a ladder by the ancients, they succeeded in reaching the summit. Clem and I went back to the large house ruins for a re-examination, and looked over the quantities of broken arrowheads of jasper and the potsherds strewing the place in search of specimens of value. On the return trip of the climbers Andy discovered an earthen jar, fifteen inches high and about twelve inches in diameter, of the " pinched-coil " type, under a sheltering rock, covered by a piece of flat stone, where it had rested for many a decade if not for a century. It contained a small coil of split-willow, such as is used in basketry, tied with cord of aboriginal make. Some one had placed it there for a few moments.

After dinner we continued down the canyon, taking the pot with us. The walls were nearly vertical on both sides, or at any rate appeared so to us from the boats, and they often came straight into the water, with here and there a few willows. They were not more than 450 feet apart. No rapids troubled us, and the current was less than three miles an hour, but we seemed to be going swiftly even without rowing. After about seven miles the trend of the chasm became easterly, and we saw the mouth of the Grand, the Junction, that hidden mystery which, unless we count D. Julien, only nine white men, the Major's first party, had ever seen before us. The Grand entered through a canyon similar to that of the Green, all the immediate walls being at least 800 feet and the summit of the plateau about 1500 feet above the river. On the right

8

was a small bench, perhaps one-third of a mile long and several rods wide, fringed by a sand-bank, on which we found the crew of the *Nell* established in Camp 62. Between the two rivers was another footing of about two acres, bearing several hackberry trees, and it was on this bank up the Grand River side that the first party camped. Across on the east shore we could see still another strip with some bushes, but there was no more horizontal land to be found here. The two rivers blended gracefully on nearly equal terms, and the doubled volume started down with reckless impetuosity. This was the end of Stillwater Canyon, with a length of 42¾ miles. At last we had finished the canyons of the Green, with every boat in good condition and not a man injured in any way, and now we stood before the grim jaws of the Colorado. Our descent from Gunnison Crossing was 215 feet, with not a rapid that was worth recording, and from the Union Pacific crossing in feet, 2215, and in miles, 539. The altitude of the Junction is 3860 feet above sea-level.

CHAPTER IX

A Wonderland of Crags and Pinnacles—Poverty Rations—Fast and Furious Plunging Waters—Boulders Boom along the Bottom—Chilly Days and Shivering—A Wild Tumultuous Chasm—A Bad Passage by Twilight and a Tornado with a Picture Moonrise—Out of one Canyon into Another—At the Mouth of the Dirty Devil at Last.

WE were on the threshold of what the Major had previously named Cataract Canyon, because the declivity within it is so great and the water descends with such tremendous velocity and continuity that he thought the term rapid failed to interpret the conditions. The addition of the almost equal volume of the Grand—indeed it was now a little greater owing to extra heavy rains along its course—doubled the depth and velocity of the river till it swirled on into the new canyon before us with a fierce, threatening intensity, sapping the flat sand-bank on which our camp was laid and rapidly eating it away. Large masses with a sudden splash would drop out of sight and dissolve like sugar in a cup of tea. We were obliged to be on the watch lest the moorings of the boats should be loosened, allowing them to sweep pell-mell before us down the gorge. The long ropes were carried back to their limit and made fast to stakes driven deep into the hard sand. Jack and I became dissatisfied with the position of our boat and dropped it down two or three hundred yards to a place where the conditions were better, and camped by it. There were a few small cottonwoods against the cliff behind the sand-bank, but they were too far off to be reached by our lines, and the ground beneath them was too irregular and rocky for a camp. These trees, with the hackberry trees across the river and numerous stramonium bushes in full blossom, composed the chief vegetation of this extraordinary locality. No more remote place

existed at that time within the United States—no place more
difficult of access. Macomb in his reconnaissance in 1859 had
tried hard to arrive here, but he got no nearer than the edge of
the plateau about thirty miles up Grand River.

It was necessary that we should secure topographic notes
and observations from the summit, and we scanned the surroundings for the most promising place for exit. The Major
was sure we could make a successful ascent to the upper regions
by way of a narrow cleft on the right or west some distance
back up the Green, which he had noted as we came along; so in
the morning of Saturday, September 16th, he and Jack, Beaman,
Clem, Jones, and I rowed up in the *Cañonita*, the current being
slow along the west bank, and started up the crevice, dragging
the cumbrous photographic outfit along. Prof. remained below
for observations for time. The cleft was filled with fallen
rocks, and we had no trouble mounting, except that the photographic boxes were like lead and the straps across one's chest
made breathing difficult. The climb was tiring, but there was
no obstacle, and we presently emerged on the surface of the
country 1300 feet above the river and 5160 above the sea.
Here was revealed a wide cyclorama that was astounding.
Nothing was in sight but barren sandstone, red, yellow, brown,
grey, carved into an amazing multitude of towers, buttes, spires,
pinnacles, some of them several hundred feet high, and all
shimmering under a dazzling sun. It was a marvellous mighty
desert of bare rock, chiselled by the ages out of the foundations
of the globe; fantastic, extraordinary, antediluvian, labyrinthian,
and slashed in all directions by crevices; crevices wide, crevices
narrow, crevices medium, some shallow, some dropping till a
falling stone clanked resounding into the far hollow depths.
Scarcely could we travel a hundred yards but we were compelled to leap some deep, dark crack. Often they were so wide
a running jump was necessary, and at times the smooth rock
sloped on both sides toward the crevice rather steeply. Once
the Major came sliding down a bare slope till at a point where
he caught sight of the edge of a sombre fissure just where he
must land. He could not see its width; he could not return,
and there he hung. Luckily I was where by another path I

could quickly reach the rock below, and I saw that the crevice
was not six inches wide, and I shouted the joyful news. Steward had not come up with us, but had succeeded in ascending
through a narrow crevice below camp. He soon arrived within
speaking distance, but there he was foiled by a crack too wide
to jump, and he had to remain a stranger to us the rest of the
day. At a little distance back from the brink these crevices
were not so numerous nor so wide, and there we discovered
a series of extremely pretty "parks" lost amidst the million
turreted rocks. I made a pencil sketch looking out into this
Sinav-to-weap, as the Major called it from information obtained
from the Utes.[1] Beaman secured a number of photographs,
but not all that were desired, and, as we did not have rations for
stopping on the summit, we went back to camp and made the
climb again the next day. Fortunately the recent rains had
filled many hollows in the bare rock, forming pockets of delicious, pure water, where we could drink, but on a hot and dry
summer's day travelling here would be intolerable, if not impossible. Fragments of arrow-heads, chips of chalcedony, and
quantities of potsherds scattered around proved that our ancient
Shinumos had known the region well. Doubtless some of their
old trails would lead to large and deep water-pockets. There
are pot-holes in this bare sandstone of enormous size, often
several feet in depth and of similar diameter, which become
filled with rain-water that lasts a long time. The Shinumos
had numerous dwellings all through this country, with trails
leading from place to place, highways and byways.

The following day the Major and Jones climbed out on the
side opposite camp, that is on the east side, where they found
an old trail and evidences of camping during the summer just
closed, probably by the Utes. That night, Jones, in attempting
to enter our boat in the moonlight, stepped on the corner of
the hatch of the middle cabin, which was not on securely; it
tipped, and he was thrown in such a way as to severely injure
his leg below the knee. This was the first mishap thus far
to any one of the party.

[1] The pencil sketches I made on this trip were taken to Washington, but I do
not know what became of them.

The Major entertained some idea of making a boat trip up the Grand, but he abandoned it, and we prepared for the work ahead. The rations, which were now fallen to poverty bulk, were carefully overhauled and evenly distributed among the boats, so that the wrecking of any one would not deprive us of more than a portion of each article. The amount for daily use was also determined; of the bacon we were to have at a meal only half the usual quantity. We knew Cataract Canyon was rough, but by this time we were in excellent training and thoroughly competent for the kind of navigation required; ready for anything that strong boats like ours could live through. At ten o'clock on Tuesday, September 19th, the cabins were all packed, the life preservers were inflated, and casting off from Camp 62 we were borne down with the swift current. The water was muddy, of a coffee-and-cream colour, and the river was falling. Not far below our camp we saw a beaten trail coming down a singular canyon on the left or east side, showing again that the natives understood the way in to the Junction.[1] We knew it was not far to rapids, as we had seen two heavy ones from the brink above, and we soon heard the familiar roar of plunging water, a sound which had been absent since the end of Gray Canyon. Presently we were bearing down on the first one, looking for the way to pass it. On landing at the head it was seen to be a rather rough place, and it was deemed advisable to avoid running it. The boats were carefully let down by lines and we went on. In a short distance we reached a second rapid, where we decided to repeat the operation that took us past the other, but these two let-downs consumed much time and gave us hard work. The water was cold, we were wet and hungry, and when we arrived at a third that was more forbidding than the ones above we halted for dinner at its beginning. The muddy water boomed and plunged over innumerable rocks—a mad, irresistible flood. So great was the declivity of the river bed that boulders were rolled along under water with a sound like distant thunder.

[1] As mentioned in a previous footnote, the name D. Julien—1836, was later found near this point and in two other places. All these inscriptions appear to be on the same side of the river, the east, and at accessible places.

Clement Powell
Cataract Canyon.
Photograph by E. O. BEAMAN, 1871

Cataract Canyon.

Photograph by E. O. BEAMAN, 1871.

We had noticed this also in Lodore, but in Cataract it was more common. The rumbling was particularly noticeable if one were standing in the water, as we so continually were. After dinner the boats were lowered past the rapid, but we had no respite, for presently we came upon another big one, then another, and another, and then still another, all following quickly and giving us plenty of extremely hard work, for we would not risk the boats in any of them. When these were behind us we went on a distance and came to one that we ran, and then, wet through and shivering till our teeth chattered, as well as being hungry and tired, every one was glad to hear the decision to go into camp when we arrived at the top of another very ugly pair of them. The canyon having a north and south trend and it being autumn, the sun disappeared early so far as we were concerned; the shadows were deep, the mountain air was penetrating. As soon as possible our soaking river garments were thrown off, the dry clothing from the rubber bags was put on, the limited bacon was sending its fragrance into the troubled air, the bread took on a nice deep brown in the Dutch oven, the coffee's aromatic steam drifted from the fire, and warm and comfortable we sat down to the welcome though meagre meal. The rule was three little strips of bacon, a chunk of bread about the size of one's fist, and coffee without stint for each man three times a day. Sugar was a scarce article, and I learned to like coffee without it so well that I have never taken it with sugar since. The " Tirtaan Aigles " needed now all the muscle and energy they could command, and an early hour found every man sound asleep. The record for the first day in Cataract Canyon was nine miles, with eight bad rapids or cataracts, as they might properly be called, and out of the eight we ran but one.[1] The river was about 250 feet wide.

The Major decided the next morning that he would try to

---

[1] The next party to pass through this canyon was the Brown Expedition, conducting a survey for the Denver, Colorado Canyon, and Pacific Railway in 1889. At the first rapid they lost a raft, with almost all their provisions, and they had much trouble. See *The Romance of the Colorado River*, Chapter xiv. Another expedition in 1891—the Best Expedition—was wrecked here.

get out on the right, and he took me with him. We had no great trouble in reaching the plateau at an elevation of eighteen hundred feet above the river, where we could see an immense area of unknown country. The broken and pinnacled character was not so marked as it had been at the Junction, but it was still a strange, barren land. We expected to find water-pockets on the top, and we had carried with us only one quart canteen of water. While the Major was taking notes from the summit of a butte, I made a zealous search for water, but not a drop could I find; every hole was dry. The sun burned down from a clear sky that melted black into eternal space. The yellow sand threw the hot rays upward, and so also did the smooth bare rock. No bird, no bee, no thing of life could be seen. I came to a whitish cliff upon which I thought there might be water-pockets, and I mounted by a steep slope of broken stones. Suddenly, almost within touch, I saw before me a golden yellow rattlesnake gliding upward in the direction I was going along the cliff wall. I killed it with a stone, and cut off the rattles and continued my reconnaissance. At length I gave up the search. By the time I had returned to the foot of the butte on which the Major was making his observations, the heat had exhausted me till I was obliged to rest a few moments before ascending the sixty feet to where he was. I had carried the canteen all the time, and the water in it was hot from exposure to the sun. The Major bade me rest while he made a little fire, and by the aid of a can and ground coffee we had brought he made a strong decoction with the whole quart. This gave us two cups apiece, and we had some bread to go with it. The effect was magical. My fatigue vanished. I felt equal to anything, and we began the return.

The Major having no right arm, he sometimes got in a difficult situation when climbing, if his right side came against a smooth surface where there was nothing opposite. We had learned to go down by the same route followed up, because otherwise one is never sure of arriving at the bottom, as a ledge half-way down might compel a return to the summit. We remembered that at one point there was no way for him to hold on, the cliff being smooth on the right, while on the left was empty air, with a sheer drop of several hundred feet. The footing too was narrow. I climbed down first, and, bracing myself below with my back to the abyss, I was able to plant my right foot securely in such a manner that my right knee formed a solid step for him at the critical moment. On this improvised step he placed his left foot, and in a twinkling had made the passage in safety.

During our absence the men below had been at work. Camp was moved down the river some three quarters of a mile, while the boats had been lowered past the ugly pair of rapids, and were moored at the camp below the second. In one the current had "got the bulge," as we called it, on the men on the line; that is, the powerful current had hit the bow in such a way that the boat took the diagonal of forces and travelled up and out into the river. For the men it was either let go or be pulled in. They let go, and the boat dashed down with her cargo on board. Fortune was on our side. She went through without injury and shot into an eddy below. With all speed the men rushed down, and Jack, plunging in, swam to her and got on before she could take a fresh start. It was a narrow escape, but it taught a lesson that was not forgotten. Prof. had succeeded in getting some observations, and all was well. It was bean day, too, according to our calendar, and all hands had a treat.

By eight o'clock the next morning, Thursday, September 21st, we were on the way again, with the boats "close reefed," as it were, for trouble, but one, two, three and one half miles slid easily behind. Then, as if to make up for this bit of leniency, six rapids came in close succession, though they were of a kind that we could safely run, and all the boats went flying through them without a mishap of any kind. The next was a plunger so mixed up with rocks that we made a let-down and again proceeded a short distance before we were halted by one more of the same sort, though we were able to run the lower portion of it. A little below this we met a friendly drop, and whizzed through its rush and roar in triumph. But there was nothing triumphant about the one which followed, so far as our work was concerned. We manoeuvred past it with much diffi-

culty only to find ourselves upon two more bad ones. Bad as
they were, they were nevertheless runable, and away we dashed
with breakneck speed, certainly not less than twenty miles an
hour, down both of them, to land on the left immediately at the
beginning of a great and forbidding descent. These let-downs
were difficult, often requiring all hands to each boat, except
the Major, whose one-armed condition made it too hard for
him to assist in the midst of rocks and rushing water, where
one had to be very nimble and leap and balance with exactness. Two good arms were barely sufficient. Sometimes, in
order to pass the gigantic boulders that stretched far off from
the shore, the boat had to be shot around and hauled in below,
an operation requiring skill, strength, and celerity.

The walls, very craggy at the top, increased in altitude till
they were now about sixteen hundred feet, separated from
each other by one third of a mile. The flaring character of the
upper miles of the canyon began to change to a narrower
gorge, the cliffs showing a nearer approach to verticality. At
the head of the forbidding plunge we had our slice of bacon,
with bread and coffee, and then we fought our way down
alongside amongst immense boulders and roaring water. It
was an exceedingly hard place to vanquish, and required two
and a half hours of the most violent exertion to accomplish it.
All were necessary to handle each boat. Hardly had we passed
beyond the turmoil of its fierce opposition than we fell upon
another scarcely less antagonistic, but yet apparently so free
from rocks that the Major concluded it could be run. At the
outset our boat struck on a concealed rock, and for a moment
it seemed that we might capsize, but luckily she righted, swung
free, and swept down with no further trouble. The *Nell* struck
the same rock and so did the *Cañonita*, but neither was injured
or even halted. These boats were somewhat lighter than ours,
having one man less in each, and therefore did not hit the
rock so hard. The boats were now heavy from being water-
soaked, for the paint was gone from the bottoms. This would
have made no difference in any ordinary waters, but it did
here, where we were obliged to lift them so constantly.

This was an extremely rough and wet day's work, and the

moment the great cliffs cut off the warmth of the direct sun
we were thrown suddenly from summer to winter, and our
saturated clothing, uncomfortably cool in sunlight, became icy
with the evaporation and the cold shadow-air. We turned
blue, and no matter how firmly I tried to shut my teeth they
rattled like a pair of castanets. Though it was only half-past
three, the Major decided to camp as soon as he saw this effect,
much as we had need to push on. We landed on the right,
and were soon revived by dry clothes and a big fire of driftwood. We had made during the day a total distance of a trifle
less than seven miles, one and three quarters since dinner.
There were fourteen rapids and cataracts, nine of which we
ran, on a river about two hundred feet wide. We had sand to
sleep on, but all around us were rocks, rocks, rocks, with the
mighty bounding cliffs lifting up to the sky. Our books for
the time being were not disturbed, but Whittier's lines, read
further up, seemed here exactly appropriate to the Colorado :

> " Hurrying down to its grave, the sea,
>   And slow through the rock its pathway hewing!
>   Far down, through the mist of the falling river,
>   Which rises up like an incense ever,
>   The splintered points of the crags are seen,
>   With water howling and vexed between,
>   While the scooping whirl of the pool beneath
>   Seems an open throat, with its granite teeth ! "

It was not long before the blankets were taken from the
rubber bags and spread on the sand, and the rapids, the rocks,
and all our troubles were forgotten.

The next day was almost a repetition of the preceding one.
We began by running a graceful little rapid, just beyond which
we came to a very bad place. The river was narrow and deep,
with a high velocity, and the channel was filled with enormous
rocks. Two hours of the hardest kind of work in and out of
the water, climbing over gigantic boulders along the bank,
lifting the boats and sliding them on driftwood skids, tugging,
pulling, shoving every minute with might and main put us at
the bottom. No sooner were we past this one than we engaged

in a similar battle with another of the same nature, and below
it we stopped for dinner, amidst some huge boulders under a
hackberry tree, near another roarer.   One of these cataracts
had a fall of not less than twenty feet in six hundred, which gave
the water terrific force and violence.   The canyon walls closed
in more and more and ran up to two thousand feet, apparently
nearly vertical as one looked up at them, but there was always
plenty of space for landings and camps.   Opposite the noon
camp we could see to a height beyond of at least three thousand
feet.   We were in the heart of another great plateau.   After
noon we attacked the very bad rapid beside whose head we
had eaten, and it was half-past three when we had finished it.
The boats had been considerably pounded and there was a hole
in the *Dean*, and a plank sprung in the *Nell* so that her middle
cabin was half full of water.   The iron strip on the *Dean's* keel
was breaking off.   Repairs were imperative, and on the right,
near the beginning of one of the worst falls we had yet seen, we
went into camp for the rest of the day.   With false ribs made
from oars we strengthened the boats and put them in condition
for another day's hammering.   It seemed as if we must have
gone this day quite a long distance, but on footing up it was
found to be no more than a mile and a quarter.   Darkness now
fell early and big driftwood fires made the evenings cheerful.
There was a vast amount of driftwood in tremendous piles,
trees, limbs, boughs, railroad ties; a great mixture of all kinds,
some of it lying full fifty feet above the present level of the
river.   There were large and small tree-trunks battered and
limbless, the ends pounded to a spongy mass of splinters.   Our
bright fires enabled us to read, or to write up notes and diaries.
I think each one but the Major and Andy kept a diary and
faithfully wrote it up.   Jack occasionally gave us a song or two
from the repertory already described, and Steward did not
forget the mouth-organ, but through the hardest part of Cataract Canyon we were usually tired enough to take to our
blankets early.

     In the morning we began the day by running a little rapid
between our camp and the big one that we saw from there, and
then we had to exert some careful engineering to pass below

by means of the lines. This accomplished we found a repetition of the same kind of work necessary almost immediately, at the next rapid. In places we had to lift the boats out and slide them along on driftwood skids. These rapids were largely formed by enormous rocks which had fallen from the cliffs, and over, around, and between these it was necessary to manœuvre the boats by lines to avoid the furious waters of the outer river. After dinner we arrived at a descent which at first glance seemed as bad as anything we had met in the morning but an examination showed a prospect of a successful run through it. The fall was nearly twenty feet in about as many yards. The Major and Prof. examined it long and carefully. A successful run would take two minutes, while a let-down would occupy us for at least two hours and it had some difficult points. They hesitated about running the place, for they would not take a risk that was not necessary, but finally they concluded it could be safely accomplished, and we pulled the *Dean* as quickly as possible into the middle of the river and swung down into it. On both sides the water was hammered to foam amidst great boulders and the roar as usual was deafening. Just through the centre was a clean, clear chute followed by a long tail of waves breaking and snapping like some demon's jaws. As we struck into them they swept over us like combers on the beach in a great storm. It seemed to me here and at other similar places that we went through some of the waves like a needle and jumped to the top of others, to balance half-length out of water for an instant before diving to another trough. Being in the very bow the waves, it appeared to me, sometimes completely submerged me and almost took my breath away with the sudden impact. At any rate it was lively work, with a current of fifteen or eighteen miles an hour. Beaman had stationed himself where he could get a negative of us ploughing through these breakers, but his wet-plates were too slow and he had no success. After this came a place which permitted no such jaunty treatment. It was in fact three or four rapids following each other so closely that, though some might be successfully run, the last was not safe, and no landing could be made at its head, so a very long let-down was obligatory; but it was an easy one, for each crew could take its own boat down without help from the others.   Then, tired, wet, and cold as usual, we landed on the left in a little cove where there was a sandy beach for our Camp 67. We had made less than four miles, in which distance there were six rapids, only two of which we ran. At another stage of water the number and character of these rapids would be changed; some would be easier at higher water, some harder, and the same would be true of lower water. Rapids also change their character from time to time as rocks are shifted along the bottom and more rocks fall from the cliffs or are brought in by side floods.   The walls were now about two thousand feet, of limestone, with a reddish stain, and they were so near together that the sun shone to the bottom only during the middle hours of the day in September.

It was now September 24th; a bright and beautiful Sunday broke, the sky above clear and tranquil, the river below foaming and fuming between the ragged walls in one continuous rapid with merely variations of descent.   In three quarters of a mile we arrived before the greatest portion of the declivity, where, though there seemed to be a clear chute, we did not consider it advisable to make the run because of conditions following; neither could we make a regular let-down or a portage. The least risky method was to carry a line down and when all was ready start the boat in at the top alone.   In this way when she had gone through, the men on the line below were able to bring her up and haul her in before reaching the next bad plunge. There was no quiet river anywhere; nothing but rushing, swirling, plunging water and rocks. We got past the bad spot successfully and went on making one let-down after another for about four miles, when we halted at noon for the rest of the day, well satisfied with our progress though in distance it appeared so slight.   The afternoon was spent in repairing boats, working up notes, and taking observations.   The cliffs were now some 2500 feet in height, ragged and broken on their faces, but close together, the narrowest deep chasm we had seen.   It was truly a terrible place, with the fierce river, the giant walls, and the separation from any known path to the outer world.   I thought of the Major's first trip, when it was not known what kind of waters were here. Vertical and impassable falls might easily have barred his way and cataracts behind prevented return, so that here in a death trap they would have been compelled to plunge into the river or wait for starvation. Happly he had encountered no such conditions.

An interesting feature of this canyon was the manner in which huge masses of rock lying in the river had been ground into each other by the force of the current. One block of sandstone, weighing not less than six hundred tons, being thirty or forty feet long by twenty feet square, had been oscillated till the limestone boulders on which it rested had ground into it at least two feet, fitting closely. Another enormous piece was slowly and regularly rocking as the furious current beat upon it, and one could feel the movement distinctly. A good night's sleep made all of us fresh again, and we began the Monday early. Some worked on the boats, while Beaman and Clem went up "Gypsum" Canyon, as Steward named it, for views, and the Major and I climbed out for topographic observations. We reached an altitude above camp of 3135 feet at a point seven or eight miles back from the brink. The view in all directions was beyond words to describe. Mountains and mountains, canyons, cliffs, pinnacles, buttes surrounded us as far as we could see, and the range was extensive. The Sierra La Sal, the Sierra Abajo, and other short ranges lay blue in the distance, while comparatively near in the south-west rose the five beautiful peaks just beyond the mouth of the Dirty Devil, composing the unknown range before mentioned. At noon we made coffee, had lunch, and then went on. It was four o'clock by the time we concluded to start back, and darkness overtook us before we were fairly down the cliffs, but there was a bright moon, and by its aid we reached camp.

At half-past eight in the morning of September 26th we were again working our way down the torrential river. Anybody who tries to go through here in any haphazard fashion will surely come to grief. It is a passage that can safely be made only with the most extreme caution. The walls grew straighter, and they grew higher till the gorge assumed proportions that seemed to me the acme of the stupendous and magnificent. The scenery may not have been beautiful in the sense that an Alpine lake is beautiful, but in the exhibition of the power and majesty of nature it was sublime. There was the same general barrenness: only a few hackberry trees, willows, and a cottonwood or two along the margin of the river made up the vegetation. Our first task was a difficult let-down, which we accomplished safely, to find that we could run two rapids following it and half of another, landing then to complete it by a let-down. Then came a very sharp drop that we ran, which put us before another easy one, that was followed by a difficult bit of navigation through a bad descent, after which we stopped for dinner on the right at the head of another rapid. The cliffs now on both sides were about 2800 feet, one quarter mile wide at top, and in places striking me as being perpendicular, especially in the outer curve of the bends. The boats seemed to be scarcely more than chips on the sweeping current and we not worth mentioning. During the afternoon we halted a number of times for Beaman to make photographs, but the proportions were almost too great for any camera. The foreground parts are always magnified, while the distances are diminished, till the view is not that which the eye perceives. Before stopping for the night we ran three more rapids, and camped on the right on a sand-bank at the head of another forbidding place. The record for the whole day was six and three quarter miles, with ten runs and two let-downs. At one bad place the *Nell* got too far over and laboured so heavily in the enormous billows that Cap., who pulled the bow oars, was completely lost to sight and the boat was filled with water. Only about thirty degrees of sky were visible as one looked directly up from our camp. A pretty canyon came in near camp, and some of us took a walk up its narrow way.

In the morning Beaman made some pictures, and it was eleven o'clock before we resumed our navigation. Our first work was a let-down, which took an hour, and about a mile below we stopped for dinner on the left. Then we continued, making eight miles more, in which distance we ran six rapids and made two line-portages. The last rapid was a bad one, and there we made one of the portages, camping at its foot on the left bank. The walls began to diminish in height and the river was less precipitous, as is apparent from the progress we were able to make. September 28th we began by running two rapids immediately below camp, and the *Nell* remained at the foot of the second to signal Beaman in the *Cañonita*, as he had stayed behind to take some views. Another mile brought us to a rather bad place, the right having a vertical cliff about 2700 feet high, but the left was composed of boulders spread over a wide stretch, so that an excellent footing was offered. The Major and Prof. concluded to climb out here, instead of a point farther down called Millecrag Bend, and, appointing Steward master of the let-down which was necessary, they left us. It was dinner-time when we got the boats below to a safe cove, and we were quite ready for the meal which Andy meanwhile had been cooking. A beautiful little brook came down a narrow canyon on the left, and it was up this stream that the Major went for a mile and a half and then climbed on the side. They were obliged to give it up and come back to the bottom. By this time it was too late to make another attempt, so they turned their backs on " Failure Creek," and, returning to us, said we would go on as soon as we had eaten the supper which Andy was preparing. They would climb out at Millecrag Bend. Andy had cooked a mess of beans, about the last we had, and what we did not eat we put on board in the kettle, which had a tight cover. The Major's manner for a day or two had been rather moody, and when Prof. intimated to me that we would have a lively time before we saw another camp, I knew some difficult passage ahead was on his mind; some place which had given him trouble on the first trip.

About five o'clock we were ready; everything was made snug and tight on the boats, nothing being left out of the cabins but a camp kettle in each standing-room for bailing, and we cast off. Each man had his life-preserver where he could get it quickly, and the Major put his on, for with only one arm he could not do this readily in case of necessity. The current

was swift. We were carried rapidly down to where the gorge
narrowed up with walls vertical on each side for a height of
fifty to one hundred feet. We soon dashed through a small
rough rapid. A splash of water over our bow dampened my
clothes and made the air feel chilly. The canyon was growing
dim with the evening light. High above our heads some
lazy clouds were flecked with the sunset glow. Not far below
the small rapid we saw before us a complicated situation at
the prevailing stage of water, and immediately landed on the
left, where there was footing to reconnoitre. A considerable
fall was divided by a rocky island, a low mass that would be
submerged with two or three feet more water, and the river
plunging down on each side boiled against the cliffs. Between
us and the island the stream was studded by immense boulders
which had dropped from the cliffs and almost like pinnacles
stood above the surface. One view was enough to show that
on this stage of water we could not safely run either side of the
cataract ; indeed destruction would surely have rewarded any
attempt. The right-hand channel from the foot of the island
swept powerfully across to meet the left-hand one and together
they boomed along the base of the left-hand cliffs before swinging sharply to the right with the trend of the chasm in that
direction. There was no choice of a course. The only way
was to manœuvre between the great boulders and keep in the
dividing line of the current till a landing could be effected on
the head of the island between the two falls. The difficulty
was to avoid being drawn to either side. Our boat went first
and we succeeded, under the Major's quick eye and fine judgment, in easily following the proposed course till the *Dean*
began to bump on the rocks some twenty yards above the
exposed part of the island. I tested the depth of water here
with an oar as Jack pulled slowly along, the current being quite
slack in the dividing line, and as soon as practicable we jumped
overboard and guided our craft safely to the island. Prof. in
the *Nell* was equally precise, and as he came in we waded out
to catch his boat ; but the *Cañonita* passed on the wrong side of
one of the pinnacles and, caught in the left current, came near
making a run of it down that side, which would have resulted

disastrously.   Luckily they were able to extricate themselves
and Beaman steered in to us.   Had the water been only high
enough to prevent landing on this island we would have been
in a bad trap, but had it been so high as to make navigation
down the centre possible the rapid might perhaps have been
run safely.

We were now on the island, with darkness falling, and the
problem was to get off.   While Prof. and the Major went down
to the foot to make a plan we sat in the diminishing light and
waited.   It was decided to pull the boats down the right-hand
side of the island as far as the foot of the worst part of the right-
hand rapid, and from there cut out into the tail of waves, pulling through as quickly as we could to avoid contact with the base
of the left wall along which the current dashed.   We must pull
fast enough to get across in the very short time it would take
the river to sweep us down to the crucial point.   The gorge by
this time was quite sombre; even the clouds above were losing
their evening colour.   We must act quickly.   Our boat as usual
made the first trial.   As we shot out, Jack and I bent to our
oars with every muscle we possessed, the boat headed slightly
upstream, and in a few seconds we were flying along the base
of the cliffs, and so close that our starboard oars had to be
quickly unshipped to prevent their being broken.   In a few
seconds more we were able to get out into the middle, and then
we halted in an eddy to wait for the other boats.   They came
on successfully and in the gloaming we continued down the
canyon looking for a place to camp, our hearts much lightened
with our triumph over the difficult rapid.   Before long night
was full upon us and our wet clothes made us shiver.   About
a mile below a warning roar dead ahead told us to make land
at once, for it would be far from prudent to attack a rapid in the
dark.   Fortunately there was here room to camp on some rocks
and sand on the right.   Scarcely had we become settled than a
tornado broke over the canyon and we were enveloped in a
blinding whirl of rain and sand.   Each man clung to his blankets to prevent their departure and waited for the wind to pass,
which it did in less than ten minutes.   The storm-clouds were
shattered and up the gorge, directly east from our position,

from behind a thousand needle-like spires that serrated the top of the cliffs, the moon like a globe of dazzling silver rolled up with serene majesty, flooding the canyon with a bright radiance. No moon-rise could have been more dramatic. The storm-clouds were edged with light and the wet cliffs sparkled and glittered as if set with jewels. Even the rapid below was resplendent and silvery, the leaping waves and the spray scintillating under the lustrous glare.

Morning brought a continuation of the rain, which fell in a deluge, driving us to the shelter of a projecting ledge, from which comparatively dry retreat we watched the rain cascades that soon began their display. Everywhere they came plunging over the walls, all sizes, and varying their volume with every variation in the downpour. Some dropped a thousand feet to vanish in spray; others were broken into many falls. By half-past eight we were able to proceed, running the rapid without any trouble, but a wave drenched me so that all my efforts to keep out of the rain went for nothing. By ten o'clock we had run four more rapids, and arrived at the place the Major had named Millecrag Bend, from the multitude of ragged pinnacles into which the cliffs broke. On the left we camped to permit the Major and Prof. to make their prospective climb to the top. A large canyon entered from the left, terminating Cataract Canyon, which we credited with forty-one miles, and in which I counted sixty-two rapids and cataracts, enough to give any set of boatmen all the work they could desire. The Major and Prof. reached the summit at an altitude of fifteen hundred feet. They had a wide view over the unknown country, and saw mountains to the west with snow on their summits. Snow in the canyons would not have surprised us now, for the nights were cold and we had warmth only in the middle of the day. Near our camp some caves were discovered, twenty feet deep and nearly six feet in height, which had once been occupied by natives. Walls had been laid across the entrances, and inside were corncobs and other evidences usual in this region, now so well known. Pottery fragments were also abundant. Another thing we found in the caves and also in other places was a species of small scorpion. These

Narrow Canyon.
Photograph by BEST EXPEDITION, 1891.

The Mouth of Fremont River (The Dirty Devil River)
Photograph by the BROWN EXPEDITION, 1889

venomous creatures were always ready to strike, and somehow one got into Andy's shoe, and when he put on the shoe he was bitten. No serious result seemed to follow, but his general health was not so good after this for a long time. He put tobacco on the wound and let it go. This was the second accident to a member of the party, which now had been out four months.

The last day of September found us up before daylight, and as soon as breakfast was eaten, a small matter these days both in preparation and consumption, we pulled away, intending to reach the mouth of the Dirty Devil as soon as possible. The morning was decidedly autumnal, and when we arrived at a small rapid, where we had to get overboard to help the boats, nothing ever came harder than this cold bath, though it was confined to our legs. Presently we saw a clear little rivulet coming in on the left, and we ran up to that shore to examine it, hoping it was drinkable. Like the first party, we were on the lookout for better water to drink than the muddy Colorado. The rivulet proved to be sulphurous and also hot, the temperature being about 91 F. We could not drink it, but we warmed our feet by standing in the water. The walls of this new canyon at their highest were about thirteen hundred feet, and so close together and straight that the Major named it Narrow Canyon. Its length is about nine miles. Through half of the next rapid we made a let-down, running the remainder, and then, running two more below which were easy, we could see through to the end of the canyon, and the picture framed by the precipices was beautiful. The world seemed suddenly to open out before us, and in the middle of it, clear and strong against a sky of azure, accented by the daylight moon, stood the Unknown Mountains, weird and silent in their untrodden mystery. By this token we knew that the river of the Satanic name was near, and we had scarcely emerged from Narrow Canyon, and noted the low bluffs of homogeneous red sandstone which took the place of the high cliffs, when we perceived a sluggish stream about 150 feet wide flowing through the barren sandstone on our right. Landing on its west bank, we instantly agreed with Jack Sumner when on the first trip he had proclaimed it a "Dirty Devil." Muddy, alkaline, undrinkable, it slipped along between the low walls of smooth sandstone to add its volume to that of the Colorado. Near us were the remains of the Major's camp-fire of the other voyage, and there Steward found a jack-knife lost at that time. At the Major's request he gave it to him as a souvenir.

Our rising had been so early and our progress from Millecrag Bend so easy that when our camp was established the hour was only nine o'clock, giving us still a whole day. The Major and Prof. started off on an old Indian trail to see if there was a way in to this place for horses, Cap. took observations for time, and the others occupied themselves in various ways, Andy counting the rations still left in our larder.

That night around our camp-fire we felt especially contented, for Cataract and Narrow canyons were behind, and never would we be called upon to battle with their rapids again. The descent from the mouth of Grand River was 430 feet, most of it in the middle stretch of Cataract Canyon.

CHAPTER X

The *Cañonita* Left Behind—Shinumo Ruins—Troublesome Ledges in the River— Alcoves and Amphitheatres—The Mouth of the San Juan—Starvation Days and a Lookout for Rations—El Vado de Los Padres—White Men Again— Given up for Lost—Navajo Visitors—Peaks with a Great Echo—At the Mouth of the Paria.

HAVING now accomplished a distance down this turbulent river of nearly six hundred miles, with a descent toward sea-level of 2645 feet, without a serious accident, we were all in a happy frame of mind, notwithstanding the exceedingly diminutive food supply that remained. We felt that we could overcome almost anything in the line of rapids the world might afford, and Steward declared our party was so efficient he would be willing to "run the Gates of Hell" with them! Barring an absence of heat Cataract Canyon had been quite a near approach to that unwelcome entrance, and the locality of the mouth of the Dirty Devil certainly resembled some of the more favoured portions of Satan's notorious realm. Circumstances would prohibit our lingering here, for our long stretch on short rations made the small amount we could allow ourselves at each meal seem almost like nothing at all, and we were desirous of reaching as soon as possible El Vado, something over a hundred miles below, where our pack-train was doubtless now waiting.

The plan of leaving a boat at this place for a party to bring down, which should penetrate the unknown country the next year and then complete what we might now be compelled to slight, was carried out. The *Cañonita* was chosen and the day after our arrival, Sunday, October 1st, we ran her down a short distance on the right, and there carried her back about two hundred feet to a low cliff and up thirty or forty feet above the prevailing stage of water, where we hid her under an enormous mass of rock which had so fallen from the top as to lodge against the wall, forming a perfect shelter somewhat longer than the boat. All of her cargo had been left at camp and we filled her cabins and standing-rooms with sand, also piling sand and stones all about her to prevent high water from carrying her off. When we were satisfied that we had done our best we turned away feeling as one might on leaving a friend, and hoping that she would be found intact the following year. As nine o'clock only had arrived, the Major and Jones then climbed out from this place, while Prof. with the *Nell* ran down about a mile and a half to the mouth of a gulch on the right where he and the Major had traced the old trail. The rest of us returned to camp. Prof. and Cap. climbed out, after following the trail up the gulch six miles, and they saw that it went toward the Unknown Mountains, which now lay very near us on the west. Steward got out by an attempt not so far up the canyon and reached an altitude of 1950 feet, where he had a clear, full view of the mountains. With his glass he was able to study their formation and determined that lava from below had spread out between the sedimentary strata, forming what he called "blisters." He could see where one side of a blister had been eroded, showing the surrounding stratification.[1]

When the Major and Jones came back we put the cargo of the *Cañonita* on the *Dean*, and all of us embarked, seven in number, and ran down to where the *Nell* was moored. Here we camped for the night. The crews were then rearranged, Beaman being assigned to my bow oars, Clem and Andy going in the *Nell*, while I was to sit on the middle cabin of the *Dean* in front of the Major, where I could carry on my sketching. We were now a shaggy-looking lot, for our clothes had been almost worn off our bodies in the rapids. Our shoes, notwithstanding that the Major had brought us a fresh supply at Gunnison Crossing, were about gone, and we were tanned till

[1] These blisters were later called laccolites by G. K. Gilbert after his careful study of the locality. See his *Geology of the Henry Mountains*, published by the government.

we could hardly have been distinguished from the old Shin-umos themselves; but we were clean. Steward was a great lover of Burns and could quote him by the page, though what he most liked to repeat just now was:

> " O wad some Power the giftie gie us
> To see coursels as others see us! "

I think the *Address to the Deil* would have been appropriate for this particular environment, but I do not remember that Steward quoted:

> " Hear me, auld Hangie, for a wee,
> An' let poor damned bodies be;
> I 'm sure sma' pleasure it can gie,
> E'en to the deil,
> To skelp an' scaud poor dogs like me,
> An' hear us squeel! "

The cargo of the *Cañonita* was distributed among the cabins of the *Dean* and the *Nell*, and Cap. was somewhat disturbed by having an addition to the bow compartment in the *Nell*. Each man had charge of a cabin and this was Cap.'s special pride. He daily packed it so methodically that it became a standing joke with us, and we often asked him whether he always placed that thermometer back of the fifth rib or in front of the third, or some such nonsensical question, which of course Cap. took in good part and only arranged his cabin still more carefully.

The next morning, the 2d of October, at eight o'clock, we continued our voyage, now entering a new canyon, then called Mound, but it was afterwards consolidated with the portion below called Monument, and together they now stand as Glen Canyon. In about three and one half miles we ran several sharp little rapids, but they were not of much consequence, and we stopped to examine a house ruin we saw standing up boldly on a cliff on the left. It could be seen for a long distance in both directions, and correspondingly its inmates in the old days could see every approach. Doubtless the trail we had seen on the right had its exit on the other side near it. The walls, neatly built of thin sandstone slabs, still stood about

fifteen feet high and fifteen inches thick. The dimensions on the
ground were 12 x 22 feet outside. It had been of two or three
stories, and exhibited considerable skill on the part of the
builders, the corners being plumb and square. Under the brink
of the cliff was a sort of gallery formed by the erosion of a soft
shale between heavy sandstone beds, forming a floor and roof
about eight or ten feet wide, separated by six or seven feet in
vertical height. A wall had been carried along the outer edge,
and the space thus made was divided by cross walls into a
number of rooms. Potsherds and arrow-heads, mostly broken
ones, were strewn everywhere. There were also numerous
picture-writings, of which I made copies.

As we pulled on and on the Major frequently recited selections from the poets, and one that he seemed to like very
much, and said sometimes half in reverie, was Longfellow's:

> " Often I think of the beautiful town
>   That is seated by the sea ;
> Often in thought go up and down
> The pleasant streets of that dear old town,
>   And my youth comes back to me.
> And a verse of a Lapland song
>   Is haunting my memory still :
>   ' A boy's will is the wind's will,
> And the thoughts of youth are long, long thoughts.' "

He would repeat several times, with much feeling:

> " A boy's will is the wind's will,
> And the thoughts of youth are long, long thoughts. "

Another thing he enjoyed repeating was Whittier's *Skip-
per Ireson's Ride*:

> " Old Floyd Ireson, for his hard heart,
>   Tarred and feathered and carried in a cart
>   By the women of Marblehead ! "

Towards evening we came to another Shinumo ruin, where
we made camp, having run altogether sixteen miles, with

ten rapids, all small, between walls of red, homogeneous sandstone, averaging about one thousand feet in height. The river, some three hundred and fifty feet wide, was low, causing many shoals, which formed the small rapids. We often had to wade alongside to lighten the boats, but otherwise these places were easy. A trifle more water would have done away with them, or at least would have enabled us to ignore them completely. The house ruin at our camp was very old and broken down and had dimensions of about 20 x 30 feet. Prof. climbed out to a point 1215 feet above the river, where he saw plainly the Unknown Mountains, Navajo Mountain, and a wide sweep of country formed largely of barren sandstone. Steward felt considerably under the weather and remained as quiet as possible.

In the morning we were quickly on the water, pushing along under conditions similar to those of the previous day, making twenty-seven miles and passing eleven very small rapids, with a river four hundred feet wide and the same walls of homogeneous red sandstone about one thousand feet high. The cliffs in the bends were often slightly overhanging, that is, the brink was outside of a perpendicular line, but the opposite side would then generally be very much cut down, usually to irregular, rounded slopes of smooth rock. The vertical portions were unbroken by cracks or crevices or ledges, being extensive flat surfaces, beautifully stained by iron, till one could imagine all manner of tapestry effects. Along the river there were large patches of alluvial soil which might easily be irrigated, though it is probable that at certain periods they would be rapidly cut to pieces by high water.

Prof. again climbed out at our noon camp, and saw little but naked orange sandstone in rounded hills, except the usual mountains. In the barren sandstone he found many pockets or pot-holes, a feature of this formation, often thirty or forty feet deep, and frequently containing water. Wherever we climbed out in this region we saw in the depressions flat beds of sand, surrounded by hundreds of small round balls of stone an inch or so in diameter, like marbles—concretions and hard fragments which had been driven round and round by the winds till they were quite true spheres.[1]

The next day, October 4th, we ran into a stratum of sandstone shale, which at this low stage of water for about five miles gave us some trouble. Ledge after ledge stretched across the swift river, which at the same time spread to at least six hundred feet, sometimes one thousand. We were obliged to walk in the water alongside for great distances to lighten the boats and ease them over the ridges. Occasionally the rock bottom was as smooth as a ballroom floor; again it would be carved in the direction of the current into thousands of narrow, sharp, polished ridges, from three to twelve inches apart, upon which the boats pounded badly in spite of all exertions to prevent it. The water was alternately shallow and ten feet deep, giving us all we could do to protect the boats and at the same time avoid sudden duckings in deep water. With all our care the *Nell* got a bad knock, and leaked so fast that one man continually bailing could barely keep the water out. We repaired her at dinner-time, and, the shales running up above the river, we escaped further annoyance from this cause. Even with this interference our progress was fairly good, and by camping-time we had made twenty-one miles.

We had a rapid shallow river again the following day, October 5th, but the water was not so widely spread out and there were fewer delays. The walls were of orange sandstone, strangely cut up by narrow side canyons some not more than twenty feet wide and twisting back for a quarter of a mile where they expanded into huge amphitheatres, domed and cave-like. Alcoves filled with trees and shrubs also opened from the river, and numerous springs were noted along the cliffs. Twelve miles below our camp we passed a stream coming in on the left through a canyon about one thousand feet deep, similar to that of the Colorado. This was the San Juan, now shallow and some eight rods wide. We did not stop till noon when we were two miles below it near one of the amphitheatres or

[1] The illustration on page 43 of *The Romance of the Colorado* well shows the character of the Glen Canyon country, and that on page 63 the nature of the pot-holes.

Glen Canyon.
Photograph by E. O. Beaman, 1871.

Looking down upon Glen Canyon.

Cut through homogeneous sandstone.
Photograph by J. K. HILLERS, U. S. Colo. Riv. Exp.

grottoes to which the first party had given the name of "Music Temple." The entrance was by a narrow gorge which after some distance widened at the bottom to about five hundred feet in diameter leaving the upper walls arching over till they formed a dome-shaped cavern about two hundred feet high with a narrow belt of sky visible above. In the farther end was a pool of clear water, while five or six green cottonwoods and some bushes marked the point of expansion. One side was covered with bright ferns, mosses, and honeysuckle. Every whisper or cough resounded. This was only one of a hundred such places but we had no time to examine them. On a smooth space of rock we found carved by themselves the names of Seneca Howland, O. G. Howland, and William Dunn, the three men of the first party who were killed by the Shewits in 1869. Prof. climbed up eight hundred feet and had a fine view of Navajo Mountain which was now very near. We then chiefly called it Mount Seneca Howland, applied by the Major in memory of that unfortunate person but later, the peak already having to some extent been known as Navajo Mountain, that name was finally adopted. No one had ever been to it, so far as we knew, and the Major was desirous of reaching the summit.

Leaving the Music Temple, which seemed to us a sort of mausoleum to the three men who had marked it with their names, we soon arrived at a pretty rapid with a clear chute. It was not large but it was the only real one we had seen in this canyon and we dashed through it with pleasure. Just below we halted to look admiringly up at Navajo Mountain which now loomed beside us on the left to an altitude of 10,416 feet above sea level or more than 7100 feet above our position, as was later determined. The Major contemplated stopping long enough for a climb to the top but on appealing to Andy for information as to the state of the supplies he found we were near the last crust and he decided that we had better pull on as steadily as possible towards El Vado. We ran down a considerable distance through some shallows and camped on the left having accomplished about twenty miles in the day towards our goal. Here the remaining food was divided into two portions, one for supper, the other for breakfast in the morning. Though we were running so close to the starvation line we felt no great concern about it. We always had confidence in our ability somehow to get through with success. Andy, particularly, never failed in his optimism. Generally he took no interest in the nature of a rapid, lying half asleep while the others examined the place, and entirely willing to run anything or make a portage or even swim; he cared not. "Nothing ever happens to any outfit I belong to," he would declare shifting to an easier position, "Let her go!" and now so far as Andy's attitude was concerned we might have possessed unlimited rations. Jack lightened the situation yet more with his jolly songs and humorous expressions and no one viewing that camp would have thought the ten men had before them a possibility of several days without food, except what they might kill in the barren country, and perhaps a walk from El Vado over an unknown trail about one hundred miles out to Kanab. In the morning, Friday, October 6th, we got away as quickly as we could and pulled down the river hoping that El Vado was not far ahead and feeling somewhat as Escalante must have felt a century before when he was trying to find it. He had the advantage of having horses which could be eaten from time to time. Of course we knew from the position of the San Juan and of Navajo Mountain, that we could reach El Vado in at most two days, but the question was, "would we find any one there with rations?" The Major apparently was unconcerned. He told me a story about a farmer's son in his neighbourhood when himself a boy who had no shoes, no good clothes, no decent hat, but who went to the father and declared he wanted a "buzzum pin," and nothing but a buzzum pin would he have, though his parent called his attention to his lack of other necessaries, one after the other. "No Pa," the boy would repeat "I want a buzzum pin."

As we rowed along the Major sang softly another of his favourites:

"Flow gently, sweet Afton! among thy green braes,
Flow gently, I 'll sing thee a song in thy praise;
My Mary 's asleep by thy murmuring stream—
Flow gently, sweet Afton, disturb not her dream."

The almost vertical walls ran from two hundred to one thousand feet in height, cut by many very narrow side canyons opening into large glens or alcoves. On and on we steadily pulled till noon, making 13½ miles when we stopped on the right on a sandstone ledge against a high cliff. Andy had a few scraps left, among them a bit of bacon which Jack enterprisingly used for baiting a hook and soon drew out several small fish, so that after all we had quite a dinner. The walls became more broken as we went on apparently with numerous opportunities for entrance from the back country, though the sandstone even where not very steep was so smooth that descent over it would be difficult. We had gone about three miles after dinner when we saw a burned place in the brush on the right where there was quite a large piece of bottom land. We thought this might be some signal for us but we found there only the tracks of two men and horses all well shod proving that they were not natives. About three miles farther down we caught a glimpse of a stick with a white rag dangling from it stuck out from the right bank, and at the same moment heard a shot. On landing and mounting the bank we found Captain Pardyn Dodds and two prospectors, George Riley and John Bonnemort, encamped beside a large pile of rations. Dodds was one of the men with Old Jacob who had tried desperately to reach the mouth of the Dirty Devil with our supplies. He thought he had arrived at a point where he could see it and went back to inform Jacob when they received an order from the Major to come to this place, El Vado de los Padres, by September 25th, and here he was. Jacob had come with him but had gone on to Fort Defiance, the Navajo Agency, to settle some Indian business, leaving him to guard the rations. Having left Kanab early in September they had no late news. They had become discouraged by our non-appearance and concluded that we would never be heard from again. Consequently they had planned to cache the rations and leave for the settlement on Sunday. That night Andy was able to summon us to "go fur" the first "square" meal we had eaten for nearly a month. There was among the supplies some plug tobacco which we cut up, all but Steward,

Prof., and Cap. who did not smoke, and rolled in cigarettes with thick yellow paper, the only kind we had, having learned to make them Spanish fashion from the Hamblins, and we smoked around the fire talking to Dodds and the prospectors over the general news. They told us they had found small quantities of gold along the river. A great many papers, magazines, and letters for everybody were in the packs supplying us with reading matter enough for weeks. Though the papers were of ancient dates they were new to us.

The whole next day was consumed in preparing maps, notes, specimens, fossils, etc., to be sent by pack-train to the settlement of Kanab one hundred miles off whither the Major himself had decided to start with the outfit the next morning and go from there to Salt Lake City about 400 miles north. None of us had a chance to write even a line to expectant relatives far away and we were naturally disappointed till Prof. persuaded the Major to hold over till Tuesday which he willingly did when he realised the situation. We wrote late by the light of a diminutive fire, wood being scarce. He then left us on October 10th with Jack, Captain Dodds, and the miners who had waited only to learn something about the river above as a place for prospecting. The trail up over the barren sandstone was so steep and smooth that two of the pack-animals lost their footing and rolled back to the bottom but received no injury except scraping the skin off their knees.

Not the least welcome articles among the supplies were a pair of good heavy shoes and a pair of strong overalls, which the foresight of the Major had secured for each one of us, our clothing, as before mentioned, having been completely worn out. My watch, which I had carried all the way in a little rubber pocket sewed to my shirt near the neck, where it seldom got wet enough to stop it, though occasionally it refused to go till I punched it up with a large pin kept for the purpose, which my wicked companions called my "starting bar," at last had stopped permanently, and I sent it out by Jack for repairs. After they had gone we settled down again to our accustomed labours. We were to run down thirty-five miles farther to the mouth of the Paria, whence there was another known trail to the settlement, and cache the boats. The pack-train was to come back to us there with additional supplies and horses and take us out to Kanab, where we were to make headquarters for our winter explorations in the practically unknown Grand Canyon region as well as in that to the eastward. During this interval we expected to discover some point between the Paria and Diamond Creek where rations could be brought in to us while working through the Grand Canyon the next season. We did not then know that the winter is the safest and best time for making the passage through that wonderful gorge.[1]

Our appetites were now enormous, and as we could eat all we wanted, the supplies diminished in an astonishing way, but as we were soon to receive more we did not care. Every man braced up; all but Steward, who felt quite sick. Jones began to feel trouble brewing in the leg which he had hurt at the Junction; Andy showed the effects of the scorpion bite by becoming thin and pale, thinner than our previous lack of rations justified; Cap., who had been shot in the Civil War through and through near the heart, now felt the effects of the long exposure; and neither Clem nor Beaman considered their health perfect. Altogether, however, we had come through very well. Our worst work was over for this year, and the maladies portending seemed not dangerous. Prof., desiring to get some notes from up the river, went on the 11th, with Cap., Beaman, and Clem, back six miles in the *Dean* to the foot of some rapid water they could not pass. Arriving there about half-past twelve, they spent all afternoon going up numerous gulches, trying to find a way out. As there was a large area of bottom land, with old camp-fires and much broken pottery, they were sure there was a path, but it was late before they discovered a place where modern natives had piled brush and stones to make a horse trail, and another where the old Shinumos for fifty feet had cut steps in the smooth rock. The party followed the Shinumo trail, finding the steps in places

---

[1] We learned later that while we were working through Cataract Canyon, Lieutenant George M. Wheeler, U. S. Engineers, was coming up from Fort Mohave. After great labour he reached the mouth of Diamond Creek. See *The Romance of the Colorado*, Chapter XII.

almost worn out by time, in others still quite good and large enough to get the toe of a shoe in. By the time they came to the top it was too late for observations, and they returned to the river for camp, making the same climb by the steps the next day and securing the observations. They got back to our Camp 79 late in the afternoon. Meanwhile Steward's illness had increased, and I spent much of the night trying to relieve his pain. The air was cold and he was most uncomfortable, the only shelter being a wickiup of boughs we had built to protect him from the sun. We had opium pills in our medicine chest, and I had the little flask of brandy referred to. With several of the pills and my brandy, which I at last persuaded him to take as medicine (he despised alcoholic drinks), his suffering was somewhat relieved, and he was able to lie still on his bed of willows. During the next day his condition was no better, and Prof. returning, was much distressed by it. By drawing further on the medicine chest, which contained numerous remedies, he was able to relieve him a little more. The exposure had brought on a trouble of the back which had originally developed during the campaigns of the Civil War.

Before leaving this point Prof. wanted some observations from the heights, and he and Cap. tried to climb the near-by cliffs, but failed. They then took a hammer and chisel, and by cutting "holds" in the sandstone after the manner of the old Shinumos, they got up 850 feet and secured the bearings Prof. desired. The following day they went out on the trail toward Kanab five miles, trying to find another point of exit to the summit, but did not succeed. While they were gone we heard a sudden shout, and saw an Indian standing on the rocks not far away. We beckoned for him to come, and thereupon he fell back to another, and together they approached. We saw by their dress, so different from the Ute (red turbans, loose unbleached cotton shirts, native woven sashes at the waist, wide unbleached cotton trousers reaching to a little below the knee and there slashed up on the outer side for seven or eight inches, bright woven garters twisted around their red buckskin leggins below the knee, and red moccasins with

turned up soles and silver buttons), that they were Navajos.[1]
They indicated that they were father and son, the father
announcing himself in a lordly way as "Agua Grande." He
was over six feet tall and apparently sixty or seventy years
old. The son was a fine young lad of about fifteen. Their
bearing was cordial, yet proud and dignified. They had not
long been with us when Prof. came in, and during the next
hour seven more Navajos arrived, all dressed very much as the
first ones were. They expressed great friendliness by embracing
us after their custom and delivering long speeches, of which
we understood not a word. One had a short black mustache
which came straight out sidewise and then turned at right
angles down past the corners of his mouth. I never had heard
of an Indian with a mustache before. They had no visible
firearms, being armed with strong bows and cougar-skin quivers
full of iron-headed arrows.[2] Old Agua Grande became much
interested in our sick man, and made signs by placing two
spread fingers of one hand inverted upon one finger held hori-
zontally of the other hand, and moving them north-westerly to
indicate that he ought to ride out to the Mormon settlement,
whither they were bound, and that they would take him along.
As the chief had exhibited a document, signed by the agent at
Fort Defiance, to the effect that he and his band were peaceable and going on a trading expedition to the Mormon settlements, we felt certain they would take good care of the invalid,
but Steward said he preferred to remain with us.

We now had no further work for this immediate locality,
and concluded to run down a mile or so to separate ourselves from the Navajos, one having disclosed a tendency to

[1] For further description of the Navajo costume, see *The North Americans of
Yesterday*, by F. S. Dellenbaugh, pp. 148, 150.

[2] Like all the tribes of the region of that time, the Navajos considered the
Mormons a different people from the Americans. They had been at war with the
Mormons, from whom they stole horses and cattle, and there had been some
bloodshed. Old Jacob had induced them to make peace, and this party now on its
way to trade was the first to try the experiment. Vanquished by our troops, a few
years before, the Navajos were very poor and anxious to acquire live stock and
firearms, for which they had blankets and other articles of their own make to
trade.

surreptitiously appropriate small articles belonging to us. A bed was made on the middle deck of one of the boats for Steward, and when all was ready we carried him down to it. The Navajos ranged themselves along the bank to see us off, and Clem, with his customary urbanity, went down the line all smiles, shaking each one cordially by the hand, and requesting him to " Give my love to all the folks at home," and " Remember me, please, to Eliza Jane," and similar expressions. The Navajos did not understand the words, but being themselves great jokers they saw that it was fun, and they all laughed, making remarks which doubtless were of the same kind. Just below was El Vado de los Padres by which these Navajos had now come across. It was also sometimes called the Ute Ford. The necessary route was indicated by a line of small piles of stones showing above water. It was not an easy crossing, feasible only at low water, and quite impossible for waggons, even had there been a road to it. A shoal was followed up the middle of the river half a mile with deep channels cutting through it, reached from the south over a steep slope of bare sandstone and from the north through a very narrow, small canyon, not over ten feet wide. Escalante in 1776, after the failure of his attempt to reach California, had great difficulty in finding the place, which for centuries has been known to all the tribes of the region. About three miles below our last camp we landed on the left on a very pretty piece of bottom land, inaccessible except by river, being bounded behind by a high, vertical, unscalable wall. Here we made Camp 80, with plenty of food, water, and wood, and all were comfortable by a fine fire; all but Steward, who, feeling very sick, was lying on the bed we had prepared for him. He had another bad night, but after this his condition seemed gradually to improve.

Prof.'s favourite quotation now was Charles Fenno Hoffman's poem:

" We were not many—we who stood
    Before the iron sleet that day;
Yet many a gallant spirit would
    Give half his years if but he could
        Have been with us at Monterey."

Tom.
A Typical Navajo.
Photograph by WITTICK.
Tom became educated and no longer looked like an Indian.

Glen Canyon.

Sentinel Rock—about 300 Feet High.
Photograph by E. O. BEAMAN, 1871.

In the morning he went with Jones across the river and climbed out while the rest of us did nothing but lie around camp doing what was possible to make Steward comfortable. It was Sunday as well and whenever practicable we rested the whole or part of that day. Monday we started late and ran only a short distance before dinner which we ate on the right. Steward still was unable to sit up and he was carried on the middle deck of the *Nell* where he had a rope to cling to so that he should not roll off into the water when the boat lurched. Toward evening we camped at the head of a small rapid near a fine little stream coming in from the left which we named Navajo Creek. The river was about four hundred feet wide with walls on each side of four hundred feet in height. The next morning Prof., Cap. and I climbed out for bearings reaching an altitude a mile or so back from the river of 875 feet. Everywhere we discovered broken pottery, fragments of arrow-heads, and other evidences of former Shinumo occupancy. Even granting only a few persons at each possible locality, the canyons of the Colorado and Green must have been the former home of a rather large population. In the afternoon we ran the little rapid and kept on for about six miles making twenty in all from El Vado, when we camped on a heavy talus on the left. The following morning, October 18th, we had not gone more than a mile when we came to a singular freak of erosion, a lone sandstone pinnacle on the right, three hundred or four hundred feet high, the river running on one side and a beautiful creek eight feet wide on the other. We named these Sentinel Rock and Sentinel Creek and camped there for Beaman to get some photographs. Prof. and I went up the creek and tried to climb out for observations, but though we made three separate attempts we had to give it up. Steward grew so much better that he was able to walk a little, but now Jones began to feel more pain in his injured leg. On Thursday, the 19th, we made nearly seven miles between walls about eight hundred feet high and one quarter of a mile apart, so nearly vertical that we could not get out.

The next day we ran six miles more with walls one thousand feet high, camping at a place where there was a wide bottom with many signs of old native camps, probably Navajo. In the morning Prof., Cap., and I climbed a steep slope of bright orange sand a little below our camp, a rather hard task as the sand was loose, causing us to slip backward at every step. After twelve hundred or fifteen hundred feet of this kind of climbing we reached the base of three rocky peaks several hundred feet higher. We had considerable difficulty in surmounting one of these, being forced around to the opposite side, where there was a sheer descent from our position of some fifteen hundred feet, with sharp black rocks at the bottom where any one slipping would fall. There were some narrow transverse crevices in the rock by means of which we got up. One man, having been pushed aloft from the solid ledge by the two below, would lie back against the slope, brace himself with one heel in a transverse fissure, and lower the free foot as a handhold for the others to mount by. The next trouble was a crevice wide enough for us to pass through to the top, but holding exactly midway a large rock lodged in such a manner that we could not crawl under and yet seeming in danger of rolling down if we went over it. It was precarious not only for the man ahead who tried to pass but for those below waiting for results, but it was more firmly wedged than it appeared to be and each one in turn climbed over it. Emerging from this crack we were on the summit 2190 feet above the river and 5360 above the sea, with standing room no more than six or eight feet square. The view was superb. The peaks formed the northern end of a long line of cliffs running back to the south at the end of Glen Canyon, and we looked out across a wonderful region, part of that on the south being the "Painted Desert," so called by Ives. Mountains solid and solitary rose up here and there and line upon line of strangely coloured cliffs broke across the wide area, while from our feet stretching off to the south-west like a great dark dragon extending miles into the blue was the deep gorge of Marble Canyon, its tributary chasms appearing like mighty sprawling legs. Far away west were the San Francisco Mountains, and the Kaibab, while behind we saw Navajo Mountain and others.

This peak, or cluster of peaks, of course had never been named, had never been climbed before, but they soon named

themselves. For amusement I tried to shoot into the river
with Cap.'s 44 Remington revolver. As I pulled the trigger
the noise was absolutely staggering. The violent report was
followed by dead silence. While we were remarking the
intensity of the crash, from far away on some distant cliffs
northward the sound waves were hurled back to us with a rattle
like that of musketry. We tried again with the same result,
the interval between the great roar and the echo being twenty-
four seconds by the watch. We could call the place nothing but
Echo Peaks, and since then the name has been applied also to
the line of cliffs breaking to the south. Our descent was easy
and we reached camp without any incident except the loss of
my sheath knife.

Nobody did anything the next day, for it was Sunday,
so when Monday morning came we were eager to be off for
the mouth of the Paria, which we had seen from the top of
Echo Peaks. Two or three miles down we reached it ; a small
river coming through a great canyon on the right. The cliffs
of Glen Canyon broke back south-westerly and south-easterly in
a V form with the point at the foot of Glen Canyon, leaving a
wide platform of different rock rising gently from under them
and mounting steadily toward the south. Into the middle of
this the river immediately slashed a narrow gorge very much as
a staircase might be cut through a floor, beginning the next canyon of the series, called Marble, through which we would not
descend till the following year. We went into camp on the
left bank of the Paria and the right of the Colorado, Camp 86,
in the tall willows. A rough scow lay there, which the Major
had built the year before when on his way from Kanab to the
Moki Towns, for there is no ford.

We were to wait here for our pack-train which the Major,
on arriving at Kanab, was to start back with rations and some
extra horses. Our altitude was 3170 feet, showing a total descent
for the season of 2905 feet, 913 feet from Gunnison Crossing.
Our work on the water for the present was now over ; we would
pursue it with mule and pack instead of with boats. As the 23d
of October had arrived we were glad to avoid daily saturation.

CHAPTER XI

More Navajos Arrive with Old Jacob—The Lost Pack-train and a Famished Guide—From Boat to Broncho—On to Kanab—Winter Arrives—Wolf Neighbours too Intimate—Preparing for Geodetic Work—Over the Kaibab to Eight-mile Spring—A Frontier Town—Camp below Kanab—A Mormon Christmas Dance.

AT the mouth of the Paria we established ourselves for a stay of several days. Not only did we have the pack-train to wait for, but there were maps to finish, boats to cache, and all manner of things to attend to before we could leave for the winter. Steward recovered so that he could slowly walk around, but to balance this Jones developed inflammatory rheumatism in both knees, but especially in the one which had been injured by the fall at the Junction. Though he was perfectly cheerful about it, he suffered excruciating pain, and was unable to move from the bed of willows which we made for him. The medicine chest was drawn on again, and we hoped that the attack would not last long. Andy remained wan and thin, but he insisted on sticking to his work. So liberally had we used our rations that we were nearing the end, and we began to look hopefully in the direction from which we expected the pack-train to arrive. Four days passed and still there was no sign of it. We had to put ourselves on half-rations once more, and Prof. declared that if the train did not soon arrive either he or I, being the only entirely well members of the party, would have to walk out to Kanab and obtain relief. None of us knew anything about the trail. On the 26th Prof. and I climbed the cliffs back of camp to a height of two thousand feet, and had a remarkable view similar to that from Echo Peaks. On Saturday, October 28th, in the morning we were surprised to hear from the opposite or south side of the river an Indian yell, and looking across we perceived what appeared to be three natives, with horses, standing on the edge of the canyon wall, here very low. We prepared one of the boats to cross and find out what was wanted, when a fourth figure joined the group, and in good English came the words, "G-o-o-d m-o-r-n-i-n-g," long drawn out. On landing we were met by a slow-moving, very quiet individual, who said he was Jacob Hamblin. His voice was so low, his manner so simple, his clothing so usual, that I could hardly believe that this was Utah's famous Indian-fighter and manager. With him were three other white men, Isaac Haight, George Adair, Joe Mangum, and nine Navajos, all on their way to the Mormon settlements. They desired to be put across the river, and we willingly offered the services of ourselves and our boats. Some of the Navajos had never before seen so large a stream, and were free to express their surprise. We took on board Jacob and one or two others, and after landing them made several trips with both boats to ferry the rest over, including all their saddles and baggage. The Navajos were rather afraid of the boats, which to them probably looked small and wobbly, but they all got on board with much hilarity, except one who preferred to swim. He struck boldly out with a sort of dog-paddle stroke. Having no confidence in his swimming ability, we followed closely. The water was cold ; the distance greater than the Navajo had imagined. Before he was one third of the way over he consented to be pulled into our boat and finish the passage that way. The horses were towed over, swimming behind the boats, a rope being held by a man sitting in the stern. There was a rapid not far below, and we feared if driven in to swim loose they might be drawn into it. One horse refused to swim or even to try, and made repeated efforts to plunge his head under, giving us a lot of trouble, but by holding his head close to the boat we towed him across in spite of his opposition. Without the boat he would surely have gone down the river. When everybody and everything were safely across the hour was so late that Jacob concluded to camp with us for the night.[1]

[1] Five years later Jacob came near being drowned in crossing here. Lorenzo

The Navajos were found to be a very jolly set of fellows, ready to take or give any amount of chaff, and perfectly honest. They were taking blankets of their manufacture to trade for horses and sheep. Their spirits ran high, they sang their wild songs for us, and we had the liveliest evening we had seen in many a month. Finally we joined in a circle with them, dancing and singing around the smouldering fire, while the chief Konéco, a noble-looking fellow, sitting at one side, with a patriarchal expression, monotonously drummed an accompaniment with a willow root on the bottom of one of the camp-kettles. When any of us would stumble on a stick they were all convulsed with laughter. The blankets they had were beautiful, and Jacob possessed one valued at $40, which had taken seventy days to make. After the Navajos had gone to rest we listened to some Mormon songs by Jacob's party. They left us the next morning, Sunday, October 29th, Prof. obtaining from Jacob some red Mexican beans to eke out our supplies; also a description of the trail. I traded a cap I happened to have to one of the Navajos for his feather plume, and a pair of shoes to one of the white men for some Mishongnuvi moccasins. Monday we took the *Dean* across the river, and some distance down we hauled her by means of ropes up high above the water under a large rock, where we concealed her well. Then we made five caches near camp of goods not needed till next year, covering our traces by fires and other devices. Jones was so much improved that he managed to hobble about on a pair of crutches I had made for him out of strong willow sticks, and we felt much encouraged as to his ability to stand riding when the time came to start for Kanab.

On Tuesday we built a shelter back of camp for the *Nell* and housed her there. The next day was the first of November and we thought surely the pack-train would come, but the sun went down behind the cliffs and no one arrived. Prof. could not understand what the trouble was, but he went on with his observations. The next morning, as we were about

---

W. Roundy was lost, as well as two waggons loaded with supplies. The scow they had tried to use tilted, throwing everything into the fierce torrent.

to eat our bean breakfast beside the fire, we were astonished
by the extremely cautious appearance through the willows,
without a word of announcement, of a single, ragged, woebe-
gone, silent old man on as skinny and tottering a pony as ever
I saw. The old man was apparently much surprised to find
himself here, and with the exclamation, "My God! I have
found you!" he dropped to the ground. When at last he
spoke he said his name was Mangum of Kanab, and that he
had been employed to guide our pack-train, of which Riley, one
of the prospectors we had met at El Vado, was leader. "Well,
where is the train?" we asked, for if he were all that remained
of it we wanted to know it soon. "Several miles back on the
trail," he said. Not having eaten a mouthful since the morning before it was no wonder he was weak and silent. We gave
him the best breakfast we could command from our meagre
stock and then like a spectre he vanished on his scrawny steed
up the Paria Canyon. All the day long we watched and waited
for his triumphal return with the longed-for supplies at his back,
but the sun departed without his approach and the twilight
died into that mystery which leaves the world formless against
the night. And still we had faith in the stranger's story. Early
the next morning Prof., Clem, and I started on his track thinking we would soon meet the train. It led us up the valley of
the Paria, between the great cliffs about three miles, and then
we had another surprise, for it swung sharply to the right and
climbed a steep sandy slope towards the only apparent place
where the two-thousand-foot cliffs could possibly be scaled with
horses. We saw that he had followed a very old Indian trail.
When we had mounted to the base of the vertical rocks we
travelled zig-zagging back and forth across the face of the
precipice till presently the trail passed through a notch out
upon the plateau. From an eminence we now scanned the
whole visible area without discovering anything that apparently
had not been there for several thousand years. Save the coming and going tracks of our strange visitor there was nothing to
show that any living animal had trod this place in centuries.
We could see to where Prof. and I previously climbed to this
same plateau, and to-day was like yesterday and yesterday like

the year before last. Time and the years were as little grains of drifting sand.

Leaving Clem as a sentinel on our observation point Prof. followed the out track and told me to follow the in till three o'clock. It was now high noon. I walked on and on through an arid, wonderful maze of sand, rocks, and cacti, feeling that the old horseman was no more than a phantom, when in half an hour I almost fell upon our lost pack-train meandering slowly and silently through a depression. I fired our signal shots and Prof. soon joined us. The situation was precarious. The animals were nearly dead from thirst, one had been abandoned, and Riley was in a state of pent-up rage that was dangerous for the spectre guide, who had nearly been the destruction of the whole outfit, for he did not know the trail and was himself lost. Of course he blamed Riley—it was his only defence. Riley broke loose in a string of fiery oaths, declaring he would shoot "the old fool," then and there. But receiving no encouragement from Prof. or me he did n't. There was a third member of the party, Joe Hamblin, a son of Jacob, a very sturdy young fellow. He said afterwards that he thought often that Riley would "sure let daylight through the old man." Our next care was to successfully manœuvre the pack-animals down the difficult trail across the face of the cliff, which had not seen a horse for many a year and probably never had been traversed by animals with packs on their backs. We had to watch that they did not crowd each other off, but with all our exertions one fell and rolled down a few feet. He was not injured and we continued the descent, finally reaching the bottom without so much as a scratch of any consequence. There, at the Paria, the horses enjoyed the first full drink for several days and we followed it down to camp. Riley had started from Kanab October 23d and had been twelve days making a journey that required at most only four or five by the regular trail. Mangum had not known the way, had led toward El Vado, and his finding the Indian trail to the mouth of the Paria was an accident.

Provisions were now plenty again, and by the light of a big fire we overhauled the mail, finding letters, newspapers and magazines enough to satisfy any party. Word was received from the Major to move to a place called House Rock Spring, and Prof. said we would leave Camp 86 on November 5th, which gave us a day intervening in which to pack up. About noon of this packing day we were not surprised when two horsemen, Haight and Riggs, galloped into camp at full speed leading a lightly laden pack-mule. They had come through in two and one half days, at top speed, by direction of Jacob, who on reaching Kanab with the Navajos learned that our pack-train had left long before, and he had seen nothing of it. On the pack-mule were fifty pounds of flour and several rolls of butter; the first time we had seen any of this latter article since the final breakfast at Field's on May 22d. They were greatly relieved to know that the train was found and that all was well. They brought news of the burning of Chicago about a month before. In the evening Isaac Haight favoured us with some Mormon songs and recited examples of the marvellous curative effects of the Mormon "laying on of hands." Heavy clouds had settled along the face of the cliffs and the air grew wintry. We felt the chill keenly, as we were not clad for cold weather. In the morning snow began to drop gently out of the leaden sky and continued all day, preventing any one from starting. Soon the cliffs and Echo Peaks were white and we knew that now autumn was gone. Toward evening the sun flared across the rocky landscape, turning everything to gold, and we believed the next day would be fair. We were not disappointed. Monday the 6th of November came sharp and cold. Haight, Riggs, Mangum, and Joe Hamblin left early and we got under way as soon as we could. With two very sick men and a new method of travel it was not easy. We had to learn the art of packing on mules and horses from Riley, who was an expert in this line and who could " sling the diamond hitch " with great skill. He was just as handy with a lasso and seldom missed if he wished to catch an animal, but Prof. did not approve of the lasso method, for it makes stock wild and unmanageable. His way was the quiet one and he was right, for we soon had the entire herd so that there was no rumpus at starting-time. With a free use of the lasso preparations to start partake of the activity of a tornado.

Steward by this time was able to walk slowly. Andy was well enough to travel on his feet, but Jones could not move at all without crutches. We did not have extra horses for all to ride, so Steward and Andy changed off, while the rest of us had to walk. Jones we lifted as gently as possible, though it was pain even to be touched in his condition, upon Riley's special horse called Doc, a well-trained, docile animal, who walked off with him. It was after noon before the start was accomplished, and meanwhile I went back on the incoming trail of the lost pack-train to the foot of the steep precipice for Riley's canteen, which had been forgotten there, and when I returned all were gone but Steward, Clem, and Beaman, who had remained behind to round up a young steer which had been driven in with the train for us to convert into beef at a convenient opportunity. As the advance party travelled very slowly we soon caught them, the steer being gentle as a kitten. The trail followed south along the foot of the cliffs which emerged from Paria Canyon, and to which the Major had given the name of Vermilion on account of their rich red colour. We wound in and out of deep alcoves, around the heads of impassable lateral canyons running to the Colorado, and past enormous rocks balanced in every conceivable position on extremely slender pedestals. After about eight miles we arrived at a diminutive spring, which gave enough water for Andy to make bread and coffee with, but none for the stock. There we camped. A few armfuls of scraggy sage-brush furnished wood for a fire, but it was not enough to make our invalids comfortable, and the night was cold and raw. We did all we could for them and they did not grumble.

In the morning a pair of bronchos—that is, recently broken wild horses—made the camp lively for a time, but they were subdued and the caravan again got under way. Our next camp was to be Jacob's Pools, so called from the fact that Jacob was the first white man to camp there. We had gone only a mile or so when we crossed in a small canyon a little stream already enjoying two names, Clear and Spring (now called Badger) Creek, and a little farther on another called

Soap Creek, still holding that name.[1] When first travellers enter a country they naturally bestow names on important objects, and two or three parties of white men who had passed this way had named these two creeks. After this we had no more water, and we pushed slowly ahead, looking for the Pools. Snow began to fall again in widely scattered, reluctant flakes, but melted on touching the ground. Late in the afternoon the trail turned the corner of the cliffs, which here broke to the west, and we saw a wide, desolate open plain stretching away to the foot of a distant table-land, which we knew to be the Kaibab Plateau or Buckskin Mountain. None of the party had been over the trail before, but it was easy to follow, especially for a man of Riley's experience. It was an old Navajo trail, and was here fairly well worn. The sun went down as we plodded on, the light faded from the west, and still we saw no Jacob's Pools. The air was biting, and with our thin, worn garments we felt it keenly and wished for a fire. At last just as the darkness began to thicken a patch of reeds on the right between some low hills was discovered, where it seemed there might be water, and we could not well go farther. The ground was moist, and by digging a hole we secured red, muddy liquid enough for Andy to make a little bread and a cup apiece of very poor coffee. The men and animals came straggling in out of the darkness. We gathered a lot of sage-brush and made a fire, and as soon as Jones came we lifted him off and put him as near the warmth as possible, for he was chilled through. There was no water for the stock, but the grass was wet and they did not suffer. Everything was damp and uncomfortable, and the fire was too small to dry anything out, so all turned in to the limited blankets and passed a cold, half-sleepless, uncomfortable night.

Morning was a relief, though the thermometer stood at 11 F. There was water enough in the holes for breakfast, and as soon as this meal was over the pack-train was on the move towards Jacob's Pools, which we found not two miles farther on. There were two of them, each seven or eight feet long, supplied by

[1] It was in the rapid in Marble Canyon near the mouth of the canyon of this creek that Frank M. Brown was drowned in July, 1889.

fine clear water oozing out of a hill-side. The lower one we turned over to the animals, reserving the upper for ourselves. We approached the plateau all day, and late in the afternoon we were within three or four miles of it, when the right-hand cliffs turned sharply to the north in a line parallel with the plateau, forming a long narrow valley. Cedars and piñons now grew about us, so that we were assured of a good fire. About sunset we passed two large boulders which had fallen together, forming a rude shelter, under which Riggs or some one else had slept, and then had jocosely printed above with charcoal the words "Rock House Hotel." Afterward this had served as identification, and Jacob and the others had spoken of "House Rock" Spring and House Rock Valley. We called it the same, and finally it went on the maps and is now permanent. A few yards beyond the House Rock the trail led into a gulch, at the head of which was a good spring. Plenty of cedars and piñons grew about, and we soon had a fire that compensated for the meagre ones of the preceding nights. The sick men became warm and dry, and we all felt much better. The whole outfit halted two days, and on the second the poor little steer, gazing sadly at us, was shot and cut up. In an hour the quarters were swinging from a tree and some of the beef was in the pan. Necessity is a sauce that makes every grist palatable. We were hungry, and nothing could have tasted better than that fresh beefsteak. The entrails and refuse were left on the ground in the neighbouring gulley where we had killed the steer, and next morning the place was about cleaned up by the lurking wolves.

Prof. decided to go on across the Kaibab to Kanab with the two very sick men, and leave Cap., Clem, Andy, and me here at House Rock Spring until the plan for the winter's campaign had been better formulated. Steward concluded that his condition was too precarious to risk further exposure, and said he would now leave the expedition permanently, which we learned with deep regret, but it was plainly imperative. Jones thought that a week or two of warmth and rest, accompanied by a change of diet, would make him whole again and enable him to stay till the end of our special task.

On Saturday, November 11th, the party started, with the invalids riding the gentlest and easiest horses, though Steward
found it less painful at times to walk. I accompanied them to
the summit of the Kaibab to bring back one of the horses we
called Thunderbolt, on which Jones was to be carried to the
top and there change to Doc. After I left them I halted many
times to look out into the wonderful land to the west and
north. When I got back to the spring, our Camp 3 of the
land operations, we immediately set up a stout 6 by 8 tent that
was in the outfit brought from Kanab, and it made a very snug
sleeping-place for the four of us. Around the fire we rolled
big stones for seats, and soon had the gulch in a homelike condition. There was an abundance of dead, fat piñon, which
burned like a candle, and we could easily extend our reading
into the evenings.

From all around us there arose the frequent bay and bark
of the wolves. They were of different kinds, numerous and
rather bold. At night they came in and cleared up what was
left of the entrails of the steer, also securing a fine, large piece
of beef which Cap. had hung in a tree, but not high enough to
escape their efforts. We took turns bringing the four horses
left with us to water, and in that way kept ourselves informed
about them. During these trips, especially in the late afternoon, the wolves were apt to trot along near by, and on one
occasion Clem was obliged to drive one out of the trail with
stones, not having his rifle. One morning, as I was riding
along not far from camp, a huge whitish fellow followed behind
like a dog about twenty yards back, licking his chaps. At first
I thought he might be the dog of some Indian camped near,
but remembering that there were none in the valley, and also
that an Indian dog, or any strange dog, would have run from
me, I saw that he was a hungry wolf unused to man. I had
no rifle with me, but I took a walk over the same ground next
morning with my Winchester, hoping to see my acquaintance
again, but he discreetly kept out of sight. We had little now
to occupy us except to examine the locality, chop wood for
our fire, and read over and over the newspapers and magazines.
The nights were very cold, the spring always freezing over, but

the days were delightful. The beef had to be jerked to preserve it. We cut it up into thin long strips, which we strung
through the ends on long withes, these in turn being hung on a
framework that left the strips swinging within two or three
feet of a slow fire. One hour's neglect of this tempting array
would have seen it vanish to the four winds, so we kept a
constant watch day and night, taking turns through the dark
hours. Every article which had grease or leather about it had
to be carefully put away to prevent its disappearance. Riley
had lost his spurs on the way out from this cause, the leather
on them making sweet morsels for the watchers.

Cap. concluded to profit by this appetite, and in an adjoining gulch he built a trap between two rocks, in which he
set his Remington six-shooter, so that a wolf picking up a
scrap of beef would pull the trigger by a string and receive the
ball in his head. That night during my watch over the beef I
roasted a piece on a stick for a lunch, and as the savory odour
drifted off on the crisp winter air howl after howl of ravenous
desire rang out from many directions, followed by the bang
of the revolver in the trap. Cap. went over, but found no
game, though later he often came back with a fine large specimen, bearing a perfect coat of fur, which Cap. always removed
by the firelight at once. About every night except Sunday,
when Cap. refused to set the trap—for he never did any work
on that day that was not absolutely necessary—there was a
fatal shot, and he accumulated a lot of excellent large skins,
which he tacked on trees to preserve them. He thought he
had put them up securely high, but one morning every skin
had disappeared. The wolf relatives had carried them away to
the last shred.

The Kaibab was too far away for us to go there to hunt
deer, and there were none around the spring, though one night
at supper-time, the western sky being a broad sweep of deep
orange, we saw a large wild animal of some sort on the crest of
the hill silhouetted against the colour. I started for it with my
rifle, but of course it did not wait; no animal ever does if
he can help it, unless he is carnivorous and famished. The
weather remained generally fair, though one day we had a wild

The Grand Canyon.
From Havasupai Point, South Rim, Showing Inner Gorge.
From a sketch in colour by F. S. DELLENBAUGH, 1907.

The Grand Canyon.
From South Rim near Bright Angel Creek.

gale that nearly relieved us of the tent in the midst of thick flurries of snow. We often climbed among the cliffs, and everywhere we found picture-writings, poles laid up, stepping-stones, fragments of pottery, arrowheads, and other evidences of former occupation. The poles and stones may have been placed by the Pai Utes as well as by the old Shinumos, who once were numerous over all this country. Cap. was by no means well. An extreme nervousness connected with the old gunshot wound developed, and he said he felt sure he could not continue the work in the field during the winter, much less go through the Grand Canyon with us the next year. Clem also felt under the weather, and besides was growing home-sick. He confided to me one day that he also had concluded not to remain with us. As there was little the matter with him I undertook to argue him out of his determination not to go through the Grand Canyon, pointing out the disappoint-ment he would feel when we had accomplished the passage and he realised that he might as well have come along. This produced some impression, but I was uncertain as to its lasting result.

By November 17th we began with confidence to look for some one to come over the mountains from Kanab, and just after sunset we heard Riley's long shrill " ee—ii—oooooooo," which he could deliver upon the air in such a fashion that it carried for miles. Presently Prof. and he rode into our camp with fresh supplies and a great bundle of mail that included papers giving the details of the burning of Chicago. Prof. with Cap. then reconnoitred the neighbourhood, and on the 21st he returned to Kanab, leaving us as before, except that Riley re-mained two days longer. The Major had not yet arrived at Kanab from Salt Lake and our winter work could not begin till he came. The days rolled by with occasional rain and snow and we began to grow impatient with our inaction, especially when November passed away. The second day of December was fading when we distinguished in the distance the familiar Riley yell, and in a little while he came into view with welcome news. We were to move at once to a spring eight miles from Kanab. He also brought some apples, native raisins and a large canteen full of fresh wine from "Dixie" as the country along the Virgin was called. These luxuries together with a number of letters from home made that night one of the most cheerful we had known for a long time. Monday morning, December 4th we left House Rock Spring behind with our pack-train, followed the trail across the open valley, climbed two thousand feet to the top of the Kaibab, and were soon traversing the forest on its broad summit. Riley having been over the trail now several times we went ahead steadily, and about sunset arrived at the farther side of a narrow longitudinal depression of the top which Cap. immediately put down in his notes as Summit Valley, a name that holds to-day. There we threw off our packs and made camp for the night. Though there was no water the ground was covered by a thin layer of snow, that made the long bunch grass palatable to the horses and for ourselves we had sufficient water in two small kegs and several canteens. A bright fire blazed cheerfully, the dense cedars broke the wind, and everybody felt that it was a fine camp. The others spent the evening playing euchre by fire-light, but I preferred to read till bedtime.

The next morning, after crossing some rough gulches, we came to the western edge of the great plateau, and emerging from the forest of pine and cedar we saw again the magnificent, kaleidoscopic, cliff country lying to the north. First about twenty miles away was a line of low chocolate-coloured cliffs, then a few miles back of this the splendid line of the Vermilion Cliffs, the same which began at the mouth of Glen Canyon and which we had skirted to House Rock Spring. From there the line continued northward till it passed around the north end of the Kaibab, when it struck southwesterly far to our left, where it turned back to the north again, forming one of the longest and finest cliff ranges anywhere to be seen. Above them and some miles still farther back, rising higher, was a line of greyish cliffs following the trend of the Vermilion, and still above these was the broken meandering face of the Pink Cliffs, frosted with snow, whose crest marks the southeastern limit of Fremont's "Great Basin," the end of the High Plateaus, and tops the country at an altitude of some 11,000 feet above sea-level.

A more extraordinary, bewildering landscape, both as to form and colour, could hardly be found in all the world. Winding our way down to the barren valley, in itself more a high plateau than a valley, we travelled the rest of the day in the direction of the great cliffs. The sun was just gone when we reached the first low line, and passing through a gap turned into a side gulch thickly studded with cedars, where we saw before us two white-covered waggons, two or three camp-fires blazing, and friends. We heard a hearty voice cry, "Tirtaan Aigles dis wai!" and we sprang from our horses to grasp Jack's welcoming hand and greet all the others, some of whom were new acquaintances. The fragrance of coffee and frying bacon filled the sharp air, while from the summits of the surrounding cliffs the hungry chorus of yelping wolves sent up their wail of disappointment.

In an alcove a large tent had been put up, which the Major's family was occupying, for Mrs. Powell and her baby daughter had come from Salt Lake with him, arriving a few days before. The daughter was but three months old and was happy in a big clothes-basket for a cradle. Mrs. Thompson, Prof.'s wife, and sister of the Major, had also come from Salt Lake and another large tent sheltered them, while still another of equal size, not yet erected, was designed for the men. It was a specially interesting camp to us who had come over from House Rock for it was novel to see so many people around. The Major himself was absent at Kanab. Before the camp was asleep the hour was late, and so soundly did every one rest that the sneaking wolves without the least molestation carried off two large sacks of the jerked beef from near our heads, where we had put it against a huge rock thinking they would not come so close; but as they had pulled a ham the night before from under the head of Captain Dodds where he had placed it for safety, we ought to have been more sensible. Two or three nights later, as I was sleeping in a special bed one of the men then absent had made by a big rock some yards from the main camp, I was awakened by a wolf crunching bones by the fire not eight feet from my head. I wanted to shoot the impertinent wretch, but his form was indistinct and my rifle lying by my side had to be trained his way. This

took some time, as I had to move cautiously, and in the midst
of my effort my elbow slipped.   Like a shadow he flitted into
the deeper gloom and I went to sleep again.   I did not want
to shoot without certainty, though some nights later I did shoot
with Riley's huge double-barrelled shotgun loaded with buck-
shot straight into our mess kit, not killing the wolf that was
there, but putting holes in numerous tin plates through which
bean soup delighted to percolate, so that I never heard the last
of this midnight effort of mine to diminish the wolf family.

The day following our arrival the Major came from Kanab
and the plans for our winter's campaign were put in operation.
A base line for our geographic work was necessary and this was
to run south from Kanab, so Prof. on December 7th, with Mrs.
Thompson, Cap., Clem, Andy, Jones (who had recovered his
health), and one of the new men named MacEntee, left us
with loaded waggons to establish another camp nearer to the
scene of this work.   Another member of the party was Fuzz,
Mrs. Thompson's dog, an intelligent Dandie Dinmont. As I
was much interested to see Kanab, of which so much had been
said, and as it was now nearly seven months since I had seen
an occupied house, I decided to take a Sunday ride in that
direction.   On the 17th, about noon, I put a saddle on a white
mule which Jack had named Nigger and was soon on my way.
Emerging from the Chocolate Cliffs the road led along the
foot of the Vermilion Cliffs, crossing long ridges covered with
cedars and piñons with a vast view to the Kaibab on the south
and east, and soon joining a road that led from a canyon to
eastward where there was a very small settlement called Johnson's, and from two or three houses which had been built where
the El Vado trail crossed the Paria River.   Nigger went along
very well and I was in Kanab by three o'clock.   The village,
which had been started only a year or two, was laid out in the
characteristic Mormon style with wide streets and regular lots
fenced by wattling willows between stakes.   Irrigating ditches
ran down each side of every street and from them the water,
derived from a creek that came down a canyon back of the
town, could be led into any of the lots, each of which was about
one quarter of an acre; that is, there were four lots to a block.

Fruit trees, shade trees, and vines had been planted and were already beginning to promise near results, while corn, potatoes, etc., gave fine crops. The original place of settlement was a square formed by one-story log houses on three sides and a stockade on the fourth. This was called the fort and was a place of refuge, though the danger from Navajo attack seemed to be over and that from any assault by the Pai Utes certainly was past. One corner of the fort was made by the walls of the schoolhouse, which was at the same time meeting-house and ball-room. Altogether there were about 100 families in the village. The houses that had been built outside the fort were quite substantially constructed, some of adobe or sun-dried brick. The entire settlement had a thrifty air, as is the case with the Mormons. Not a grog-shop, or gambling saloon, or dance-hall was to be seen; quite in contrast with the usual disgraceful accompaniments of the ordinary frontier towns. A perfectly orderly government existed, headed by a bishop appointed by the church authorities in Salt Lake, the then incumbent of this office being an excellent man, Bishop Stewart. I rode to the fort, where I found Clem and Beaman domiciled with their photographic outfit, with a swarm of children peeping through every chink and crevice of the logs to get a view of the " Gentiles," a kind of animal they had seldom seen. Every one was cordial. Beaman even offered me a drink made with sugar-water and photographic alcohol, but it did not appeal to my taste. It was after sunset when I started Nigger towards Eight Mile Spring and I enjoyed the ride in the edge of night with not a living thing, besides Nigger (and Nigger was a mule), to disturb my reveries.

I had as yet seen none of the natives of the locality. They were now very friendly and considered harmless, thanks to Jacob's wise management. The only Indians the settlers dreaded were some renegades, a band of Utes and Navajos, collected by a bold and skillful chief named Patnish, whose " country " was south of the Colorado around Navajo Mountain. He was reputed to be highly dangerous, and the Kanab people were constantly prepared against his unwelcome visits. He had several handsome stalwart sons, who dressed in white and who generally accompanied him. Though Patnish was so much feared, I do not remember to have heard that he committed any depredations after this time. There had been much trouble with the Navajos, but Jacob, growing tired of the constant warfare, had resolved to go to them and see if he could not change the state of affairs. When he had guided the Major to the Moki Towns and Fort Defiance the year before (1870), about six thousand Navajos were assembled at the Agency. The chiefs were invited to meet in council on the 2d of November, and all the principal chiefs but one and all subchiefs but two were there. The Major led the way by introducing Jacob and speaking in highly complimentary terms of the Mormons; and Jacob then gave a long talk in his low-voiced way, illustrating the great evils of such warfare as had existed, and closed by saying:

"What shall I tell my people the 'Mormons' when I return home? That we may expect to live in peace, live as friends, and trade with one another? Or shall we look for you to come prowling around our weak settlements, like wolves in the night? I hope we may live in peace in time to come. I have now grey hairs on my head, and from my boyhood I have been on the frontiers doing all I could to preserve peace between white men and Indians. I despise this killing, this shedding of blood. I hope you will stop this and come and visit and trade with our people. We would like to hear what you have got to say before we go home."

Barbenceta, the principal chief, slowly approached as Jacob ended, and putting his arms around him said: " My friend and brother, I will do all that I can to bring about what you have advised. We will not give all our answer now. Many of the Navajos are here. We will talk to them to-night and will see you on your way home." Several days later Jacob met him and the chiefs who had been absent; he said they would all really like to see peace with the Mormons carried out, and continued:

"We have some bad men among us, but if some do wrong, the wise ones must not act foolishly, like children, but let it be settled according to the spirit of your talk at Fort Defiance. Here is

Hastele. I wish you would take a good look at him, so you will not be mistaken in the man. He never lies or steals. He is a truthful man; we wish all difficult matters settled before him. He lives on the frontier nearest to the river; you can find him by inquiry. We hope we may be able to eat at one table, warm by one fire, smoke one pipe, and sleep under one blanket."

Jacob proceeded towards home, taking a Moki, named Tuba, and his wife back with him so that they might see the Mormon country. Arriving at the crossing of the Colorado Tuba was sad. He said his people had once lived on the other side, and their fathers had told them they never again would go west of the river to live. " I am now going on a visit to see my friends. I have worshipped the Father of us all in the way you believe to be right; now I wish you would do as the Hopees think is right before we cross." Jacob assented, and Tuba, he said,

" then took his medicine bag from under his shirt and offered me a little of its contents. I offered my left hand to take it; he requested me to take it with my right. He then knelt with his face to the east, and asked the Great Father of us all to preserve us in crossing the river. He said that he and his wife had left many friends at home, and if they never lived to return their friends would weep much. He prayed for pity upon his friends the Mormons, that none of them might drown in crossing; and that all the animals we had with us might be spared, for we needed them all, and to preserve unto us all our food and clothing, that we need not suffer hunger nor cold on our journey. He then arose to his feet. We scattered the ingredients from the medicine bag into the air, on to the land, and into the water of the river."

When they were all safely over Tuba gave thanks that his prayer had been answered.[1]

The last white men to be killed by the Navajos in the Kanab region were Dr. Whitmore and his herder at Pipe Springs, twenty miles west, five years before in the winter of 1865–66. The raiders were pursued by a strong party, and some of them, turning down the Kanab Canyon, perhaps think-

[1] *Jacob Hamblin*, a Narrative, etc. Faith-promoting Series—Juvenile Instructor Office, Salt Lake City—1881.

ing the river could be crossed there, were surprised and fired on at dawn. Some escaped, though wounded. Jacob kept a close watch on all the passes, and especially at El Vado. Several raiders were intercepted and shot. In 1869 a raiding band successfully drove off twelve hundred head of horses and cattle from northern settlements, and the winter of 1869–70 was one of the worst, requiring Jacob's presence in the field almost constantly. He was accompanied by friendly Pai Utes, who hated the Navajos. One Navajo was shot in a band who had stolen cattle, but the others were allowed to leave on giving up the stock. The shot did not kill the Navajo, and they followed to see what became of him. He was carried along by his friends to where another raiding party was encamped. The Pai Utes then killed two of this party, scalping one, but refraining from taking the scalp of the other because he had sandy hair and looked too much like a white man. Later three more Navajos were killed in a fight, but the rest escaped with ten horses. Jacob grew heartily sick of this kind of work, and made the resolve to appeal to the Navajos, with the result stated. He also visited the Red Lake Utes to the north, and all the Indians along the Sevier. Beginning with the band of Navajos under Agua Grande, which we had met at El Vado, they came north in numerous parties with perfect confidence that the Mormons would receive them peacefully. But they continued to despise the Pai Utes, considering them beneath notice.

In September of the year 1870 the Major, by Brigham Young's advice, had engaged Jacob to go with him to Mt. Trumbull in the Uinkaret region adjoining the Shewits country. Jacob, wishing to see these Indians himself, was very willing to go. They made a camp by a spring, and finding some natives near, Jacob asked them to bring in some of the party who had taken part in the killing of the Howlands and Dunn the year before. Twelve or fifteen finally came, and they had a talk.

"I commenced [said Jacob] by explaining to the Indians Professor Powell's business. I endeavoured to get them to understand that he did not visit their country for any purpose that would work evil to them, that he was not hunting gold or silver or other metals; that he would be along the river next season with a party of men, and if they found any of them away from the river in the hills, they must be their friends and show them places where there was water if necessary."

They replied that friends of theirs from across the river had declared the men were miners and advised killing them, for if they found mines it would bring great evil among them. The men were followed and killed while asleep. They declared that had they been correctly informed about the men they would not have killed them. Kapurats (" No-arm," meaning the Major), they said, could travel and sleep in their country unmolested and they would show him and his men the watering-places.[1]

On December 19th we moved our camp from Eight Mile Spring to a place below the gap in the Chocolate Cliffs south of Kanab and not far below the Utah-Arizona boundary; the 37th parallel. Bonnemort and I remained behind to gather up the last articles and it was dark when we reached the new ground. Our large tent was pitched in the creek bottom with the others not far off, making quite a settlement. The weather was rainy and cold, but a conical sheet-iron stove heated the tent well and there we had dry comfortable evenings, some of the men singing, some writing letters or plotting notes, others reading and still others perhaps playing a game. Bonnemort was something of a singer and was specially fond of *Beautiful Isle of the Sea*, but Jack still maintained his complete supremacy as a tenor. His repertory always increased and he was ever ready to entertain us. One of his selections I remember was the ballad :

> " I wandered by the brookside,
> I wandered by the mill;
> I could not hear the brook flow,
> The noisy wheel was still,

[1] In 1864 the danger from the Pai Utes, who had not been well treated, increased till Jacob had to take the matter in hand and made a visit to the place where they were gathering for attack. He was asked how many men he wanted to go with him, and he answered, " One, and no arms; not even a knife in sight."

There was no burr of grasshopper
No chirp of any bird,
But the beating of my own heart
Was all the sound I heard."

Mrs. Thompson had a sweet voice and knew a lot of songs, which were frequently heard issuing from her tent, and this, with the presence of Mrs. Powell and the baby, added to the locality a pleasant homelike air.   Both Mrs. Thompson and Mrs. Powell had been familiar with camp life, Mrs. Powell having spent a winter, 1868–69, with the Major in Middle Park, Colorado, near the camp of Chief Douglas, the father of our friend Douglas Boy.

Andy cooked all the meals on a fire out of doors, and they were no longer served in our "go fur it boys" canyon style, but a large canvas, showing by its colour the effects of exposure, was elegantly spread on the ground and around its edges the tin plates, cups, etc., were arranged, with the beanpot and other provender in the middle.   This method continued henceforth.   The company would sit around on the ground, each in whatever position was comfortable.   Liberal portions of bread and sorghum molasses formed the dessert, and after a while so indispensable did the sorghum grow that we dubbed it the "staff of life."   It was easy to get, quantities being produced in "Dixie."   Kanab besides being favoured with two mails a week had a telegraph line connecting with the settlements of the Virgin region and with Salt Lake, and we now felt that once more we had a grip on the world.

On the 22d of December the Major, accompanied by Captain Dodds, Riley, and one of the Kanab men, John Stewart, a son of the bishop, started for the Kaibab to find a way to get rations to the Colorado next year near the mouth of the Little Colorado.   The weather now was rather stormy but Prof. continued his observations as well as he could, and parties were sent out in a number of directions to place flags and monuments for the geodetic work.   The base line was to be measured south from near Kanab for about ten miles.   Christmas day came with rain and small prospect of special enjoyment, and we all kept the shelter of the tent after hunting up the horses in mud ankle-deep. But our dinner was a royal feast, for Mrs. Thompson herself made a huge plum-pudding and Prof. supplied butter and milk from Kanab, making this feature of the holiday an immense success. In the evening a number of us rode up to the settlement to witness a dance that had been announced to take place in the schoolhouse, tabernacle, or town hall—the stone building in the corner of the fort which answered all these functions. The room was about 15 by 30 feet and was lighted by three candles, a kerosene lamp, and a blazing fire of pitch pine. Two violins were in lively operation, one being played by Lyman Hamblin, a son of Old Jacob, and there was a refreshing air of decorous gaiety about the whole assemblage. Dancing is a regular amusement among the Mormons and is encouraged by the authorities as a harmless and beneficial recreation. At that time the dances were always opened with prayer. Two sets could occupy the floor at one time and to even things up, and prevent any one being left out, each man on entering was given a number, the numbers being called in rotation. None of our party joined as we were such strangers, but we were made welcome in every respect. It was ten o'clock before we left, and the way being dim and muddy, midnight was on before we threw off saddles at our camp.

The next morning work was begun on the base line, but for some days the weather was so bad that little was accomplished. The year 1871 ended in this way and we hoped the new one would be more propitious.

CHAPTER XII

Reconnoitring and Triangulating—A Pai Ute New Year's Dance—The Major
   Goes to Salt Lake—Snowy Days on the Kaibab—At Pipe Spring—Gold
   Hunters to the Colorado—Visits to the Uinkaret Country—Craters and
   Lava—Finding the Hurricane Ledge—An Interview with a Cougar—Back
   to Kanab.

NEW-YEAR'S DAY, 1872, passed with nothing more event-
ful than the return of John Stewart in advance of the
Major with the news that they had succeeded in reaching
the Colorado at the foot of Kanab Canyon. They had given
up the Kaibab direction because of snow which interfered with
their advance. He also said that Riley had found gold at the
mouth of the Kanab. The telegraph operator was so deeply impressed with this statement that it was telegraphed as an item of
news to Salt Lake. Work on the base line went on daily by
our topographical staff, but presently it was turned over to a
special gang under Captain Dodds, so that the rest of us
might be freed to carry on the triangulation. On Monday
the 15th, Prof., Jones, Mac, and I started with some pack
animals on a ten days' reconnaissance trip over the Kaibab, first
going to Kanab for some supplies and taking dinner with Jacob
at the house of his wife Louisa. According to the Mormon
custom, though it was not universal, Jacob had several wives,
I do not know how many. I met two, and he was besides that
" sealed " to one or two Pai Ute women. Sister Louisa was
the one I came to know best and she was a good woman. We
had an excellent dinner with rich cream for the coffee which
was an unusual treat. In all Mormon settlements the domestic
animals were incorporated at once and they received special
care; butter, milk, and cheese were consequently abundant; but
in a " Gentile " frontier town all milk, if procurable at all, was

drawn from a sealed tin. The same was true of vegetables.
The empty tin was the chief decoration of such advance settlements, and with the entire absence of any attempt at arrangement, at order, or to start fruit or shade trees, or do any other
sensible thing, the " Gentile" frontier town was a ghastly
hodge-podge of shacks in the midst of a sea of refuse. As
pioneers the Mormons were superior to any class I have ever-
come in contact with, their idea being home-making and not
skimming the cream off the country with a six-shooter and a
whiskey bottle.   Jacob's home was simple but it was comfortable. He was a poor man for he did his work for the people
with very slight compensation.

From Jacob's we proceeded to our old camp ground at
Eight-Mile Spring and there spent the night.   Prof. had
forgotten his sextant and rode back to our main camp for it.
We continued in the morning without him to a place farther
east called Navajo Well, a deep spring in a sort of natural
hole, somewhat aided by native hands, in the midst of some
sloping, barren rocks, the last spot where one would look for
water.   A large flat stone covered the top, the water being
dipped out at one side where there was a depression leading
down to it.   A careless man, or one not familiar with the
country, might ride within a few yards of this spring without
noticing its existence.   Prof. came along towards night and
the next day we went on eastward to the top of the Kaibab
Plateau and there put up a geodetic monument.   Here we
made a dry camp having water for ourselves in a keg and some
canteens, while the animals got along very well as there was a
little snow on the ground.   Proceeding from this place eastward we bame to the edge of the plateau opposite the largest
of a series of four or five peculiar red sandstone peaks.   The
Mormons had explored a waggon road across at this place and
the grades were easy.   We followed the road and reached
House Rock Valley about ten miles north of House Rock Spring
where we went to get water and camp.   We had started late
and by the time we got down into the valley darkness had
fallen but a bright moon compensated for the absence of daylight, enabling us to see plainly our landmarks.   We jogged

along toward the spring and I sang *Oh the Lone Starry Hours, Give Me Love*, when I was suddenly interrupted by old Thunderbolt's pack loosening. Thunderbolt was a horse that waited for such an event with remarkable docility and when it arrived he made the best of the opportunity to get even with us for drawing the lash-rope so tight. Before I could dismount and lay hands on him the pack slipped back over his rump which was the signal he watched for. Joyously flinging his heels in the moonlit air, jumping high off the ground the next instant, and then darting off into the misty night with a clatter and a whirl he spread the contents of that pack to all points of the compass. This revenge adequately accomplished we were permitted to catch him. A long search was necessary before we had gathered up all the things and replaced the pack on the now meek and patient Thunderbolt, and half-past eight by the watch arrived as we got to water and supper.

We put up another "station" back of House Rock Spring and spent a day reconnoitring. On Sunday, January 21st, we went to Red Cliff and made a camp under some cedars, as we wished to put a station on the highest peak. The camp was a dry one, but we had the usual supply of water in the keg and canteens, and as the temperature was very low we did not get thirsty. There was an abundance of wood for the camp, but Mac and I concluded we wanted more warmth and light, so we set fire to two large cedars that stood alone, and they made a superb illumination, burning all night. In the morning we got to the top of the cliff, and built a monument, with a high pole and flag, to which to "sight" from other geodetic points, while Prof. took observations for time and latitude. When our work was finished we went back to House Rock Spring, arriving just before sunset. In the morning Jones and I went across and climbed the Kaibab, intending to put up a monument there, but we could find no proper site and returned to camp. Prof. and Mac had been off in another direction, but they got in just before supper-time. We had not finished this meal when, night having come on, we heard through the darkness sounds of some one approaching, and thirteen Navajos one after the other came into the light of our fire, with their greeting of "Bueno heh!" and camped just below us. Some were mounted, some were on foot. The chief was Ashtishkal, whom we had met before at the Crossing of the Fathers (El Vado). They were all friendly, and did not intrude upon us. They were on their way north to trade with the Mormons, having come across at the Paria. The night was very cold, and a heavy, dry snow began to fall, so that in the morning when we arose we could see but a short distance. The Navajos about sunrise stood silently in a circle till at a signal they all sat down and began singing, continuing for several minutes a low musical refrain, and then all rose to their feet again. They left us early, with friendly demonstrations, and went on their way towards Kanab, while we moved to another spring in a gulch farther up the valley, where we made a tent out of a pair of blankets to keep off the snow. During the stormy night our animals started to leave us, travelling before the wind, but we suspected their intention and got out and headed them back, much to their disgust, no doubt. Thursday, January 25th, came bright and clear, but still extremely cold. Prof. with Mac started across the Kaibab by the trail, while Jones and I went farther north by the waggon road referred to, camping near the station we had made on the way out. The next morning we did some work there, and then went on to the Navajo Well, reaching it at sunset, where we watered our stock and continued by moonlight through a piercing wind to Eight-Mile Spring, which enabled us to reach our main camp in time for dinner on Saturday the 27th. Prof. got back the evening before at 7.30, having made another station on the Kaibab on the way over and travelled twenty-five miles.

About a mile from Kanab the Kaibab band of Pai Utes were encamped, and we had a good opportunity to visit them and study their ways.[1] The Major was specially interested and made voluminous notes. They came to the village and our camp a great deal. While they were dirty, they were not more dishonest than white men, so far as I could learn. Their wickiups, about seven feet high, were merely a lot of cedar

[1] For the linguistic classification of stocks and tribes of the United States, see Appendix, *The North Americans of Yesterday*, by F. S. Dellenbaugh.

boughs, set around a three-quarter circle, forming a conical
shelter, the opening towards the south.   In front they had
their fire, with a mealing-stone or two, and round about were
their conical and other baskets, used for collecting grass seeds,
piñon nuts, and similar vegetable food, which in addition to
rabbits formed their principal subsistence.   At certain times
they all went to the Kaibab deer-hunting.   Their guns, where
they had any, were of the old muzzle-loading type, with outside hammers to fire the caps.   Many still used the bow-and-
arrow, and some knew how to make stone arrow-heads.   We
learned the process, which is not difficult.   Their clothing was,
to some extent, deerskin, but mainly old clothes obtained from
the whites.   They made a very warm robe out of rabbit skins,
twisted into a long rope and then sewed side to side into the
desired size and shape.   But when we traded for one of these
as a curiosity we placed it beside a large ant hill for some days
before bringing it into camp.   They obtained fire by the use of
matches when they could get them, but otherwise they used
the single stick or "palm" drill.   We went to the camp one
moonlight night, January 6th, to see a sort of New-Year's
dance.   They had stripped a cedar tree of all branches but a
small tuft at the top, and around this the whole band formed
a large circle, dancing and singing.   The dancing was the usual
hippity-hop or "lope" sideways, each holding hands with his
or her neighbours.   In the centre stood a man, seeming to be
the custodian of the songs and a poet himself.   He would first
recite the piece, and then all would sing it, circling round at
the same time.   We accepted their cordial invitation to join
in the ceremony, and had a lot of fun out of our efforts, which
greatly amused them too, our mistakes raising shouts of laughter.   The poet seemed to originate some of the songs, but
they had others that were handed down.   One of these, which
I learned later, was:

> " Montee-ree-ai-ma, mo-quontee-kai-ma
> Umpa-shu-shu-ra-ga-va
> Umpa-shu-shu-ra-ga-va
> Umpa-ga-va, shu-ra-ga-va
> Montee-ree-ai-ma."

This, being translated, signifies that a long talk is enough to bore a hole in a cliff; at least, that was the interpretation we obtained. Another popular one was:

> " Ca, shakum, poo kai
> Ca, shakum poo kai
> Ca, shakum tee kai
> Ca, shakum tee kai,"

these lines being repeated like the others over and over and over again. They were highly philosophical, for they explain that you must kill your rabbit (shakum) before you eat him. I do not remember that they sang these particular songs on that occasion, but they will serve as examples.

On February 1st the Major left camp for Salt Lake with Mrs. Powell and the baby. Jack went along to accompany them as far as Tokerville on the Virgin River. Before leaving, the Major settled up with Beaman, who was now to separate from the party. The Major intended to go to Washington to ask Congress for another appropriation to continue the work of exploration and map-making when we had finished that already planned. On the 6th Clem and Bonnemort arrived from an expedition to make photographs down the Kanab Canyon, where the Major had been with Riley and Dodds. They had met with bad luck, and did not get a single negative. The silver bath got out of order, and the horse bearing the camera fell off a cliff and landed on top of the camera, which had been tied on the outside of the pack, with a result that need not be described. Bonnemort's time was now up; he wanted to go back to prospecting, and we reluctantly said good-bye to him. On the 16th of February, finding our central camp no longer practicable, we abandoned it and operated in small parties from various nearby points, finally returning again in three or four days to near the site of the old camp. MacEntee then wanted to go to prospecting also, and he departed. He was an interesting, companionable young man, educated at the University of Michigan, seeking a fortune, and he was desirous of striking it rich. Whether he ever did or not I have not learned.

While camped below Kanab, Clem and I in walking one day saw a place where the creek which flowed on a level with the surroundings suddenly plunged into a deep mud canyon. This canyon had been cut back from far below by the under-mining action of the falling water, and it was plain to see that it would continue its retrogression till it eventually reached the mouth of the great canyon several miles above, but I did not dream that it could accomplish this work as rapidly as it actually did years after. During a great flood it washed a canyon not only to Kanab but for miles up the gorge, sweeping away at one master stroke hundreds of acres of arable land and leaving a mud chasm forty feet deep. Had the fall we examined been arranged then so that the water might glide down, the fearful washout would not have occurred. There are thousands of places in the West to-day that require treatment to conserve arable land, and in time the task may be undertaken by the Government.

Cap's health being such that he deemed it inadvisable to continue work in the field, he had severed his connection with the expedition, after finishing the preliminary map of Green River, and was temporarily settled in Kanab, where he had been for some time. On Wednesday, February 21st, Prof., Mrs. Thompson, and I took supper with him in one of the log houses at the fort, and on the 22d several of us accepted his invitation to dinner, a sort of farewell, for on the following day we started with our whole outfit for the Kaibab. We were extremely sorry to lose Cap, with his generous spirit and cheery ways, but when one has been punctured by a minie-ball he has to heed warnings. All day long we travelled through sandy hills gradually rising toward the plateau, the foot-hills of which we reached late in the afternoon. We had followed a waggon road with our pack-train up to this point, but here we struck off on a trail that was said to be a shorter way to the canyon we were aiming for, and a little before sunset we came to the brink of a steep slope, almost a cliff, where a picturesque, a romantic view opened before us. Below stretched away to the south a narrow, deep, and sharply defined valley or canyon one-eighth mile wide, the bottom of which seemed perfectly flat. A light snow which had fallen the night before whitened the sharp slopes, but from the valley bottom it had melted away, leaving a clear line of demarkation on either side and producing an extremely beautiful effect under the evening glow. Tall pine trees accented the scene, which was one of the most inviting I had ever beheld. One of our helpers from Kanab had been over the trail, and led us down to a small but excellent spring, within a quarter of a mile of which we camped, passing a most comfortable night.

Before we had finished slinging the last pack in the morning, a heavy grey sky began to sift down thickly falling snowflakes gently as if not wishing to give alarm. But when we were fairly under way this mildness vanished, and the storm smote our caravan with fierce and blinding gusts, amidst which progress was difficult. After four miles up the valley through beautiful pine trees of great height, we came to a deserted log cabin only half roofed over, and there we stopped to make our temporary headquarters. The Stewarts of Kanab had started a saw-mill at this place, but as yet the work had not gone very far. The snow ceased by the time we had thrown off the packs, and we made ourselves as comfortable as circumstances permitted. Prof. had a tent put up for Mrs. Thompson, while some took possession of the half-roofed house, for by keeping on the side where the board cover was they were slightly sheltered. With two or three of the others I pitched a small tent. There was plenty of fat pine, and rousing fires made the valley seem habitable. A fine little brook swept full grown fifteen inches in diameter from under a cliff two hundred feet above the valley bottom, and there was no lack of good water. Our trouble was with the horses and mules, for we had no grain for them, and if the snow got very deep they would not be able to paw down to the bunch grass. The snow soon began again, and all night it fell with aggravating facility. Sunday morning opened as leaden and dark as a February day could be, and there was no cessation of the showers of whiteness that were rapidly building up on the ground a formidable barrier to our operations. As I was wearing rather low brogans, having discarded top-boots as too close-fitting and uncomfortable around camp, I now made for myself a pair of leggins out of pieces of a common but heavy seamless sack. When these were buttoned in place they answered perfectly to protect my legs from the snow. We hoped Monday would begin the week with a clear sky, but we were disappointed. We had to sally out to hunt horses, hoping at the same time to come across a deer, but that hope was not realised. As I got far from camp in the midst of the tall pines and the unbroken snow sheet, I suddenly became aware of a whispering sound, which I could not at first account for, as I did not believe in fairies. Standing perfectly still, I perceived that it was produced by the friction of the snow-flakes upon the pine needles. It was a weird, ghost-like language which I had never listened to before.

Prof. went up one thousand feet on the mountain and climbed a tree 125 feet high with a determination to see something in spite of the snow. He caught a glimpse of the south wall of the Grand Canyon near Mt. Trumbull, miles to the west. On Tuesday he started George Adair, one of our Mormon assistants, back to Kanab for more rations, and directed Jones and Captain Dodds to get ready to start the next day for the south-east corner of the plateau, while Andy and I were to go to the south-west corner. Wednesday, February 28th, came clear, with the snow lying twelve inches on the level, but some of the horses were missing, and the day was spent in hunting this wayward stock, so it was not till Thursday afternoon that we got started. Our paths lying for a distance in the same direction, we four travelled together along a divide on the right or west of camp. It was slow work in the deep drifts, and we had not made many miles when night came on. We went into camp where we were. The horses bothered us by trying to go back searching for grass, and nobody could blame them. Finally we tied the worst offender to a tree in a bare place where he might pick up a few mouthfuls of food, and we managed to sleep the rest of the night. The only sound I heard when I woke up at one time was the satirical voice of an owl in the far distance. It seemed to be saying very deliberately " poo-poo, poo-poo," and that did not sound respectful. The next morning was March 1st, and it brought a fine sky, which would have put us quickly on the way, or rather in motion toward our respective goals, as there was no road or trail, but one of our animals which bore the mysterious name of Yawger, and which was the pack-horse of Andy and me, could not be found. Jones and Dodds went on, as they would probably soon have to separate from us anyhow, while we took Yawger's track, and at last found him browsing happily in a bare spot about a mile from our stopping place. It was two o'clock by the time we started on, floundering through the drifts in the trail of Jones and Dodds. Some drifts were so high it was all we could do to wallow through them even after the others had in a measure broken the way. After two hours of hard work in this line we came to the edge of a wide gully, where the advance party had halted. The slope was towards the south and the ground was somewhat bare, with good bunch grass, where the other horses were feeding, while Jones and Dodds were just descending from a tall pine tree. They declared nothing but snow could be seen in all directions on the mountain and they were going back. Besides it was impossible, they told me, to cross the gulch ahead. I did not want to turn back till I was compelled to, and I appealed to Andy as to whether or not he wanted to give up, not wishing to drag him along unwillingly. With his characteristic nonchalance he said, "Go ahead if you want to." Dodds had one of his own horses with him, and he said he would bet me that horse I could not cross the gulch. I made a trial, wading ahead of my horse, the pack animal following and Andy driving from behind. When I got into the middle it was all I could do to move, but I continued my efforts till suddenly the bottom seemed to rise, and then in a few yards the going grew easier and we emerged triumphantly on the other side, where we waved an adieu to the others. By keeping close to the boles of the large pine trees, where the wind had swept circular places, leaving the snow shallow, we were soon out of sight of our late companions.

After two or three miles of tiring work the day began to fade, but we reached a beautiful south slope where there was little snow, with a rich crop of bunch grass just starting green under the vernal influence that was a feast for the famished horses, the snow relieving their thirst. While Andy the ever-faithful got supper I reconnoitred and made up my mind that I could reach the locality I was trying for, by following a ridge I saw ahead where the snow seemed moderate. We were up and off early. The snow was deep but we got on quite rapidly and finally reached the ridge, crossing two big gulches to get to it. At eleven o'clock we were at the end of its summit and I could see a wide area to the west and north. The point appeared to be one of several similar projections though the one we were on was the most prominent. I selected a spot for a monument where we dug a hole in the rocks and dirt, and then cutting a tall slim pine and trimming it clean we hitched Yawger to it and made him drag it to the hole, where by a combination of science and strength we got it upright. While Andy, who had great strength, lifted and pushed after we had together got it half way, I propped it with a strong pole with a Y on the end, and in a few moments we saw the flag waving triumphantly from its tip at least thirty feet above our heads. Around its base we piled the rocks, which were exceptionally heavy, waist high, first cutting a notch in the pine and placing therein a can containing a record, and our "Point F" was finished. The rest of the day I spent in triangulating to various other stations, and we went to bed under a clear sky and a milder atmosphere. In the morning I completed my triangulating work and by that time the snow had settled and melted so that the back track was much easier than the outward march, enabling us to get to headquarters at the spring before dark. I had been a little afraid that a heavy snow would come on top of the large drifts which would have held us prisoners for a day or two.

On Wednesday, March 6th, the whole party packed up and left the valley by its narrow canyon outlet, a tributary of the Kanab Canyon. It began eight hundred feet deep and continually increased. We called it Shinumo Canyon because we found everywhere indications of the former presence of that tribe. Snow fell at intervals and we were alternately frozen and melted till we reached an altitude where the warmth was continuous and the snow became rain. Grass fresh and green and shrubs with the feeling of early spring surrounded us at the junction with Kanab Canyon where the walls were twelve hundred feet high. A mile below we camped by a lone cedar tree where there were "pockets" of rain-water in the rocks. The next day our course was laid up Kanab Canyon through thick willows that pulled the packs loose. One horse fell upside down in a gully, but he was not hurt and we pried him out and went on, camping near a large pool of intensely alkaline water. On the 8th going up a branch on the left called Pipe Spring Wash we came out on the surface, very much as one might reach a second floor by a staircase. This is a feature of the country and as one goes northward he arrives on successive platforms, in this manner passing through the several cliff ranges by means of transverse gorges that usually begin in small "box" canyons and rapidly deepen till they reach the full height of the cliff walls. At two o'clock we came to Pipe Spring. A vacant stone house of one very large room and a great fireplace was put at our disposal by Mr. Winsor the proprietor, and it was occupied by the men while Prof. had a tent put up for Mrs. Thompson. We found a party of miners here who had heard of the gold discovery at the mouth of the Kanab on the Colorado and were heading that way to reap the first-fruits. They were soon followed by hundreds more, making a steady stream down the narrow Kanab and out again for some time, for on reaching the river the limited opportunity to do any mining was at once apparent and they immediately took the back track swearing vengeance on the originator of the story.

For protection against raiders Mr. Winsor was building a solid double house of blocks of sandstone, making walls three feet thick. The two buildings were placed about twenty feet apart, thus forming an interior court the length of the houses, protected at the ends by high walls and heavy gates. No windows opened on the exterior, but there were plenty of loopholes commanding every approach. A fine large spring was conducted subterraneously into the corner of one of the buildings and out again, insuring plenty of water in case of a siege. Brigham Young was part owner of this establishment, and it was one of the most effective places of defence on a small scale, that I have ever seen.   It was never needed so far as I have heard, and even at the time I marvelled that it should be so elaborately prepared—far beyond anything else in the whole country.   The cut opposite shows this fort as it was in 1903.   Clem here told Prof. he did not care to stay with us any longer.   Ill success with his photographs had discouraged him, but Prof. persuaded him to remain for a time.

Until March 21st we operated around Pipe Spring triangulating and recording the topography, and other data, when we packed our animals again and laid our course across the open country towards a range of blue mountains seen in the southwest.   One of these had been named after Senator Trumbull by the Major in the autumn of 1870.   They were the home of the Uinkarets and we called the whole group by that name, discarding North Side Mountains, the name Ives had given when he sighted them in 1858 from far to the south.   Adjoining the Uinkaret region on the west was the Shewits territory where the Howlands and Dunn were killed.   Travelling across the dry plains we came to a well defined trail about sunset and followed it hoping that it would lead to water.   We were not disappointed for it took us to a pool of rain-water in a little gulley at the foot of some low hills.   A band of wild horses roamed the plain and as we had been told about a pool called the Wild Band Pocket, we had no doubt this was the place. There was no wood anywhere, but a diligent search produced enough small brush to cook by, though Andy had a hard time of it.   Clem's horse ran away from him and lost his gun, so he remained behind at Pipe Spring to hunt for the weapon.

The next day we travelled on over hilly country, following a moccasin trail, with here and there cedar groves as we approached nearer to the mountains.   On the edge of night traces of water were found in a gulch near the foot of Trumbull, and while Jack and a new member of our force, Will Johnson of Kanab, dug for more, Prof., Jones, and I scoured the vicinity in search of a spring or pocket, but though we found many old wickiups there was no water.   The Uinkarets had evidently camped here in wet weather.   When we returned we were told

The Grand Canyon.

From Part Way down South Side above Bright Angel Creek.

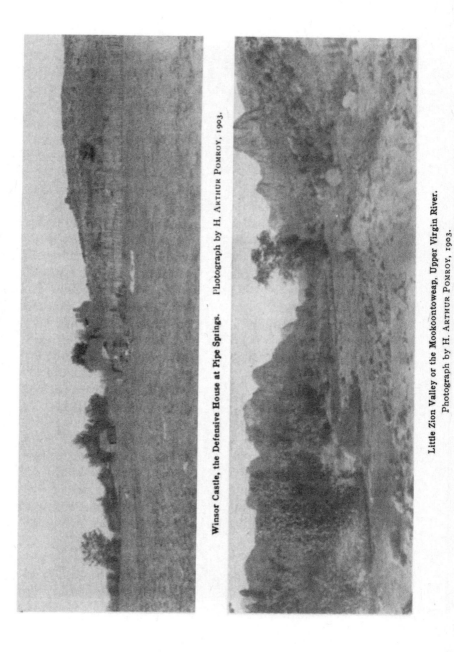

Winsor Castle, the Defensive House at Pipe Springs.   Photograph by H. ARTHUR POMROY, 1903.

Little Zion Valley or the Mookoontoweap, Upper Virgin River.
Photograph by H. ARTHUR POMROY, 1903.

that the little trace of water in the gulch had disappeared completely after the digging, a sad development which was accepted by all but one old white horse which stood on the edge of the hole for an hour or more patiently waiting. Our kegs and canteens provided enough to make bread which we ate with sorghum, and as early as possible in the morning we pushed on without breakfast, three men scouting ahead to discover the pool where the Major in the autumn of 1870 had camped. Prof. finally found it, a large pool of about a hundred barrels of clear, clean water, in a lava gulch, surrounded by cedar and piñon trees. Andy then gave us breakfast and dinner at the same time, eleven o'clock. Another new member of our party was Beaman's successor, Fennemore, from Salt Lake, who had joined us at Pipe Spring on March 19th, and he was prepared to photograph the region. We reconnoitred the neighbourhood during the afternoon, and the next morning Jones and I rode in one direction around Mount Trumbull, while Prof. and Captain Dodds rode the other way, to ascertain the lay of the land, and especially to find a ranch which some St. George men had started in this locality. Jones and I met Whitmore, the proprietor of the ranch, and a friend of his, who informed us the ranch was six miles farther on. We concluded not to go to it, but when Prof. and Captain Dodds got in after dark they told us they had gone the whole way. The following day, Monday March 25th, all the party except Andy and a new member, Alf Young of Kanab, climbed to the summit of Mount Trumbull, finding the ascent very gradual and easy and taking the horses to the top, which was 2440 feet above the pool and 8650 above sea level, commanding a magnificent view in every direction, as far to the south-east as Mount San Francisco. Jones, Jack, Fennemore, and I remained there all night while the rest returned to camp. Jones and I wanted to do some topographical work and get sights to some of our other stations, and Fennemore, assisted by Jack, wanted pictures.

Descending the opposite side the next day we went to a spring in an oak grove which Prof. had seen, where the others were already encamped. On the 27th, Prof. and I climbed a high cinder peak, of which there were many, to get a view, and then went to Whitmore's Ranch, where we had a talk with him to get points on the region. He told us he had followed a trail to the Colorado, about twelve miles, to what he called the Ute Crossing. If I remember correctly he had taken a horse down at that point. The next day Johnson and I put a signal flag on one of the high mountains, afterwards named Logan, forming Signal Station Number 7.   This was a volcanic district and there were many old craters. Near the Oak Spring camp was an extensive sheet of lava, seeming to have cooled but a year or two before. Its surface was all fractured, but there were no trees on its lower extremity and where it had flowed around a hill its recent plasticity was exceedingly distinct. It had come from a crater, about five hundred feet high, two miles north. This had once been a cone but it was now disrupted, the lava having burst through to the north and to the south, leaving two sections standing, the stream to the south being one quarter mile wide and a mile and a half long, that on the north one mile wide and about the same in length. The depth of these streams was not far from thirty feet, and in spite of the exceedingly rugged surface the southern stream was marked by deeply worn trails running to and from a small spring situated in the middle of it. Beside this spring one of the men from the ranch had found a human skeleton, covered with fragments of lava, with the decayed remains of a wicker water-jug between the ribs, marking some unrecorded tragedy. We estimated that less than three hundred years had passed since the last outburst from the crater. As there were pine trees a hundred years old on the lava where it was more disintegrated near the point of outpour, the age of the flow could not have been less than that.

Friday the 29th being cloudy and stormy nothing in the line of geodetic work was done and we could only rest in camp. Dodds and Jones who had gone to explore a way to the Grand Canyon came in reporting success. Saturday morning Jones and Fennemore started for Kanab to bring out more rations and meet us either at Fort Pierce or at Berry's Spring near St. George, while Prof. with Dodds and Johnson went to try to

follow the trail Whitmore had told about to the river, but after
four miles they gave it up and climbed by a side trail to the
plateau again. They made a dry camp and the next day went
on till they found water enough for the horses in some pools
on the rocks, and here, leaving the others to continue the reconnaissance, Prof. came back to our camp, arriving in a snow-
storm. It had been snowing with us at intervals all day. The
next day was April first, and with it came still heavier snow.
We planned to move down to the edge of the Grand Canyon,
and Jack and Andy started as Jack wished to make some
photographs there, but the snow continuing we concluded to
wait till another day. When that came the snow was quite
deep on the ground and was still falling hard, which it continued
to do most of the time, preventing us from moving. Fennemore had brought with him a copy of *The Count of Monte
Cristo*, which I had never read, and in its pages I soon became
oblivious to the surroundings. The snow kept on the next day
also and all the men out returned to the main camp, Dodds
and Johnson having reached the river bank. When another
morning dawned and showed no cessation of the aggravating
storm, with the snow fifteen inches on the level, Prof. said he
would pack up Friday the 5th and get down to lower country
around St. George. The day came clear and sunny and the
snow began to melt. We headed for the Pine Valley Mountains back of St. George and made about twenty miles with no
snow after the first six, the altitude dropping to where the
temperature was milder. Prof. had inquired at the ranch about
trails, but there were so many cattle trails that we did not get
on the right one. We made a dry camp and early the following
morning went on, not being able to see any landmarks because
of the clouds. Half an hour after starting a thick snow-storm
set in but we kept going, till in about a mile and a half the
world seemed suddenly to end. Above, below, and around us
was a great blank whiteness. Dismounting and cautiously ad-
vancing on foot we discovered that we were on the brink of a
very high cliff. As we did not know which way to turn we
threw off the packs and stopped where we were. Spreading
out blankets we scraped the snow from them into the kettles to

melt for water.   Then by holding a blanket up over Andy by
the four corners he was able, with some chips he had previously
chopped out of the side of a dead pine, to start a fire, by which
he proceeded to cook dinner.

When the snow fell less heavily we could peer down and
then saw that the cliff was continuous in both directions.   By
half-past two, with our kegs and canteens filled with the snow
water, we were again on the way following along to find a place
to go down, but we saw none that seemed practicable, and at
last, having made altogether five miles, we halted for the night
in a grove of cedars, where we had a good fire and were comfortable though our rations were now growing scarce.   Snow
at intervals continued all day up to bedtime.   The next day
was Sunday.   We travelled twenty miles along the line of
cliffs and camped near a canyon in which we found pools of
good water.   We saw an antelope during the day but could
not get it.   Andy baked up the last of our flour for supper and
put on a pot of beans and one of dried peaches to cook for
breakfast.   The beans were edible in the morning and we disposed of them and the peaches and went on our way.   After a
day of many ups and downs we arrived about two o'clock at a
ranch called Gould's or Workman's, where we bought five
dollars, worth of corn-meal and milk.   We were now on what
the inhabitants of the region called Hurricane Hill, and from this
we applied the name Hurricane Ledge to the long line of sharp
cliffs we had followed, which begin at the Virgin River and extend, almost unbroken and eight hundred to a thousand feet
high, south to the Grand Canyon, forming the western boundary
of the Uinkaret Plateau.   From Gould's we had a waggon road
and following it we were led to the brink of the Hurricane
Ledge, where a road had been constructed to the bottom.   Before descending we took a final look at the enchanting view
opening away to the north and north-west.   At our feet was
the Virgin Valley with the green fields of Tokerville, while
beyond rose magnificent cliffs culminating to the north-west in
the giant buttes and precipices of the Mookoontoweap, or, as
the Mormons call it, Little Zion Valley.   Topping the whole
sweep of magnificent kaleidoscopic topography were the Pine

Valley Mountains and the lofty cliffs of the Colob and Markargunt plateaus. It has ever since been my opinion that few
outlooks in all the world are superior for colour and form to
that stretching north from the northern part of the Hurricane
Ledge.[1]

Descending to the valley we arrived just at dusk at Berry's
Spring, where our waggon under the direction of Jones had
come with supplies. The spring was an excellent one and the
rivulet flowing away from it was bordered with large wild-rose
bushes. Though the waggon and supplies were there Jones
was not, for we had expected to come in from farther west past
Fort Pierce, and he had gone on to that place to tell us where he
had decided to camp. Clem had found his gun and come out
with them, the others of the party being Fennemore and George
Adair. Jones came back the next day and prepared to start
with Andy, and Johnson for several days' work in the Pine
Valley Mountains, while Jack, Captain Dodds, Fennemore,
and I were to return to the Uinkaret region to complete certain work there. Some goods to be distributed to the natives
from the Indian Bureau arrived at St. George and Prof. went
there with George Adair to have a talk with the Indians to be
found, and distribute goods. We had seen no Indians at all
in the Uinkaret region. He discovered the Shewits who came
in to be afraid of us, thinking we wanted to kill them, but they
were willing to accept anything they could get in the line of
presents. Hardly any would acknowledge themselves to be
either Uinkarets or Shewits.

On April 12th, according to the plan, Jack, Dodds, Fennemore, and I started back to the Uinkaret Mountains, following
the trail we had tried to strike coming out. It led past a place
called Fort Pierce, a small stone building the settlers had
formerly used as an advance post against the Shewits and
Uinkarets. There we spent the night, and the next day after
some trouble we got on the right trail, and on Monday, the
15th of April, we again reached what we had called Oak Spring,
near Mount Trumbull, and the southern flow of lava already

[1] For a description of Little Zion Valley, see "A New Valley of Wonders," by
F. S. Dellenbaugh, *Scribner's Magazine*, January, 1904.

described. The following day Jack and Fennemore went down to the brink of the Grand Canyon, at the foot of a sort of valley the Uinkarets called Toroweap, while with Dodds I climbed the peak later named after Senator Logan, and attempted some triangulation, but the air was so murky I could not get my sights and had to return for them the next morning. The day after that we climbed Mount Trumbull, and I triangulated from there. One of my sights from Logan was to a conical butte near which we had camped as we came out, and near which we had found a large ant-hill covered with small, perfect quartz crystals that sparkled in the sun like diamonds. When I sighted to this butte, for want of a better name, I recorded it temporarily as Diamond Butte, remembering the crystals, and the name became fixed, which shows how unintentionally names are sometimes bestowed. We examined the lava flows and the crater again, and I made a sketch in pencil from another point of view from one I had made during our former sojourn. Then we joined Jack and Fennemore, who had been taking negatives at the canyon edge. On the 20th Dodds and I climbed down the cliffs about three thousand feet to the water at a rapid called Lava Falls. Across the river we could see a very large spring, but of course we could not get over to it. Returning to Oak Spring, we spent there another night, and in the morning, while the others started for headquarters, I rode around to the ranch to inquire about a spring I had heard something about existing on the St. George trail; but the solitary man I found there, who came out of the woods in response to my shout, a walking arsenal, did not know anything concerning it. After drinking a quart or two of milk, which he kindly offered me, I rode on to join my companions by continuing around the mountain, "running in" the trail as I went with a prismatic compass. Presently I saw a cougar sitting upright behind a big log, calmly staring at me, so I dismounted and sent a Winchester bullet in his direction. My mule was highly nervous about firearms, and having to restrain her antics by putting my arm through the bridle rein, her snorting skittishness both at the rifle and the cougar disturbed my aim and my shot went a trifle under. The bullet

seemed to clip the log, but if it hit the cougar the effect was
not what I expected, for with a rush like a sky-rocket the
animal disappeared in the top of the pine tree overhead, and I
could see nothing more of it though I rode about looking
for it. Not wishing to dally here, I spurred on to overtake
my party, but in trying a short cut I passed beyond them, as
they had by that time halted in some cedars for lunch. The
man at the ranch had told me that Whitmore was due to arrive
that day, and having missed a part of the trail by the short
cut, I could not judge by the tracks as to where my party
were, and not caring to waste time, I rode on and on till I had
gone so far I did not want to turn back. Evening came, but
there was a good moon, and I did not stop till eight o'clock.
The night was cold; the plain was barren and bleak. I had
no coat, but with the saddle blanket and a handful of dead
brush, which I burned by installments, I managed to warm
myself enough to sleep by short intervals. I was on my feet
with the dawn, but my mule was nowhere to be seen, though I
had hoppled her well with my bridle reins. I tracked the mule
about five miles to a muddy place where there had been water,
caught her, and rode back to my saddle, when I continued my
journey, running in the trail as I went. I became pretty thirsty
and hungry, but the only thing for me to do was to continue
to our main camp. Had I gone back I might have missed our
men again, for there had been some talk about a short-cut
trail, and I feared they might try it. At two o'clock I reached
Black Rock Canyon, where there was a water-pocket full of
warm and dirty water, but both the mule and I took a drink
and I rode on, passing Fort Pierce at sunset. Off on my
right I perceived ten or twelve Shewits Indians on foot
travelling rapidly along in Indian file, and as the darkness
fell and I had to go through some wooded gulches I con-
fess I was a little uncomfortable and kept my rifle in readiness; but I was not molested and reached camp about ten
o'clock, where I ate a large piece of bread with molasses,
after a good drink of water, and went to bed. The others
arrived the following afternoon. I had left notes for them
by the trail in cleft-sticks, so they knew that I was ahead.

13

This was the longest trip I ever made without water or food.

We prepared to start out again in different directions; one party was to go to the Pine Valley Mountains, another to Pipe Spring and the mouth of the Paria to look after our property there, a third up the Virgin Valley for photographs, and a fourth to St. George and the Virgin range of mountains south-west of that town. Prof. headed this last party, and he took me as his topographical assistant. April 27th we rode into St. George, a town I was much interested to see. I found a very pretty, neat, well-ordered little city of about fifteen hundred population, with a good schoolhouse, a stone tabernacle with a spire, and a court house, the water running in ditches along the streets for irrigating purposes as well as for drinking. About a mile below the town we camped, and we could hear the band playing a serenade to one of the officials who was to start the next day on a long journey. After several days of feeling our way about in the rugged and dry region below St. George, we finally discovered a good water-pocket, from which Prof. and I made a long, hard ride and climb, and about sunset camped at the base of what is now called Mount Bangs, the highest peak of the Virgin Mountains, for which we were aiming. The next day we climbed an additional eleven hundred feet to its summit, and completed our work in time by swift riding to get to our main camp at the water-pocket by half-past six.

It was an easy trip back to St. George, following an old trail, and then we made our way to Kanab again, where we put all our notes in shape and fitted out for the journey to the mouth of the Dirty Devil across the unknown country.

In the Unknown Country.

Photograph by J. K. Hillers. 1872.

CHAPTER XIII

Off for the unknown Country—A lonely Grave—Climbing a Hog-back to a green grassy Valley—Surprising a Ute Camp—Towich-a-tick-a-boo—Following a Blind Trail—The Unknown Mountains Become Known—Down a deep Canyon—To the Paria with the *Cañonita*—John D. Lee and Lonely Dell.

ANDY and Captain Dodds, who had gone to the mouth of the Paria to ascertain the condition of our boats, returned May 15th, reporting the boats all right, but the caches we had left torn up by wolves and prospectors. The latter had stolen oars and other things, and gone down on a raft to be wrecked at the first rapid in Marble Canyon, where they just escaped with their lives. A settler had established himself there a short time before, the notorious John D. Lee, who was reputed to have led the massacre of the unfortunate Missourians at Mountain Meadows in 1857, and who had eluded capture all these years. He had been "cut off," nominally at least, from the Mormon Church, and had lived in the most out-of-the-way places, constantly on his guard. Our men took all our ropes and remaining materials from the caches to his cabin, where they would be safe till our arrival. We prepared for the trip eastward across the unknown country to the mouth of the Dirty Devil River, and by the 22d of May I had completed the preliminary map of the region to westward which we had just reconnoitred. Mrs. Thompson was to stay in Kanab, for Prof. decided that it would not be advisable for her to accompany him on this journey, although she was the most cheerful and resolute explorer of the whole company. A large tent was erected for her in the corner of Jacob's garden, and she was to take her meals with Sister Louisa, whose house stood close by. With Fuzz, a most intelligent dog, for a companion in her tent and the genial Sister Louisa for a near neighbour she was satisfactorily settled.   Fuzz had the peculiarity of sympathising with the Navajos in their contempt for the Pai Utes.   The latter roused his ire on the instant, but when a Navajo came up, with his confident step, Fuzz would lie still, with merely a roll of the eye to signify that he was on guard.

Saturday, May 25th, our caravan of riders, pack animals, and a waggon moved slowly toward Eight-Mile Spring, the first stop in prospect.   I rode a brisk little horse which had received the lofty name of Aaron.   When we reached Eight-Mile Spring about noon there was barely enough water for our animals and for cooking dinner, which compelled our going elsewhere to put on the finishing touches to our outfit before cutting loose from the settlements, and Prof. directed the caravan to continue to Johnson, farther east and up one of the canyons of the Vermilion Cliffs.   He returned to Kanab to make some final arrangements there, while we kept on to Johnson, passing the little settlement of two or three houses, and making a camp two miles above, where the canyon bottom was wide and level.   Here we went over everything to be sure that all was in good order and nothing left behind.   The animals were reshod where necessary, which operation kept Andy and Dodds busy all of Sunday, the 26th.   By thus making a start and proceeding a few miles all defects and neglects become apparent before it is too late to remedy them. On Monday Jack went back to Kanab with the waggon, returning toward night with George Adair.   Fennemore had started with them, but he had turned back after something forgotten, and they did not know whether or not he had come on.   In the morning George went off to look for him, and met him down at the settlement.   He had followed on the day before, but instead of turning up the Johnson road, according to instructions, he had gone ahead on the road towards the Paria settlement.   Finally concluding that he was wrong he had tried to correct his mistake by moonlight, but after a while gave it up, tied his mule, unsaddled, to a cedar, and claimed the protection of another for himself.   During the night the mule chewed the bridle in two and departed for Kanab, leaving

Fennemore, when daylight came, to walk some eight miles under a hot sun without water or breakfast to Johnson. He was considerably used up by this episode, and put in the remainder of the day in recuperating. The evenings were wonderfully beautiful, and looking from a height the scene was exceptionally picturesque, with the red rocks, the warm sky, the camp equipage, and the air so still that the smoke of the camp-fires rose slender and unbroken till lost in the zenith.

Early Wednesday morning Prof. rode up on his powerful buckskin-coloured horse, and with Johnson and me went over to our Point B some miles away for some bearings, while Fennemore rode in search of his abandoned saddle. By night there was nothing to interfere with our making the final start, which we did May 30th, proceeding up the canyon without Mormon, one of our strongest horses, which by an accident had been injured so badly that he had to be left behind at Johnson. He was a fractious, unruly beast, but with so great vitality that we were sorry not to have his services. He died a week or two later. Towards night we passed another very small settlement called Clarkston, and camped near it, the last houses we would see for some time. Several Pai Utes hung around, and Prof. engaged one called Tom to accompany us as interpreter and, so far as he might know the country, as guide.

The next day, after sixteen miles north-easterly up canyons, we entered about three o'clock an exceedingly beautiful little valley, with a fine spring and a small lake or pond at the lower end. George Adair instantly declared that he meant to come back here to live, and after dinner when we reconnoitred the place he staked out his claim. All the next morning, June 1st, our way led over rolling meadows covered with fine grass, but about noon this ended and we entered the broken country of the upper Paria, with gullies and gulches barren and dry the rest of the day, except two, in which we crossed small branches of the Paria. In one of the dry gulches we passed a grave, marked by a sandstone slab with E. A. cut on it, which the wolves had dug out, leaving the human bones scattered all around. We could not stop to reinter them. They were the remains of Elijah Averett, a young Mormon, who was killed

while pursuing Pai Utes in 1866. Just before sunset we arrived
at the banks of the Paria, where we made camp, with plenty of
wood, water, and grass. Captain Dodds during the afternoon
recognised a place he had been in when hunting a way the
autumn before, and we followed his old trail for a time. Leaving
the Paria the following day where it branches, we followed the
east fork to its head, twelve miles, climbing rapidly through a
narrow valley. We could plainly see on the left a high, flat, cliff-
bounded summit, which was called Table Mountain, and early
in the afternoon we reached a series of "hog-backs," up one of
which the old Indian trail we were now following took its precarious way. The hog-backs were narrow ridges of half-disin-
tegrated clay-shale, with sides like the roof a house, the trail
following the sharp summit-line. Before we had fairly begun
this very steep, slippery, and narrow climb, the thunder boomed
and the heavens threw down upon us fierce torrents of rain,
soaking everything and chilling us through and through, while
making the trail like wet soap. Part way up, at one of the
worst places, a pack came loose, and, slipping back, hung on
the rump of the horse. There was no room for bucking it off,
and there was no trouble so far as the beast of burden was concerned, for he realised fully his own danger. Two of us managed to climb along past the other animals to where he meekly
stood waiting on the narrow ridge, with a descent on each side
of eight hundred or nine hundred feet, and set things in order
once more, when the cavalcade continued the ascent, the total
amount of which was some twelve hundred feet.

Arriving at the top we found ourselves almost immediately on the edge of a delightful little valley, mossy and green
with a fresh June dress, down which we proceeded two or three
miles to a spring where Dodds and Jacob had made a cache of
some flour the year before. The flour had disappeared. We
made a camp and dried out our clothes, blankets, etc., by
means of large fires. Though it was summer the air was decidedly chilly, for we were at an altitude of nearly 6000 feet.
Our interpreter that was to be did not enjoy the situation and
I think he dreaded meeting with the stranger Indians we might
encounter. He declared he was "heap sick," and begged to

be allowed to return, so Prof. gave him several days' rations
and we saw him no more. There was a pretty creek in this
valley flowing eastward, which Dodds said was the head of the
Dirty Devil, the same stream he had followed down the year
before in the attempt to find a way to bring us rations. The
weather was very bad but we kept on down Potato Valley as it
had been named, crossing three or four swift tributaries. About
four o'clock we stopped beside a raging torrent and went into
camp to reconnoitre. There were signs of some one having
been here about a month before, and as the animals were shod
we judged it was some prospector. The next day was so
wet and Prof. was feeling so sick that we kept our camp, having
made tents out of paulins and pack-covers, which gave me a
chance to plot up the trail from Kanab to this point, one hundred and three miles. Instead of crossing the torrent the
following day, June 5th, we went over the chief stream before the union and travelled down the right-hand side till we
arrived within half a mile of the place where the river canyoned and received a tributary from the left. It cut into the
rocks very abruptly and being high we could not enter the
canyon as Dodds had done. While the party camped here,
Prof. and Dodds rode away to the south on a dim trail to find
out what move to make; how far we might be able to go down
the Dirty Devil the next day. When they got back they reported finding a canyon twelve miles farther on, with many
water-pockets, and concluded to go there. We arrived about
noon Thursday, June 6th, making camp. Prof. and Dodds
then climbed to where they could get a wide view, and Dodds
pointed out the locality he had before reached when he
thought himself so near the mouth of the Dirty Devil. No
sooner had he done so than Prof. perceived at once that we
were not on the river we thought we were on, for by this explanation he saw that the stream we were trying to descend
flowed into the Colorado far to the south-west of the Unknown
Mountains, whereas he knew positively that the Dirty Devil
came in on the north-east. Then the question was, "What
river is this?" for we had not noted a tributary of any size
between the Dirty Devil and the San Juan. It was a new river

whose identity had not been fathomed. This discovery put a different complexion on everything. The problem was more complicated than Dodds had imagined when he was trying to reach the mouth the year before.

Prof. declared it was impossible to proceed farther in this direction towards our goal. The canyon of the river was narrow, and with the stream swimming high it was out of the question as a path for us now, and even had we been able to go down far enough to get out on the other side, the region intervening between it and the distant mountains was a heterogeneous conglomeration of unknown mesas and canyons that appeared impassable. He concluded the only thing to do was to go north to the summit of the Wasatch cliffs and keep along the high land north-east to an angle where these slopes vanished to the north. From that point we might be able to cross to the Dirty Devil or Unknown Mountains. Once at these mountains we felt certain of finding a way to our former camp-ground at the mouth of the Dirty Devil River. We retraced our path to the foot of Potato Valley, and there Jones, Clem, and George Adair were sent out to Kanab for additional rations, it being plain that we were in for a longer effort than had been contemplated. They were to be here again in twelve days to meet Prof. with his party, on the return from starting down the *Cañonita* with a crew selected from the seven remaining men. This seven, which included Prof., were now to strike up a branch creek and reach the upper slopes of what he later called the Aquarius Plateau, and along its verdant slopes continue our effort to reach the Unknown Mountains. The two parties separated on Saturday, June 8th, our contingent travelling about eighteen miles nearly due north, till just at sunset we entered a high valley in which flowed two splendid creeks. There we camped with an abundance of everything needed to make a comfortable rest for man and beast. In such travel as this the beast is almost the first consideration, for without him movement is slow and difficult and distance limited. We had gone up in altitude a great deal, 1800 or 2000 feet, and the next day, which was Sunday, we continued this upward course, seeing signs of deer and elk with an occasional sight of a fat "pine

Navajo Mountain from near Kaiparowits Peak.
Photograph by J. K. HILLERS, 1872.

Example of Lakes on the Aquarius Plateau.

Photograph by J. K. HILLERS.

hen" winging its heavy flight from tree to tree. The pines
were very tall and thick, interspersed with fir and balsam as
well as with the usual accompaniment of high altitude in the
West, the aspen. Our aneroids indicated 10,000 feet above sea-
level, and we could look down upon the vast canyoned desert
to the south as on a map. Descending into a deep canyon
where a clear torrent was foaming down at the rate of five
hundred feet to the mile, we went up a branch and finally
passing over a sudden crest discovered before us a very beautiful lake of an extent of some two hundred acres. It was now
late, and though we had come only ten miles we went into
camp for the night. There were several smaller lagoons nearby
and we named the group the Aspen Lakes. Around them
in the dense groves huge snowbanks still lingered from the
heart of winter. A prettier mountain region than this could
not be imagined, while the magnificent outlook to the south
and east across the broken country was a bewildering sight,
especially as the night enveloped it, deepening the mystery of
its entangled gorges and cliffs. From every point we could see
the Navajo Mountain and at least we knew what there was at
the foot of its majestic northern slope. I climbed far above
camp and crossing over a promontory looked down upon the
nebulous region to the eastward that we were to fathom, and it
seemed to me one of the most interesting sights I had ever
beheld. The night was so cold that ice formed in our kettles,
for our altitude in feet above sea was in the ten thousand still.

All the next morning, Monday, June 10th, we rode through
a delightful region of rolling meadows, beautiful groves of
pines and aspens, and cool, clear creeks. Near noon we descended into a fertile valley where we crossed two superb
torrential streams and camped at the second under a giant
pine. Fennemore felt very sick, which prevented further progress this day, and we put in the afternoon exploring as far as
we could the neighbourhood. More lakes were found and as
they were in a cup-like depression we called them the " Hidden
Lakes." Jack made some fine negatives of several of these
pretty bodies of water, two of which I have added to the illustrations of this volume. Not far from our camp two more

splendid creeks came together to form one, which Dodds said he thought was that named by them Big Boulder, where it joined the main stream down below. The next morning, Tuesday, we began our day's work by soon crossing Cataract and Cascade creeks before they united to form the Big Boulder, rushing down with an impetuosity that was forbidding. The two forming creeks were much alike, but we could see back in the distance a beautiful cascade of fully 1000 feet in which the second stream originated, and we distinguished it by that name. All day we travelled over a rancher's paradise, meeting no Indians and seeing no recent signs of any except in some filmy smoke mounting mysteriously from canyons in the tangled sandstone labyrinth below. Who were they, how many, and what might be their temper? were questions that came to us as we reflected on the presence there of unknown human beings, and furthermore would we meet them, and if so when? As on the preceding day we crossed many fine brooks which in the dry season probably would not make so vigorous a showing. Late in the afternoon, having travelled fifteen miles, we reached the point where the end of the Wasatch or Aquarius Plateau, the high slope of which we were using as a bridge from Potato Valley to the Unknown Mountains, broke back to the north, cutting us off once more from our objective, for a wide stretch, twenty-five miles in an airline, of ragged desert apparently impassable still intervened. We camped there at a convenient little spring. In the morning I was sent with Johnson for my companion in one direction down the mountain to look for some old trail, while Prof. with Dodds went in another. Scarcely had I gone half a mile when I found tolerably fresh Indian sign, and a mile or two farther on we struck a recently travelled trail. The horses that had gone over it were unshod and there were moccasin tracks indicating Indians without a doubt, but what kind of course the track did not reveal. The trail led towards the Dirty Devil Mountains, and we followed it three or four miles to ascertain with certainty its general course. There was a possibility of our stumbling upon the Indians in camp at some bend, and as this was not desirable for only two of us we turned back as soon as we felt sure of the direction. Prof. had

seen no trail at all, and he said we would take the one I had
found and follow it.   That night was disagreeable and rainy
with numberless mosquitoes, but worst of all one of our new
men always snored till the ground shook, and owing to the rain
we could not get away from him, for we had to remain in the
improvised tent to keep dry.

The morning light never was more welcome and we were
all up early.   The day was fair.   We were soon off and made
our way down from the grassy heights to the trail, tracing its
wearisome twists and turns, sometimes thinking it was not
going our way at all when the next turn would be exactly right.
In general its course was about east.   The land was desolate
and dry, and exactly as the region appeared from above, a
complete labyrinth of variously coloured cliffs and canyons.
Besides being very crooked on account of the nature of the
topography, the trail at times was indistinct because of the
barren rocks, smooth as a floor, with nothing to take an imprint.
In these places we were obliged to make the best guess we
could.   We came to a place where a valley lay about 1800
feet below us, with the descent to it over bare, smooth, white
sandstone almost as steep as a horse could stand on.   We
travelled a mile and a half over this and then found ourselves
in a better looking region where, after a few miles, we discovered
a beautiful creek flowing rapidly.   There was plenty of good
grass and we made our camp beneath some cottonwood trees,
having accomplished twenty miles the way we came.   Smoke
of an Indian fire was rolling up about three miles below us, but
we paid little attention to it.   Every man delayed putting
down his blankets till the champion snorer had selected the site
of his bed, and then we all got as far away as the locality would
permit.   Having slept little the night before, we hardly stirred
till morning, and in gratitude we called the stream Pleasant
Creek without an attempt at originality.

It was Friday, May 14th, and our long cavalcade proceeded
in the usual single file down along the creek in the direction of
the Indian smoke.   Scarcely had we gone three miles when suddenly we heard a yell and the bark of a dog.   Then we discovered
two squaws on the other side who had been gathering seeds,

and who were now giving the alarm, for we were close upon an Indian camp set on the edge of a low hill on the opposite side of the creek. Our outfit presented rather a formidable appearance, especially as we were an unexpected apparition, and we could see them all running to hide, though I thought for a moment we might have a battle. Without a halt, Prof. led the way across the creek to the foot of the hill, and as we reached the place one poor old man left as a sacrifice came tottering down, so overcome by fear that he could barely articulate, "Hah-ro-ro-roo, towich-a-tick-a-boo," meaning very friendly he was, and extending his trembling hand. Doubtless he expected to be shot on the instant. With a laugh we each shook his hand in turn saying "towich-a-tick-a-boo, old man," and rode up the hill into the camp, where we found all the wickiups with everything lying about just as they had been using it at the moment of receiving the alarm. We dismounted and inducing the terrified old man to sit down in one of the wickiups, Prof. sat with him and we rolled cigarettes, giving him one, and when all were smoking, except Prof. who never used tobacco, we urged him in English and Pai Ute and by signs to call the others back. I walked a few yards out on the hill and just then, with a rush and a clatter of language I could not understand, except "Impoo immy pshakai?" (What do you want?) the two squaws who had been up the creek arrived. The foremost one, frothing at the mouth with excitement and effort, dashed at me with an uplifted butcher knife as if she would enjoy sending it into me, but I laughed at her and she halted immediately in front of me. She broke into a maniacal laugh then and shouted something to the hidden refugees. We persuaded the old man also to call them, and he stepped out from the cedars which grew on the point and spoke a loud sentence. At last they began to appear silently and one by one. There were eight of the men, all well dressed in buckskin, and a number of women and children. When they became confident that we really meant to be friendly they relaxed their vigilance. With the hope of securing a guide and also to study them a little we went into camp in the creek bottom under the hill where they came to visit us. Their language and appearance showed them to be Utes.

When Prof. got back to Kanab he heard that a party of Red Lake Utes had killed a white boy near the Sevier settlements, and he concluded this band must have been the one. They probably thought we were pursuing them into their secret lair to punish them. Their great anxiety to trade for powder indicated their lack of that article and partly explained the precipitousness of their retreat. They had numbers of well dressed buckskins and a very small amount of powder would buy one, but as we had only metallic cartridges we could do little in the line of exchange. To satisfy one of them that we had no loose powder I removed the spring from the magazine of my Winchester and poured the sixteen cartridges out. He had never seen such a gun before and was greatly astonished, though he hardly understood how it worked. Prof. tried his best to persuade one to go with us as a guide, for the labyrinth ahead was a puzzle, but whether through fear or disinclination to leave friends not one would go. The chief gave us a minute description of the trail to the Unknown or Dirty Devil Mountains as well as he could by signs and words, some of which we could not understand, and long afterwards we learned that his information was exactly correct, though at the time through misunderstanding we were not able to follow it. They also told us there was a trail to the big river beyond the mountains.

There was a little canyon in the creek nearby and the water rushed down over a bed of bare rock at an angle of about twenty degrees. We were surprised to discover hundreds of fish six to nine inches long wriggling up the stream along one edge where the water was very shallow. They formed a line from top to bottom.

Unable to secure the guide, we left at six o'clock in the morning, Saturday, June 15th, with all our relations cordial, the Utes going away before we did, and struck out on the trail which led south-eastward from this camp. Travelling twelve miles, we passed through a narrow canyon into a larger one, believing that we were following the chief's direction. Recent heavy rains had washed out the trail, and not knowing its course it was impossible to keep even its general direction. Going up a left-hand branch of the canyon—that is, to the north—we found no exit, so we came down and followed a trail up the right-hand branch till it disappeared, then going back once more to the entrance we again went up the left-hand branch till we came to a vertical wall one thousand feet high, which turned us around. The right-hand one was entered another time, and towards its head where the cliffs could not be climbed we made camp, with an abundance of water which was so strongly alkaline we could not use it and had to keep the stock from it also. Our kegs were full and we did not suffer except by limitation. In the morning we continued up the same canyon till it ended in vertical cliffs, beneath which there was a large pool of pure cool water, with ferns clinging above it to the rocks and rank vegetation all around. This was an immense relief, and we found it hard to turn our backs on so attractive a spot and go down the gorge once more to a point not far below our last camp. Here the walls were about a thousand feet and very precipitous, though somewhat broken. Prof., Jack, Dodds, and I climbed out on the north and hunted for water in different directions on the top. I kept on and on down a dry wash, persisting against the objection of Dodds, who thought it useless, and was at last rewarded by discovering a pocket among the rocks containing several barrels of water, with another that was larger a short distance below in a crevice on a rock-shelf at the brink of a canyon.

We returned to camp with this news, where Prof. and Jack soon joined us. They had found no pockets, but had seen the divide between the waters of the Colorado and the Dirty Devil, which we could follow to the mountains if we could scale the cliffs. Prof. had selected a point where he thought we could mount. With a liberal use of axe, shovel, and pick we succeeded in gaining the summit in an hour and a half. With all the cliff-climbing we had done with horses this seemed to me our paramount achievement. The day was ending by this time, and I led the way with some trepidation towards the pocket I had found, for in my haste to get back I had not carefully noted the topography. The cedars and piñons all looked

Tantalus Creek.
Tributary of Frémont River.
Photograph by J. K Hillers.

alike in the twilight shades, and as I went on and on the men behind began to lose faith and made joking remarks about my mental status. I felt certain I was right, yet the distance seemed so much greater in the dusk than when I had traversed it on foot that I was a little disturbed. By the time we at last got to the pocket darkness was upon us, though nobody cared for anything but water, and there it was fresh and pure. The animals and ourselves (Andy filling the kettles first) consumed the entire amount, but it gave each a full drink, and we held the second pool in reserve.

When morning came we engineered a way for the animals down to the shelf where the other pocket was, twenty or thirty feet below, by pulling rocks away in places and piling them up in others. The shelf was perhaps fifty or sixty feet wide, with a sheer plunge of one thousand feet at the outer end into the first canyon we had followed. The animals could not get to the water, but we dipped it out for them in the camp kettles. The way up from the shelf was so very steep that at one point two of us had to put our shoulders to the haunches of some of the horses to "boost" them, while other men pulled on a strong halter from above, and in this way we soon had them all watered and ready for pack and saddle. Keeping along the divide we had comparatively easy going, with the Unknown Mountains ever looming nearer, till their blue mystery vanished and we could discern ordinary rocks and trees composing their slopes. About noon we arrived at the edge of an intervening valley, with the wind blowing so fierce a gale that we could barely see. Crossing this depression we reached a small creek at the foot of the second mountain from the north (now Mt. Pennell), and climbed its slope seventeen hundred feet to a beautiful spring, where we camped, with plenty of fine grass for the famished horses. We had at last traversed the unknown to the unknown, and felt well satisfied with our success. If it had ever been done before by white men there was no knowledge of it.

The temperature was so low that water froze in the camp kettles, and next morning, June 13th, the thermometer stood at 28° F., with the water of the little brook running from the spring at 37° F. After breakfast Prof., Jack, and Dodds climbed the mountain on which we were camped, running their aneroid out, while with Johnson I went down the slope north, crossed the pass, and climbed the first mountain (now Mt. Ellen, after Mrs. Thompson). A severe snow-storm set in, and when we had finally attained a point where our aneroid indicated 11,200 feet above sea-level, we were obliged to turn back because of the lateness of the hour and having no coats, no food, or water. When we reached camp on the other mountain night had come. Andy had been trying to cook some beans, but the high altitude prevented the water from getting hot enough and the operation was incomplete.[1] I foolishly ate some of the beans, being very hungry, with the result that I was sick for the first time on the expedition, suffering a horrible stomach-ache. Though not disabled I was extremely uncomfortable. In the morning we started to go around north through the pass to the east side of the mountain, and I ran in the trail as usual, mounting and dismounting many times, till I was extremely glad after eight miles when we came to the head of a little creek and stopped to enable Prof. to climb the third peak (Mt. Hillers) for observations. While he was gone I was content to lie still in the shade of a bush, and finally lost my pain in sleep. Prof. got back so late that we camped where we were, much to my satisfaction. The view from our camp was extensive and magnificent, the whole Dirty Devil region lying open, like a book, below us.

We were striking for the creek up which Prof. and Cap. had come the year before from the river, for we knew that from its mouth we could easily get to where our *Cañonita* was cached. The next day, June 20th, we continued down Trachyte Creek, as Prof. called it, till four o'clock, passing many old camps and grazing grounds, when we halted for Prof. to climb to a height. The outlook there showed him that this was not the stream whose canyon below we wanted to descend to the river, so the following morning he took Dodds and recon-

[1] We had not yet learned to put a tight cover on the bean pot, and then by means of a big stone on the cover and a hot fire create an artificial atmosphere within it, thus raising the temperature.

noitred, the latter after a while returning with orders for us to
come on eastward to another canyon. We left Trachyte Creek
and reached Prof. at two o'clock. He had prospected a trail,
or rather a way, to descend into the canyon over the smooth
bare sandstone across which we wound back and forth for a
mile, constantly going down into the strange, weird depths till at
last we reached the creek bed, where a short distance below we
went into camp in a beautiful green cottonwood grove, with
enormous pockets of good water close by. By seven o'clock
in the morning of the 22d we were going on down the deep,
narrow canyon, and arrived at the Colorado at half-past ten.
The river was at least fifteen feet higher than last year, and
rushed by with a majestic power that was impressive. Our
first unusual incident was when Prof.'s horse, in trying to drink
from a soft bank, dropped down into the swift current and
gave us half an hour's difficult work to get him out. When
we had eaten dinner we all went up to the mouth of the Dirty
Devil, where we had stored the *Cañonita*, and rejoiced to find
her lying just as we left her, except that the water had risen
to that level and washed away one of the oars. We caulked
the boat temporarily, launched her once more on the sweeping
tide, and in two minutes were at our camp, where we hauled
her out for the repairs necessary to make her sound for the
run to the Paria.

Sunday was the next day, June 23d, and while the others
rested I plotted in the trail by which we had crossed to this
place so that Prof. could take it out with him, as he decided
that Jack, Johnson, Fennemore, and I were to take the boat
down, while he, Andy, and Dodds would go back overland
to meet Jones and George Adair at the foot of Potato Valley.
At five o'clock they left us, going up the same canyon we had
come down and which we called Lost Creek Canyon, now
Crescent Creek. The next day we recaulked and painted the
boat, and I put the name *Cañonita* in red letters on the stern
and a red star on each side of the bow. By Wednesday the
26th she was all ready and we put her in the water and ran
down four miles to the large Shinumo house. Jack rowed the
stern oars, Johnson the bow, I steered, while Fennemore sat on

the middle deck.   The high water completely obliterated the aggravating shoals which had bothered us the year before, and we had no work at all except to steer or to land, the current carrying us along at a good pace.   We stopped occasionally for pictures and notes and got about everything that Jack and Fennemore wanted in the line of photographs.   The Fourth of July we celebrated by firing fourteen rounds, and I made a lemon cake and a peach-pie for dinner.   On Sunday the 8th we passed the mouth of the stream that had been mistaken for the Dirty Devil, and which Prof. had named Escalante River.   It was narrow and shallow and would not be taken at its mouth for so important a tributary.   The next day we passed the San Juan which was running a very large stream, and camped at the Music Temple, where I cut Jack's name and mine under those of the Howlands and Dunn.   The rapid below was dashing but easy and we ran it without stopping to examine.   On Friday the 12th we came to El Vado and dug up a cache we had made there the year before.   Our rations for some time were nothing but bread and coffee, and we were glad to see the Echo Peaks and then run in at the mouth of the Paria on Saturday, July 13th, with the expectation of finding men and supplies.   The *Dean* was lying high and dry on the bank and we wondered who had taken her from her hiding-place.   Firing our signal shots and receiving no answer, Jack and I went up the Paria, crossing it on a log, and saw a cabin and a farm on the west side.   This we knew must be Lee's.   He was ploughing in a field, and when he first sighted us he seemed a little startled, doubtless thinking we might be officers to arrest him.   One of his wives, Rachel, went into the cabin not far off and peered out at us.   She was a fine shot as I afterwards learned.   Lee received us pleasantly and invited us to take our meals at his house till our party came.   As we had nothing but bread and coffee and not much of these we accepted.   The fresh vegetables out of the garden, which his other wife, Mrs. Lee XVIII., served nicely cooked, seemed the most delicious food that could be prepared.   Mrs. Lee XVIII. was a stout, comely young woman of about twenty-five, with two small children, and seemed to be entirely happy in the situation.   The other wife, whose number I did not learn, left before dark for a house they had at Jacob's Pool and I never saw her again.

Lee had worked hard since his arrival early in the year and now had his farm in fairly good order with crops growing, well irrigated by the water he took out of the Paria. He called the place Lonely Dell, and it was not a misnomer. Johnson made arrangements to go to Kanab the next day, as he concluded that his health would not permit him to go through the Grand Canyon with us, so this was our last night with him. Lee gave me his own version of the Mountain Meadows Massacre claiming that he really had nothing to do with it and had tried to stop it, and when he could not do so he went to his house and cried. The Pai Utes ever after called him Naguts or Crybaby.[1]

In the morning, Sunday, July 14th, Johnson departed with Lee and we expected someone to arrive to bring us news of the Major and Prof., but the sun went down once more without any message. We felt sure that Prof. got out of the Dirty Devil country without accident, but we wanted some definite information of it and we also desired to know when we would resume the canyon voyage. On Monday having nothing else to do we took some hoes and worked in Lee's garden till near noon, when we heard yells which proved to come from Andy and Clem with a waggon needing some help over bad places. We soon had the waggon in a good spot under some willows and there speedily ransacked it for mail, spending the rest of the day reading letters and newspapers. Andy told us that Prof. had reached Kanab with no trouble of any kind. Mrs. Lee XVIII., or Sister Emma, as she would in Utah properly be called, invited us to dinner and supper, and the next day we worked in the garden again, repaired the irrigating ditch, and helped about the place in a general way, glad enough to have some occupation even though the sun was burning hot and the thermometer stood at 110° in the shade. Almost every day we did some work in the garden and we also repaired the irrigating dam.

Our camp was across the Paria down by the Colorado, and

[1] Lee was executed for the crime five years later, 1877. Others implicated were not punished, the execution of Lee "closing the incident."

when Brother Lee came back the following Sunday he called to give us a lengthy dissertation on the faith of the Latter-Day Saints (Mormons), while Andy, always up to mischief, in his quiet way, delighted to get behind him and cock a rifle. At the sound of the ominous click Lee would wheel like a flash to see what was up. We had no intention of capturing him, of course, but it amused Andy to act in a way that kept Lee on the *qui vive*. We got the *Nell* out of her shed and found her in very bad condition, while the *Dean* was about as we had left her. Andy and Jack went to work on the *Dean* and in a few days had her in excellent trim. On July 24th, which is the day the Mormons celebrate for the settlement of Salt Lake Valley, Lee invited us to dinner and supper, which gave us a very pleasant time. So far as our intercourse with Lee was concerned we had no cause for complaint. He was genial, courteous, and generous.

A copy of DeForrest's *Overland* was in camp and I whiled away some hours reading it, but time began to hang heavily upon us and we daily longed for the appearance of the rest of the party so that we might push out on the great red flood that moved irresistibly down into the maw of Marble Canyon, and end the uncertainty that lay before us. August the first came and still no message. Fennemore now felt so sick that Jack took him to Lee's with rations in order that he might have vegetables with his meals with the hope that he would recover, but he grew worse, and on August 4th he decided that he would return to his home in Salt Lake. We concluded that one of us must go to Kanab to inform Prof. of the state of affairs, and Clem in his big-hearted way offered to do this, but we knew that his sense of locality was defective and that he might get lost. Consequently we played on him an innocent trick which I may now tell as he long ago went "across the range." I planned with Andy that we three were to draw cuts for the honour of the ride and that Andy was to let me draw the fatal one. Clem was greatly disappointed. Jack went on a chase after Nig and ran him down about sunset, for Nig was the most diplomatic mule that ever lived   Having no saddle I borrowed one from Lee who let me have it dubiously as he feared we might be laying some trap. I gave him my word that while I had his saddle no man of ours would molest him, and furthermore that they would befriend him. I rode away while he remarked that in the rocks he could defy an army, with regret still in his eyes, though he accepted my pledge. I got out a few miles before dark and slept by the roadside, with the distant murmur of rapids speaking to me of the turmoil we were soon to pass through. By noon of the next day I was at Jacob's Pool, by half-past three at House Rock Spring, and at night in Summit Valley where I camped. The day was so hot that I could hardly bear my hand on my rifle barrel as it lay across my saddle. My lunch of jerked beef and bread I ate as I rode along thus losing no time.

The trail across the Kaibab was not often travelled, and it was dim and hard to follow, a faint horse track showing here and there, so I lost it several times but quickly picked it up again, and finally came out of the forest where I could see all the now familiar country to the west and north. About two o'clock I arrived at Kanab and rode to Jacob's house where Sister Louisa told me that the Major, Prof., Mrs. Thompson, Professor De Motte, and George Adair had left that very morning for the south end of the Kaibab on the way to the Paria, and that Jones and Lyman Hamblin the day before had started for the Paria with a waggon load of supplies drawn by a team of four broncho mules. Nig being very tired I thought I would rest till morning, when he rewarded my consideration by eluding me till ten o'clock. This gave me so late a start that it was dark and rainy when I descended the east side of the Kaibab, and I had to drag Nig down the 2000 feet in the gloom over boulders, bushes, ledges, or anything else that came, for I could see only a few feet and could not keep the trail. I reached House Rock Spring at last and camped there. In the morning I discovered Jones and Lyman down in the valley and joined them for breakfast, after which I helped them start. This was no easy matter, for the four mules they had in harness, with one exception, were as wild as mountain sheep, having only recently been broken. Jones had been badly kicked three times, his hands were burned by the ropes, and there was a lively time whenever the excited animals were put to the waggon. The road was new, only a waggon track in reality, and the mules became more and more docile through exhaustion as the day went on. At night they were far safer to handle than in the morning.

July 9th about dark we arrived at Lonely Dell, Lee stealing suspiciously in behind where I was walking, to ask me who the men were and what they wanted. We had a joyful time, especially as Steward had sent out a large box of fine candy which we found in the mail and opened at once. Four days later the Major and his party came from the Kaibab and we had venison for supper. The Major said we would go on down the Colorado as soon as possible though the water was still very high.

CHAPTER XIV

A Company of Seven.—The *Nellie Powell* Abandoned.—Into Marble Canyon.—
Vasey's Paradise.—A Furious Descent to the Little Colorado.—A Mighty
Fall in the Dismal Granite Gorge.—Caught in a Trap.—Upside Down.—A
Deep Plunge and a Predicament.—At the Mouth of the Kanab.

WE now missed Steward, Cap, and Beaman more than ever, for we had been unable to get anyone to take their places. The fact was our prospective voyage through Marble and Grand canyons was considered almost a forlorn hope and nobody cared to take the risk. The plan had been to give me the steering of the *Cañonita*, but now with three boats and only seven to man them it was plain that one must be abandoned. An examination of them all showed that the *Nellie Powell* was in the poorest condition and she was chosen for the sacrifice. She was put back in her shelter being afterwards used by Lee for a desultory ferry business, that developed. About ten days before our arrival, the *Dean* had been discovered by a newspaper man named J. H. Beadle, and used to cross to the north side where he left her. This was how she happened to be there when we came. Beadle had denounced Lee and the Mormons in print and tried to conceal his identity by assuming the name of Hanson, a plan frustrated by his having some clothes, marked with his own name, laundered by Sister Emma. Lee was only amused by the incident. The *Dean* was to be manned by the same crew as before; Jones to steer, Jack at the after oars, I at the forward pair, and the Major in his usual place on the middle deck. The *Cañonita* was to have Prof. as steersman, Andy at the stroke oars, and Clem in the bow, Clem having gotten all over his inclination to leave and being determined now to see the end of the voyage before he departed.

The same day that the Major and his party arrived, Jack and
I, with Jones steering, tried the *Dean* by taking Mrs. Thompson, Professor DeMotte, and Lyman Hamblin up the river so
that they might see what a canyon was like from a boat.   Mrs.
Thompson was so enthusiastic that she declared she wanted to
accompany us.   Prof. took her as passenger on the *Cañonita*
about half-past four on Wednesday, August 14th, when we had
completed the sacking and packing of provisions, and with both
boats ran down through a small rapid or two about a mile and
a half, where we camped at the mouth of a little canyon down
which the waggon-road came.   Mrs. Thompson enjoyed the
exhilaration of descending the swift rushing water and still
thought it attractive.   I went to Lee's and brought down the
Major's arm-chair for our boat, and saw Fennemore who was
very sick.   We made our final preparations at this point, and I
spent most of Thursday morning helping the Major get his
papers in order so that if we did not appear again his affairs
could be readily settled.   This required considerable writing,
which I did, for the Major wrote slowly with his left hand, the
only one he had.   We dined with Lee, having the first watermelon of the season for dessert.   Lee was most cordial and we
could not have asked better treatment than he gave us the
whole time we were at Lonely Dell.   In the afternoon our land
outfit left for Kanab and we said a last good-bye to the men,
who looked as if they never expected to see us again.   Only
the "Tirtaan Aigles" remained, and there were but seven of
these now.   The next day we put the finishing touches on the
boats, and while we were doing this our late fellow voyageur
Beaman, and a companion named Carleton, passed on their
way to the Moki Towns where Beaman wanted to make photographs.   All being ready the next day, Saturday, August 17th,
we pushed out on the mighty Colorado about nine o'clock and
by noon ran into Marble Canyon, nearly five miles, passing one
small rapid and another of considerable size on a river about
one hundred feet wide and extremely swift, with straight walls
rapidly increasing from the fifty feet or so at the Paria.   Marble
Canyon while differing in name is but the upper continuation
of the Grand Canyon, there being no line of demarkation other

than a change in geological structure and the entrance of the canyon of the Little Colorado. The combined length of the two divisions is 283 miles and the declivity is very great. The altitude of the mouth of the Paria is 3170 feet, while the Grand Wash at the end of the Grand Canyon is 840 feet, leaving a descent of 2330 feet still before us.

At our dinner camp, which was on a talus on the left, the walls were about 500 feet and quite precipitous, but I was able to climb out on the right to get a view of the surroundings. After dinner we went on in our usual order, our boat the *Dean* in advance and the *Cañonita* following. The photographing now devolved entirely on Jack and Clem ; Andy as usual ran the culinary branch of the expedition, Jones and Prof. meandered the river. We had not gone far after dinner before we were close upon a bad-looking rapid, a drop of about eighteen feet in a distance of 225, which we concluded to defeat by means of a portage on the right-hand bank. As we knew exactly what to do no time was wasted and we were soon below, sweeping on with a stiff current which brought us, in about ten miles from our morning start and five from the noon halt, to a far worse rapid than the last, a fall of twenty-five feet in four or five hundred, with very straight walls six hundred feet high on both sides. The Major concluded to leave the passage of it till the next day, and we went into camp at the head. This was the rapid where disaster fell on the miners, ten in number, who in the spring had stolen a lot of our things at the Paria and started down prospecting on a raft. They saved their lives but not another thing, and after a great deal of hard work they succeeded by means of driftwood ladders in climbing to the top of the walls and made their way to the settlement. This is now called Soap Creek Rapid, being at the mouth of the canyon by which the little stream of that name reaches the river,—a little stream which at times is a mighty torrent. In a small rapid following or in the final portion of this, I believe, is the place where Frank M. Brown, leader of the Denver, Colorado Canyon, and Pacific Railway Survey, was drowned in 1889.

We began work on Sunday, August 18th, by making the

portage and had no trouble of any kind, Jack and Clem making some photographs before we finally said good-bye to the place. Continuing on our way we found the river very narrow, not over seventy-five feet in many places and ranging from that to two hundred, with frequent whirlpools strong enough to swing our boats entirely around. Before dinner-time we had put five large rapids behind, and then we halted under a ledge on the left a short distance above a very ugly and difficult prospect. There was an exceedingly heavy descent and a soft sandstone being at the river margin it was worn away, giving little chance for a footing by which to make a portage. The Major and Prof. decided that we could run it safely, and after dinner we shot into it, both boats going through in fine style. Just below was another smaller one that was vanquished easily, and we went swiftly on down the swirling, booming current. Rain fell at intervals to continue our saturation, and with four more rapids, all of which we ran, one having quite a heavy fall, there was little chance for us to dry out. At one point we passed an enormous rock which had dropped from the cliffs overhead and almost blocked the whole river. Then we arrived at a huge rapid whose angry tones cried so distinctly, " No running through here," that we did not hesitate but began a let down forthwith, and when that was accomplished we camped at the foot of it for the night, having come eleven and three-eighths miles during the day. The rapid was extremely noisy and the roaring reverberated back and forth from cliff to cliff as it ascended to the top, 1800 feet, to escape into the larger air. The walls had two or three terraces and were not over three quarters of a mile apart at the summit, the cliff portions being nearly or quite perpendicular. The rocks, of all sizes, which were legion at each rapid, were frequently dovetailed into each other by the action of the current and so neatly joined in a serrated line that they were practically one.

The rapidity with which the water went down and the walls went up as we cut into the plateau gave a vivid impression of descending into the very bowels of the earth, and this impression seemed daily to intensify. On Monday, August 19th, the same conditions prevailed, the walls being of marble mostly

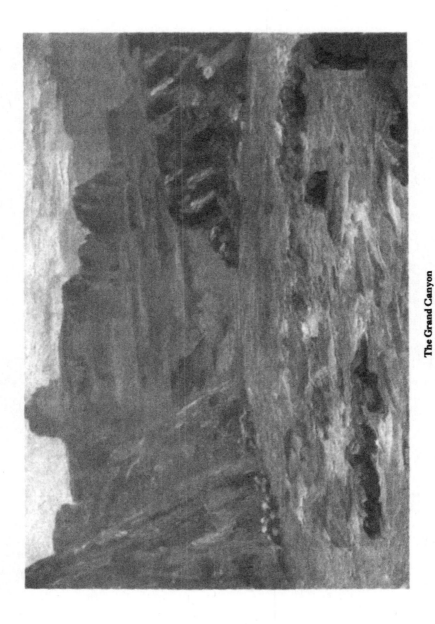

The Grand Canyon

Near mouth of Shinumo Creek

The river is in flood and the water is "colorado." Sketch made in colour on the spot by F. S. Dellenbaugh. July 26, 1907.

Thompson

Marble Canyon.

Photograph by J. K. HILLERS, 1872.

vertical from the water's edge for about seven hundred feet, and then rising by four terraces to two thousand feet, all stained red by the disintegration of iron-stained rocks overhead though the marble is a grey colour. We only made four and one-quarter miles and established Camp 90 on the left, just below a big rapid and in sight of another, with a record for the whole day of four rapids run, three passed by let-downs, and one overcome by a portage. The next day we did not accomplish a much greater distance, only about nine miles, but we were highly successful in our encounters with the enemy, running no less than twelve big rapids and making a portage at another to round out the dozen on the baker's proverbial basis. The average width of the canyon at the top was about one and a quarter miles, while the breadth of the water itself plunging along the bottom was not more than 125 feet, and the total height of wall was 2500 feet. We had marble at the river margin most of the day, a greyish crystalline rock fluted multitudinously in places by the action of high water and sometimes polished like glass. While this was a grey rock the entire effect of the canyon, for the reason stated above, was red. On the right bank we made our camp on some sand at the mouth of a gulch, and immediately put on our dry clothes from the boats. Not far below on the same side was what appeared to be a vast ruined tower. Around the indentations which answered for crumbling windows bunches of mosses and ferns were draped, while from the side, about one hundred feet up from the river, clear springs broke forth to dash down amidst verdure in silvery skeins. The whole affair formed a striking and unusual picture, the only green that so far had been visible in the canyon landscape, for the walls from brink to river were absolutely barren of trees or any apparent vegetation. On the former trip the Major had named the place after a botanist friend of his, Vasey's (Vaysey) Paradise, and this was now recorded in our notes. All day long we had seen in the magnificent walls besides caverns and galleries resemblances to every form of architectural design, turrets, forts, balconies, castles, and a thousand strange and fantastic suggestions from the dark tower against which Childe Roland with his slug-horn blew defiance, to the airy structures evolved by the wonderful lamp of Aladdin.

Starting down again on Wednesday morning we ran past the Paradise and heard a little bird singing there amidst the spray and mosses, a delicate note seeming out of place amidst such gigantic desolation. Only the boom of great cannon or the tone of some enormous organ pipe would be correct with the surroundings. The walls at the water's edge were vertical for long distances up to eight hundred feet, and being now in all about three thousand feet and not a great ways apart, the out-look ahead was something almost overpowering in its deep suggestion of mysterious and untold realms to come. On the first voyage it would have been easy to persuade oneself that the river was soon to become subterranean, but the Major having solved the enigma, we could look with indifference on the threatening prospect. Yet the walls nevertheless seemed to have a determination to close together overhead as we looked down the descending waters before us, with cliff mounting on cliff and the distance from one to the other appearing so very small. Deep and sombre were the shadows at the bends, and the imagination needed no spur to picture there rapids, falls, cataracts, of giant proportions. We made nearly eleven miles and ran ten very big rapids, meeting with no accident, though one was particularly violent and filled us half full of water in the fierce breakers. The stage of water was exactly right for this stretch; a lower stage would certainly have given us far more trouble. Our stop for the night, Camp 92, was made on a wide sandbank on the left, with some mesquite growing nearby, our first acquaintance with this tree on the river. We now were getting on so well and were so comfortable that we felt quite happy and Jack as usual entertained us with several songs. The next day, Thursday the 22d, Jack and Clem took some photographs in the morning and I hunted fossils for the Major in the limestone shales which had run up under the marble. By nine o'clock we were packed up again in our usual good form, everything in the rubber sacks, hatches firmly bat-battened down, life-preservers ready, and we set forth for an-other day's battle. There were numerous large rapids and the impetuous river, turbid and grim, rushed down with a continuity that kept us alert every instant. Though we descended with terrific velocity, nothing gave us any particular trouble before dinner, which we ate in the shade of a mesquite on the right at the mouth of a couple of giant gulches. Here we discovered a large patch of cacti loaded with the red prickly pears or cactus apples, as we called them. They were ripe,—seeming to me to be half way between a fig and a tomato,—and very welcome for dessert, as we had eaten no fresh fruit since a watermelon brought along as far as the first noon camp. All the vegetation was different from that of the upper canyons and of a kind indicating a hotter climate; cacti, yucca, etc. In the afternoon the walls became greater, the river ran swifter, the descent seemed almost without a break, for rapid followed rapid in such quick succession that it was next to impossible to separate them one from another. At times we could barely maintain control of the boats so powerful and uninterrupted was the turbulent sweep of the great narrow flood. At one place as we were being hurled along at a tremendous speed we suddenly perceived immediately ahead of us and in such a position that we could not avoid dashing into it, a fearful commotion of the waters, indicating many large rocks near the surface. The Major stood on the middle deck, his life-preserver in place, and holding by his left hand to the arm of the well secured chair to prevent being thrown off by the lurching of the boat, peered into the approaching maelstrom. It looked to him like the end for us and he exclaimed calmly, " By God, boys, we 're gone ! " With terrific impetus we sped into the seething, boiling turmoil, expecting to feel a crash and to have the *Dean* crumble beneath us, but instead of that unfortunate result she shot through smoothly without a scratch, the rocks being deeper than appeared by the disturbance on the surface. We had no time to think over this agreeable delivery, for on came the rapids or rather other rough portions of the unending declivity requiring instant and continuous attention, the Major rapidly giving the orders, Left, right, hard on the right, steady, hard on the left, *hard on the left*, H-A-R-D ON THE LEFT, pull away strong, etc., Jones aiding our oars by his long steering sweep. Rowing for progress was unnecessary ; the oars were required only for steering or for pulling as fast as we could to avoid some bad place.

At the same time the walls constantly gained height as the torrent cut down its bed till both together, with the rapidity of our movement, fairly made one dizzy. In turning a bend we saw back through a gulch the summit of the Kaibab's huge cliffs, the total height above our heads being over five thousand feet ; a sublime vista. The immediate walls of Marble Canyon were here about 3500 feet, not all vertical but rising in buttresses, terraces, and perpendicular faces, while immediately at the river they were now generally flanked by talus or broken ledges giving ample footing, as seen in the illustration opposite page 219. Words are not adequate to describe this particular day in Marble Canyon ; it must be experienced to be appreciated and I will not strive further to convey my impressions. As the sun sank to the western edge of the outer world we were rushing down a long straight stretch of canyon, and the colossal precipices looming on all sides, as well as dead ahead across our pathway, positively appeared about to overwhelm the entire river by their ponderous magnificence, burnished at their summits by the dying sun. On, down the headlong flood our faithful boats carried us to the gloom that seemed to be the termination of all except subterranean progress, but at the very bottom of this course there was a bend to the west, and we found ourselves at the mouth of a deep side canyon coming in from the east, with a small stream flowing into the big river. This was the mouth of the Little Colorado and the end at last of Marble Canyon, one of the straightest, deepest, narrowest, and most majestic chasms of the whole long series. It also had more wall rising vertically from the water's edge than any other canyon we had encountered.

Our distance for the day was eighteen miles with eighteen rapids, one nearly three miles long and all following each other so closely they were well-nigh continuous. We ran seventeen and made one let-down. It was a glorious day and a fitting preparation for our entrance into the next stupendous canyon which the Major styled the " Sockdologer of the World,"

Canyon of the Little Colorado.
Photograph by C. BARTHELMESS.

The Grand Canyon.

From just below the Little Colorado.
Photograph by J. K. HILLERS, 1872.

the now famous Grand Canyon.[1] Our altitude was 2690 feet,
giving a descent in the sixty-five and one-half miles of Marble
Canyon of 480 feet, leaving 1850 feet still to be overcome before we could reach the mouth of the Grand Wash and the
end of the Grand Canyon.   I counted sixty-three rapids in
Marble Canyon, Prof. sixty-nine.   We made four portages and
let down by line six times.

Our Camp 93 was on the left bank of the Little Colorado,
and there we remained for Friday, August 23d, to reconnoitre
the neighbourhood, and to give Prof. an opportunity to get the
latitude and longitude.   The Little Colorado was a red stream
about sixty feet wide and four or five deep, salty and impossible
to drink.   The Great Colorado was also muddy and not altogether palatable, for one's hand dipped in and allowed to dry
became encrusted with sediment; but the water otherwise was
pure.   The river had been rapidly rising for several days and
was still coming up so that we were likely to have in the Grand
Canyon more water than we required.   I climbed up the wall
on the north side of the Little Colorado thinking I might be
able to reach the summit, but when about half-way up I met
vast and vertical heights that were impossible and returned to
camp.   The next morning, Saturday, August 24th, we packed
up and entered the Grand Canyon proper on an easy river,
making about five miles in half an hour and putting behind six
rapids all small, camping at the head of one that was more
threatening.   Here a little creek came in from the right, or
west, near camp.   The canyon was wider than above, and
we could see the summits around that were six thousand
feet above the river, but some miles back.   In the morning
I made a geological sketch, and in the afternoon I climbed
a high peak and put in some of the topography.   The next
morning we crossed the river to examine a large igneous
butte where we found a small vein of copper ore, and after
dinner Prof. and I climbed a couple of peaks and did some

[1] There is but one Grand Canyon—the one here referred to.   Persons unfamil-
iar with Western geography frequently confound the Canyon of the Arkansas
with that of the Colorado because the former is in the STATE of Colorado.   The
Grand Canyon is in Arizona but on the *Colorado* River.

triangulating. Monday the 26th found us still at Camp 94 to further investigate the surroundings, and the Major, Prof., Jones, and I climbed up on the north about 2600 feet in order to get a better idea of the several valleys which here seemed to compose the bottom of the great chasm, and did not reach camp till after dark. Everything now developed on a still larger and grander scale; we saw before us an enormous gorge, very wide at the top, which could engulf an ordinary mountain range and lose it within its vast depths and ramifications. Multitudinous lofty mesas, buttes, and pinnacles began to appear, each a mighty mountain in itself, but more or less overwhelmed by the greater grandeur of the Cyclopean environment.

Tuesday, August 27th, after Prof. had put a new tube in the second barometer which had somehow been broken, we pushed off once more to see what the day would develop. The rapid just below camp we ran through easily and then made swift progress for seven miles, running nine more rapids, two rather bad ones. The *Cañonita* grounded once on a shoal but got off without damage. Where we stopped for dinner we caught sight of two mountain sheep drinking, and Andy and I got our guns out of the cabins as quickly as possible and started after them, but they flew away like birds of the air. Near this point there was a small abandoned hut of mesquite logs. We went into camp farther down on the left for investigations, the Major and I going up the river and finding a small salty creek which we followed for a time on an old trail, the Major studying the geology and collecting specimens of the rocks, which we carried back to camp, arriving after dark. The geology and topography here were complicated and particularly interesting, and we ought to have been able to spend more days, but the food question, as well as time, was a determining factor in our movements, and with only two boats our rations would carry us with necessary stops only to the mouth of the Kanab Canyon where our pack-train would meet us on September 4th. There was no other place above Diamond Creek known at that time, except perhaps the spot near Mount Trumbull, where supplies could be brought in. On Wednesday we ran two or three miles and stopped for our photographers to get some views opposite a rust-coloured sandstone. We also had dinner at this place and then continued the descent. After running four rapids successfully, making a let-down at another, and a portage over the upper end of a sixth we were ready, having made in all six miles, to go into camp part way down the last, one of the heaviest falls we had so far encountered. It was perhaps half a mile long, with a declivity of at least forty feet, studded by numerous enormous boulders. A heavy rain began during our work of getting below, and our clothes being already wet the air became very chilly. We had to carry the cargoes only a short distance, with no climbing, and there was ample room so the portage was not difficult in that respect. But though we could manœuvre the empty boats down along the shore amidst the big rocks, they were exceedingly heavy for our small band, and in sliding them down between the huge masses, with the water pouring around and often into them, we sometimes had as much as we could do to manage them, each man being obliged to strain his muscle to the limit. Jack from this cause hurt his back so badly that he could not lift at all, and overcome by the sudden weakness and pain he came near sinking into the swift river at the stern of the *Dean* where he happened at the moment to be working. I heard his cry and clambered over to seize him as quickly as I could, helping him to shore, where we did all that was possible for his comfort. As we were going no farther that day he was able to rest, and in the morning felt much better, though his back was still weak. Andy took his place in our boat to run the lower end of the rapid, which was easily done. We landed below on the same side, enabling Andy to go back to help bring down the *Cañonita*, while Jack walked along the rocks to where we were. Here we remained for a couple of hours while I climbed up for the Major and measured the " Red Beds," and Jack rested again, improving very fast. When we were ready to go on his trouble had almost disappeared.

A dark granite formation had run up at the foot of the last fall and it rose rapidly higher, hemming the water in with steep, forbidding cliffs close together. The river became much narrower and swirled with an oily-looking current around the

buttresses of granite that thrust themselves from one side or
the other into it. The declivity was not great and the torrent
was otherwise placid. After three miles of this ominous docility, just as the dinner hour was near and the threatening black
granite had risen to one thousand feet above the water, we
heard a deep, sullen roar ahead and from the boats the whole
river seemed to vanish instantly from earth. At once we ran
in on the right to a small area of great broken rocks that pro-
truded above the water at the foot of the wall, and stepping out
on these we could look down on one of the most fearful places
I ever saw or ever hope to see under like circumstances,—a
place that might have been the Gate to Hell that Steward had
mentioned. We were near the beginning of a tremendous fall.
The narrow river dropped suddenly and smoothly away, and
then, beaten to foam, plunged and boomed for a third of a mile
through a descent of from eighty to one hundred feet, the
enormous waves leaping twenty or thirty feet into the air and
sending spray twice as high.[1] On each side were the steep,
ragged granitic walls, with the tumultuous waters lashing and
pounding against them in a way that precluded all idea of
portage or let-down. It needed no second glance to tell us
that there was only one way of getting below. If the rocks
did not stop us we could " cross to Killiloo," and when a driving
rain had ceased Andy gathered the few sticks of driftwood
available for a fire, by which he prepared some dinner in advance of the experiment. Jack and Clem took three negatives,
and when the dinner was disposed of we stowed all loose
articles snugly away in the cabins, except a camp-kettle in
each standing-room to bail with, and then battening down the
hatches with extra care, and making everything shipshape, we
pulled the *Dean* up-stream, leaving the *Cañonita* and her crew
to watch our success or failure and profit by it. The Major
had on his life-preserver and so had Jones, but Jack and I put
ours behind our seats, where we could catch them up quickly,
for they were so large we thought they impeded the handling
of the oars. Jack's back had fortunately now recovered, so

[1] Professor Thompson in his diary calls the descent 130 feet in three-quarters
of a mile.

The Grand Canyon.
Running the Sockdologer.
From a sketch afterwards by F. S. DELLENBAUGH.

The Grand Canyon.

From Top of Granite, South Side near Bright Angel Creek.

that he was able to row almost his usual stroke. We pulled up-stream about a quarter of a mile close to the right-hand wall, in order that we might get well into the middle of the river before making the great plunge, and then we turned our bow out and secured the desired position as speedily as possible, heading down upon the roaring enemy—roaring as if it would surely swallow us at one gulp.

My back being towards the fall I could not see it, for I could not turn round while waiting every instant for orders. Nearer and nearer came the angry tumult; the Major shouted "Back water!" there was a sudden dropping away of all support; then the mighty waves smote us. The boat rose to them well, but we were flying at twenty-five miles an hour and at every leap the breakers rolled over us. "Bail!" shouted the Major,—"Bail for your lives!" and we dropped the oars to bail, though bailing was almost useless. The oars could not get away, for they had rawhide rings nailed around near the handle to prevent them from slipping through the rowlocks. The boat rolled and pitched like a ship in a tornado, and as she flew along Jack and I, who faced backwards, could look up under the canopies of foam pouring over gigantic black boulders, first on one side, then on the other. Why we did not land on top of one of these and turn over I don't know, unless it might be that the very fury of the current causes a recoil. However that may be, we struck nothing but the waves, the boats riding finely and certainly leaping at times almost half their length out of water, to bury themselves quite as far at the next lunge. If you will take a watch and count by it ninety seconds, you will probably have about the time we were in this chaos, though it seemed much longer to me. Then we were through, and immediately took advantage of an eddy on one side to lie to and bail out, for the boat was full of water. Setting her to rights as quickly as we could, we got ready to make a dash for the crew of the *Cañonita* in case she fared worse than we did. We looked anxiously for her to appear, and presently, at the top of what seemed to us now to be a straight wall of foam, her small white bulk hung for an instant and then vanished from our sight in the mad flood. Soon appearing at the bottom uninjured, she ran in to where we were waiting. The *Cañonita*, being lighter than our boat, did not ship as much water as in some other places, and altogether we agreed that notwithstanding its great descent and furious aspect the passage was not more difficult than we had made in several previous rapids.

Continuing on down the narrow and gloomy granite gorge, we encountered about a mile farther down a singular rapid, which turned the *Cañonita* completely around. About four o'clock we found ourselves before another tremendous fall, and a very ugly one. Landing on the left, we discovered that to be the wrong side, and crossed over to a little cove where there was a patch of gravel, surrounded by vertical walls, the crossing being easily made because the water seemed to slacken before the plunge. We did not intend to run the place if it could be avoided, and the south side gave no opportunity whatever for a portage, while the north side offered no very easy course. Prof. declared this to be one of the worst rapids we had seen, and we were now about two hundred feet above the head of it, with the vertical cliffs between. Immediately at the beginning of the drop on the same side that we were on was a pile of boulders, and our plan was to engineer the boats by lines from where we had landed down to these rocks, from which we believed we could work around over the rocks into an alcove there was there, and thence go down till we reached the lower part of the descent, through which we could navigate. Consequently several of the men entered one boat, and we lowered her from the stern of the second as far as her line would reach, and then lowered the second till the first lodged in the rocks at the desired point at the head of the fall. Then, pulling up the second boat, we who had remained got on board, and by clinging to the projections of the wall, the current close in being quite slow, we succeeded in arriving alongside the first boat. The next thing was to get around into the alcove. The sky above was heavy and rain began to come down steadily, making the dark granite blacker and intensifying the gloomy character of the locality. By hard work we finally got our boats across the rocks and down about two hundred feet farther into a cove, where they rested easily.   Up to this time we had made in all, during the day, seven and one-quarter miles.   As night was now dropping fast we had to make camp on a pile of broken granite, where a close search yielded an armful or two of small pieces of driftwood, all wet.   Under a rock several dry sticks were discovered, and by their aid a fire soon blazed up by which the indomitable Andy proceeded to get supper.   There was no use changing wet clothes for dry ones from the rubber bags as long as the rain fell, and it increased till water was dashig off the walls in streams.   The thunder roared and crashed as if it were knocking the cliffs about to rearrange them all, and a deluge swept down in which Andy's struggling little fire died with hardly a sputter.   The only thing remaining for us to do was to all stand with our backs against the foot of the wall, which was still warm from the day, and wait for something else to happen.   The bread-pan seen through the dim and dismal light was a tempestuous lake, with an island of dough in it, while Andy the undaunted stood grimly gazing at it, the rain dribbling from his hat and shoulders till he resembled the fabled ferryman of the River Styx.   The situation was so ludicrous that every one laughed, and the Weather God finding that we were not downcast slackened the downpour immediately.   Then we put some oars against the wall and stretched a paulin to protect our noble chef, who finally got the wet firewood once more ignited, and succeeded in getting the bread almost baked and the coffee nearly hot and some dried peaches almost stewed.   The rain ceasing, we hurriedly donned dry clothes and applied ourselves to the destruction of these viands, which tasted better than might be imagined. Each man then took his blankets, and, selecting rocks that in his judgment were the softest, he went to sleep.

There was another alcove about three hundred yards below our camp, and in the morning, Friday, August 30th, we proceeded to work our way down to this, several men clambering along a ledge about 150 feet above the water with the line, while I remained each time in the boat below with an oar to keep the bow in against the wall, so that she could not take the current on the wrong side—that is, on the side next to the wall—and cut out into the river. In this way we got both boats down to the alcove, whence we intended to pull out into the current and run the lower portion of the rapid. It was only noon when we reached the place, but then we discovered that both boats had been so pounded that they badly needed repairs—in fact, it was imperative to halt there for this purpose,—and we hauled them out on a patch of broken rocks, thirty or forty feet square, filling the curve of the alcove and bounded by vertical rocks and the river. While at work on them we happened to notice that the river was rapidly rising, and, setting a mark, the rate was found to be three feet an hour. The rocks on which we were standing and where all the cargo was lying were being submerged. We looked around for some way to get up the cliff, as it was now too late to think of leaving. About fifteen feet above the top of the rocks on which we were working there was a shelf five or six feet wide, to which some of the men climbed, and we passed up every article to them. When the repairs were done darkness was filling the great gorge. By means of lines from above and much hard lifting we succeeded in raising the boats up the side of the cliff, till they were four or five feet above the highest rocks of the patch on which we stood. This insured their safety for the time being, and if the river mounted to them we intended to haul them still higher. The next thing was to find a place to sleep. By walking out on a ledge from the shelf where our goods were we could turn a jutting point above the rushing river by clinging closely to the rocks, and walk back on a shelf on the other side to a considerable area of finely broken rocks, thirty feet above the torrent, where there was room enough for a camp. Rain fell at intervals, and the situation was decidedly unpromising. While Andy and the others were getting the cook outfit and rations around the point, I climbed the cliffs hunting for wood. I found small pieces of driftwood lodged behind mesquite bushes fully one hundred feet above the prevailing stage of water. I collected quite an armful of half-dead mesquite, which has the advantage of being so compact that it makes a fire hot as coal, and little is needed to cook by. Supper was not long in being despatched, and then, every man feeling about worn out, we put on dry clothes, the rain having ceased, and went to sleep on the rocks. Before doing so we climbed back to examine the boats, and found the river was not coming up farther, though it had almost completely covered the rocks.

Saturday, the 21st of August, 1872, was about the gloomiest morning I ever saw. Rain was falling, the clouds hung low over our heads like a lid to the box-like chasm in the black, funereal granite enclosing us, while the roar of the big rapid seemed to be intensified. We felt like rats in a trap. Eating breakfast as quickly as possible, we got everything together again on the shelf and lowered the boats. Though the river was not rising, it beat and surged into the cove in a way that made the boats jump and bounce the moment they touched the water. To prevent their being broken by pounding, one man at each steadied them while the others passed down the sacks and instrument boxes. Then it was seen that either a new leak had sprung in the *Dean* amidships or a hole had not been caulked, for a stream as wide as two fingers was spurting into the middle cabin. To repair her now meant hauling both boats back against the side of the cliff and spending another day in this trap, with the chance of the river rising much higher before night so that we might not be able to get away at all—at least not for days. For an instant the Major thought of pulling the boats out again, but as his quick judgment reviewed the conditions he exclaimed, "By God, we 'll start! Load up!" It was the rarest thing for him to use an oath, and I remember only one other occasion when he did so—in Marble Canyon when he thought we were going to smash. We threw the things in as fast as we could, jammed a bag of flour against the leak in the *Dean*, battened down the hatches, threw our rifles into the bottom of the standing rooms where the water and sand washed unheeded over them, and jumped to our oars. The crew of the *Cañonita* held our stern till the bow swung out into the river, and then at the signal Jack and I laid to with all our strength—to shoot clear of an enormous rock about fifty feet below against which the fierce current was dashing. The *Dean* was so nearly water-logged that she was sluggish in responding to the oars, but we swept past the rock safely and rolled along down the river in the tail of the rapid with barely an inch of gunwale to spare,—in fact I thought the boat might sink. As soon as we saw a narrow talus on the right we ran in and landed.

When the *Cañonita* was ready to start one of Clem's oars could not be found, and Prof. had to delay to cut down one of the extras for him. Then they got their boat up as far as they could, and while Prof. and Andy kept her from pounding to pieces, Clem got in, bailed out, and took his oars. Prof. then climbed in at the stern, but the current was so strong that it pulled Andy off his feet and he was just able to get on, the boat drifting down stern first toward the big rock. Prof. concluded to let the stern strike and then try to throw the boat around into the river. By this time Andy had got hold of his oars, and the eddy seemed to carry them up-stream some twenty-five feet, so perverse and capricious is the Colorado. They swung the bow to starboard into the main current, and with a couple of strong oar-strokes the dreaded rock was cleared, and down the *Cañonita* came to us over the long waves like a hunted deer. We unloaded the *Dean* and pulled her out for repairs, but it was after four o'clock when we were able to go on again with a fairly tight boat. Then for eight miles the river was a continuous rapid broken by eight heavy falls, but luckily there were no rocks in any of them at this stage of water, and we were able to dash through one after another at top speed, stopping only once for examination. Two of these rapids were portages on the former trip, proving the ease and advantage of high water in some places ; but the disadvantages are much greater. Through a very narrow canyon on the right we caught a glimpse of a pretty creek, but we were going so fast the view was brief and imperfect. At 5:15 o'clock we ran up to a wide sandbank on which grew a solitary willow tree and there Camp 99 was made. For a space the inner canyon was much wider than above and the mouth of Bright Angel Creek was just below us ; a locality now well known because a trail from the Hotel Tovar on the south rim comes down at this point. The name was applied by the Major on his first trip to offset the name Dirty Devil applied farther up.

The next day was Sunday, September 1st, and after the Major had climbed the south wall for observations we started once more on a powerful current. For the first three miles there was a continuous rapid with no opportunity to land. We dashed through waves that tossed us badly and filled the boats half full and then half full again before we had a chance to bail. In fifteen minutes we made the three miles and a half mile more, to arrive at a heavy rapid, which we ran and in two miles reached another with fearful waves, which we also ran. In one Jones was overbalanced by his oar hitting the top of a big wave behind the boat and he was knocked out. He clung by his knees and hands, his back in the water, and the boat careened till I thought she would go over. We could not move to help him without upsetting and were compelled to leave him to his own resources. In some way he succeeded in scrambling back. The waves were tremendous and sometimes seemed to come from all directions at once. There were whirlpools, too, that turned us round in spite of every effort to prevent it. The river was about one hundred and fifty feet wide. After an extremely strenuous morning we halted on the right for dinner, continuing as soon as we had disposed of it. Presently we arrived at a sharp fall of about twenty feet, where we made a portage, and waited at the foot for the photographers to take some negatives and also for repairing the *Cañonita*. Finally it was decided to camp on the spot. It was Camp 100. Our record for the day was a trifle over seven miles with nine rapids run and one portage.

Almost the first thing in the morning of September 2d was a portage, after which we had fair water for two or three miles, and then reached a very heavy fall where we landed on the left and had dinner before making another portage. This accomplished, we proceeded on a river still rising and ran a great many bad rapids, some of them having tremendous falls. In one the fierce current set against the cliff so strongly that we were carried within an oar's length of it, notwithstanding our severe effort to avoid so close an acquaintance with the rough wall. Even between rapids the velocity of the water was extremely high and we flew along at terrific speed, while in the huge waves of the rapids the boats leaped and plunged with startling violence. Toward night a sudden halt was made on the left to examine a bad-looking place half a mile below. The Major and Prof. tried to climb where they could get a good view of it, but they failed. The Major said we would run it in the morning, though Prof. was dubious about the feasibility of doing so successfully and said he thought it about the worst place we had yet seen. We camped on a rocky talus where we were. A small sandbank was found nearby for our beds, and we made another discovery, a small pool of clear, pure water, a rare treat after the muddy Colorado which we had been drinking for so long. Twenty rapids were placed to our credit for this one day in a trifle over fifteen miles, and we felt that we were vanquishing the Grand Canyon with considerable success.

Our life now was so strenuous every hour of the day that our songs were forgotten, and when night came every man was so used up that as soon as supper was over rest and sleep were the only things that interested us. Though our beds were as hard and rough as anything could be, we slept with the intensity of the rocks themselves, and it never seemed more than a few minutes before we were aroused by the Major's rising signal " Oh-ho, boys! " and rose to our feet to pack the blankets in the rubber bags, sometimes with a passing thought as to whether we would ever take them out again. For my part, never before nor since have I been so tired. One night when the Major called us to look out for the boats I did not hear him and no one waked me so I slept on, learning about it only the next morning. Our food supply was composed partly of jerked beef, and as this could not be put in rubber because of the grease it became more or less damp and there developed in it a peculiar kind of worm, the largest about an inch long, with multitudinous legs. There were a great many of them and they gave the beef a queer taste. In order to clear the sacks as far as possible of these undesirable denizens I several times emptied them on wide smooth rocks, and while the worms were scrambling around I scraped up the beef without many of them, but could not get rid of all. Andy's method of cooking this beef was to make a gravy with bacon fat and scorched flour and then for a few moments stew the beef in the gravy. Ordinarily this made a very palatable dish but the peculiar flavour of the beef now detracted from it, though we were so hungry that we could eat anything without a query, and our diminishing supply of rations forbade the abandonment of the valuable beef.

When we arose on the morning of September 3d the dubious rapid was tossing its huge waves exactly as on the night before and humanity seemed to be out of the reckoning. By eight o'clock we were ready for it, and with everything in good trim we pushed off. The current was strong from the start, and a small rapid just below camp gave additional speed, so that we were soon bearing down on the big one with wild velocity. The river dropped away abruptly, to rise again in a succession of fearful billows whose crests leaped and danced high in air as if rejoicing at the prospect of annihilating us. Just then the Major changed his mind as to running the place, for now standing on the boat's deck he could see it better than before from the region of our camp. He ordered us to pull hard on our left, intending to land at a spot that was propitious on the left or south bank, but no sooner had he given this command than he perceived that no landing above the fall was possible. He gave another order which put us straight in the middle again and down we flew upon the descent. The Major as usual had put on his life-preserver and I think Jones had on his, but Jack and I, as was our custom, placed ours inflated immediately behind our seats, not wishing to be hampered by them. The plunge was exceedingly sharp and deep, and then we found ourselves tossing like a chip in a frightful chaos of breakers which almost buried us, though the boats rose to them as well as any craft possibly could. I bailed with a camp kettle rapidly and Jack did the same, but the boat remained full to the gunwales as we were swept on. We had passed the worst of it when, just as the *Dean* mounted a giant wave at an angle perhaps of forty or fifty degrees, the crest broke in a deluge against the port bow with a loud slap. In an instant we were upside-down going over to starboard. I threw up my hand instinctively to grasp something, and luckily caught hold of a spare oar which was carried slung on the side, and by this means I pulled myself above water. My hat was pasted down over my eyes. Freeing myself from this I looked about. Bottom up the boat was clear of the rapid and sweeping on down with the swift, boiling current toward a dark bend. The *Cañonita* was nowhere to be seen. No living thing was visible. The narrow black gorge rose in sombre majesty to the everlasting sky. What was a mere human life or two in the span of eternity? I was about preparing to climb up on the bottom of the boat when I perceived Jones clinging to the ring in the stern, and in another second the Major and Jack shot up alongside as if from a gun. The whole party had been kept together in a kind of whirlpool, and the Major and Jack had been pulled down head first till, as is the nature of these suctions on the Colorado, it suddenly changed to an upward force and threw them out into the air.

There was no time to lose, for we did not wish to go far in this condition; another rapid might be in waiting around the corner. Jack and I carefully got up on the bottom, leaving the Major at the bow and Jones at the stern, and leaning over we took hold of the starboard gunwale under water, and throwing ourselves back quickly together we brought the *Dean* up on her keel, though she came near rolling clear over the other way. She was even full of water, but the cabins supported her. Jack helped me in and then I balanced his effort so as not to capsize again. The bailing kettles were gone, but as our hats had strangely enough remained on our heads through it all we bailed with them as fast as possible for a few seconds till we lowered the water sufficiently to make it safe to get the others on board. The Major came aft along the gunwale and I helped him in, then Jack helped Jones. The oars, fortunately, had not come out of the locks, thanks to our excellent arrangement, and grasping them, without trying to haul in the bow line trailing a hundred feet in the water, we pulled hard for a slight eddy on the left where we perceived a footing on the rocks, and as soon as we were near enough I caught up the rope, made the leap, and threw the bight over a projection, where I held the boat while Jack and Jones bailed rapidly and set things in order so that we could go to the assistance of the *Cañonita*. The Major's Jurgenssen chronometer had stopped at 8 : 26 :30 from the wetting.

The *Cañonita*, being more lightly laden than the *Dean*, and also not meeting the peculiar coincidence of mounting a wave at the instant it broke, came down with no more damage than the loss of three oars and the breaking of a rowlock. Probably if the Major had sat down on the deck instead of in the chair we might also have weathered the storm.[1] About a mile and a half below we made a landing at a favourable spot on the right, where the cargoes were spread out to dry and the boats were overhauled, while the Major and I climbed up the wall to where he desired to make a geological investigation. We joked him a good deal about his zeal in going to examine the geology at the bottom of the river, but as a matter of fact he came near departing by that road to another world.

We were now in an exceedingly difficult part of the granite gorge, for, at the prevailing stage of water, landings were either highly precarious or not possible at all, so we could not examine places before running, and could not always make a portage where we deemed it necessary. There were also all manner of whirlpools and bad places. Starting on about three o'clock we descended several rapids in about six miles, when we saw one ahead that looked particularly forbidding. The granite came down almost vertically to the water, projecting in huge buttresses that formed a succession of little bays, especially on the left, where we manœuvred in and out, keeping close against the rocks, the current there being slack. The plan was for me to be ready, on turning the last point, to jump out on some rocks we had noticed from above not far from the beginning of the rapid. As we crept around the wall I stood up with the bight of the line in one hand, while Jack pulled in till we began to drift down stern foremost alongshore. At the proper moment I made my leap exactly calculated. Unluckily at the instant the capricious Colorado threw a

[1] For the benefit of any one who contemplates descending the Colorado I would state that unsinkable boats are the only kind to use and the centre of gravity should be kept low. Cork life-jackets are indispensable.

" boil " up between the bow and the flat rock I was aiming at, turning the bow out several feet, and instead of landing where I intended I disappeared in deep water. I clung to the line and the acceleration of the boat's descent quickly pulled me back to the surface. She was gliding rapidly past more rocks and the Major jumped for them with the purpose of catching the rope, but they were so isolated and covered with rushing water that he had all he could do to take care of himself. Jones then tried the same thing, but with the same result. Jack stuck to his post. I went hand over hand to the bow as fast as I could, and reaching the gunwale I was on board in a second. One of my oars had somehow come loose, but Jack had caught it and now handed it to me. We took our places and surveyed the chances. Apparently we were in for running the rapid stern foremost and we prepared for it, but in the middle of the stream there was a rock of most gigantic proportions sloping up the river in such a way that the surges alternately rolled upon it and then slid back. Partly up the slope we were drawn by this power, and on the down rush the boat turned and headed diagonally just right for reaching the left bank. We saw our opportunity and, pulling with every muscle, lodged the *Dean* behind a huge boulder at the very beginning of the main rapid, where I made the line fast in the twinkle of an eye. Meanwhile the Major had hastily scrambled up to where he could see down the canyon, and he heard Jack's hearty shout of " All right!" Lowering the *Dean* a couple of rods farther to a sandbank at the mouth of a gulch we went into camp feeling that we had done enough river work for one day, and the *Cañonita's* crew without accident lowered down to the same place before Andy had supper ready. My hat had come off in my deep plunge and beyond this I did not have one. Near by was a small clear spring that gave us another treat of palatable water, the Colorado now being muddier than ever, as it was still on the rise, coming up three feet more while we were here. The entire day's run was eight and one-eighth miles. The Major and Prof. succeeded in getting down three miles on foot to reconnoitre.

Continuing in the morning, September 4th, we lowered the

The Grand Canyon.
Character of River in Rapids.
Photograph by F. S. DELLENBAUGH, 1907.

boats past the remainder of the rapid and then shoved out into the terrific current once more. Water could hardly run faster than it now did, except in a fall or rapid. The canyon was narrow and for five miles we encountered the worst whirlpools we had anywhere seen. The descent was swift and continuous, but the river was broken only by the whirlpools and " boils " as we called them, the surface suddenly seeming to boil up and run over. These upshoots, as a rule, seemed to follow whirlpools. In the latter the water for a diameter of twenty or twenty-five feet would revolve around a centre with great rapidity, the surface inclining to the vortex, the top of which was perhaps eighteen or twenty inches lower than the general level. The vortex itself was perfectly formed, like a large funnel, and about six or eight inches in diameter, where it began to be a hole in the water, tapering thence down in four or five feet to a mere point. The same effect is often seen when the water is flowing out of a round wash-basin through a pipe at the bottom. These were the most perfect whirlpools I have ever seen, those above having been lacking in so distinct a vortex. There were many and we could often see them ahead, but try as we would to cleave through without a complete revolution or two of the boat we could not do it. The boats sank down into the hollow, enabling one to look over the side into the spinning opening, but the boats, being almost as long as the whirlpool's usual diameter, could not be pulled in and we were not alarmed. We found it rather interesting to see if we could get through without turning, but we never did. Any ordinary short object or one that could be tipped on end would surely go out of sight. So furious ran the river along this stretch that we found it impossible to stop, the boats being like bits of paper in a mill-race, swinging from one side to the other, and whirling round and round as we were swept along between the narrow walls till we ran the granite under about five miles from our last camp. Finally, after a run all told of fourteen miles with twenty-three rapids, we made Camp 103 with walls of friendly sandstone about us. Here again we discovered a small clear spring for drinking and cooking purposes. There was no rain this day and at night we put on our dry clothes with confidence and had a warm comfortable camp with a good sound sleep.

Thursday morning found us early on the river, which to our surprise turned suddenly in a north-north-east direction. When we had gone about nine miles and had run the granite up and down again, it began to turn to the west. At one point the river was not more than fifty feet wide; the current was everywhere exceedingly strong and there were many rapids, of which we ran twelve, and made a portage at another, and a let-down at still another. We camped at the end of the nine miles on a small sandbank, with the total height of walls about four thousand feet, breaking back in terraces after about eight hundred feet. Clem and Jack made a number of photographs wherever practicable, and altogether they had succeeded in securing a representative collection.

During the morning of Friday, September 6th, we ran two rapids in two miles, which brought us to one which we thought required a let-down and we made it. As it was easy, Jack and Clem busied themselves photographing while we were doing it, and we also had dinner here. About two o'clock we went on and in less than three miles ran four rapids, the fourth being an exceedingly heavy fall, at the foot of which we went into camp on the right bank. A little distance above on the same side of the river was a fine clear cold creek larger than the Paria in quantity of water. We called it Tapeats Creek, because a Pai Ute of that name, who had pointed it out to the Major from the Kaibab, claimed it. During the day the work had been far less strenuous, there were few whirlpools, the river was falling, and it was in every way much easier than above in the granite. A morning was spent at Tapeats Creek for examinations, and we found there some ancient house ruins not far up the side canyon. I discovered a fine large metate or Indian mill, deeply hollowed out, and foolishly attempted to take it to camp. On arriving there it was so heavy I had to drop it and it broke in two, much to the Major's disgust, who told me I ought to have let it alone, a fact which I realised then also. Our rations were now running very low again, for we had taken more days for this passage than were planned, and as soon as we launched forth after dinner we began to look longingly for the mouth of Kanab Canyon and the pack-train. The river was much easier in every respect, and after our experience of the previous days it seemed mere play. The granite ran up for a mile or two, but then we entered sedimentary strata and came to a pretty little cascade falling through a crevice on the right from a valley hidden behind a low wall. We at once recognised it as one which Beaman had photographed when he and Riley had made their way up along the rocks from.the mouth of the Kanab during the winter. We remembered that they had called it ten miles to the Kanab from this place, and after we had climbed up to examine what they had named Surprise Valley we went on expecting to reach the Kanab before night. Running several small and one fairly large rapid, we saw, after twelve miles from the last camp, a seeming crack on the right, and a few seconds later heard a wild yelling. In a little while we landed and lowered to the head of a rapid, and running to the right up the backwater into the mouth of the Kanab Canyon, we found George Adair, Nathan Adams, and Joe Hamblin, our three faithful packers, waiting there for us with the rations. They had grown very anxious, for we were several days overdue, and they feared we had been destroyed,—a fear that was emphasised by one of Andy's discarded shirts washing ashore at their feet. We pulled the boats a short distance up the Kanab on the backwater and made a comfortable camp, 106, on its right bank, where we were soon lost in letters and papers the pack-train had brought down.

Our altitude was now 1800 feet above sea-level, showing a descent from the Little Colorado, in about 70 miles, of 890 feet, with 131 rapids run, besides six let-downs and seven portages. The total descent from the Paria was 1370 feet.

16

CHAPTER XV

A New Departure—Farewell to the Boats—Out to the World through Kanab
Canyon—A Midnight Ride—At the Innupin Picavu—Prof. Reconnoitres
the Shewits Country—Winter Quarters in Kanab—Making the Preliminary
Map—Another New Year—Across a high Divide in a Snow-storm—Down
the Sevier in Winter—The Last Summons.

THE day following our arrival at the mouth of the Kanab
Canyon was Sunday, September 8th, and with the
exception of some observations taken by Prof., and the writing
of notes, the whole camp was in a state of rest. After our trying work in the granite we enjoyed immensely the lying around
warm and dry with plenty to eat. Monday morning everybody expected to begin preparations for the descent to the
Grand Wash. We were surprised just as we were about to
rise from our places around the canvas on which breakfast had
been spread, when the Major, who was sitting in his chair thinking,
suddenly exclaimed, "Well, boys, our voyage is done!" In a
way these words were a disappointment, for we all wanted to
complete the task and we were entirely ready to go on, notwithstanding that our recent experience with high water in the
granite indicated great hazard ahead, where there was more
granite; but on the whole the disappointment was agreeable.
We knew the second granite gorge toward the lower end of
the chasm to be nearly as bad as the first one. There was
besides one exceedingly difficult passage there, which Prof.
called Catastrophe Rapid, where the Howlands and Dunn had
left the first party, which on the prevailing stage of water the
Major believed would be foolhardy to attempt. Prof. in his
diary says, "It is nonsense to think of trying the lower bend
with this water." He and the Major had talked the matter

The Grand Canyon.
At a Rapid—Low Water.

The Grand Canyon.
At the Bottom near Foot of Bass Trail.

over Saturday night and thought of stopping about forty miles down at Mount Trumbull, where we knew we could climb out; then they thought of sending only one boat that far, but by Sunday night they decided to end all river work here. Prof. said he could map the course from the notes of the first party and that he would rather explore the adjacent country by land.[1] There were some breaks in the notes from here down to Catastrophe Rapid, due to the fact that when the papers were divided on that memorable day on which the Howlands and Dunn left the party, instead of each division having a full copy of all the notes, by a mistake they had only portions of both sets. In addition to the difficulty of the forbidding Catastrophe Rapid there was a possibility of an attack on us by the Shewits. Jacob through one of his Pai Ute friends had information that they were preparing to lay an ambush, and he sent warning to that effect. Jacob knew the natives too well to have given us this notice unless he thought it a real danger, but we did not allow it much consideration at the time. Yet it would have been an easy matter for the Shewits to secrete themselves where they could fall upon us in the night when we were used up by working through some bad rapid, and then, hiding the goods, throw our bodies into the river and burn the boats, or even turn them loose, thus leaving no proof of their action, our disappearance naturally being laid to destruction by the river, a termination generally anticipated. I have sometimes thought that when they killed the Howlands and Dunn they did it deliberately to get their guns and clothes, thinking it would not be found out, or at least that they could put forth a good excuse, as they did.

We were in the field to accomplish certain work and not to perform a spectacular feat, and the Major and Prof. having decided that the descent of the remainder of the canyon, considering all the circumstances, was for us impracticable and unnecessary, we prepared to leave for Kanab. We unpacked

[1] Professor Thompson declared to me not long before his death that the river was accurate as far as Catastrophe Rapid, (about where longitude 113.39 intersects the river) but from there to the Virgin it might need some corrections.

the good old boats rather reluctantly. They had come to possess a personality as such inanimate objects will, having been our faithful companions and our reliance for many a hundred difficult miles, and it seemed like desertion to abandon them so carelessly to destruction. We ought to have had a funeral pyre. The flags of the boats, which Mrs. Thompson had made and which had been carried in them the entire way, were still to be disposed of, and that of the *Dean* was generously voted to me by the Major, Jack, and Jones, who had crew claims to it; that of the *Nellie Powell* was awarded to Steward; while Clem received the *Cañonita's*. I tried to persuade the Major to pack the *Dean* out in sections and send her east to be kept as a souvenir of the voyage, but he would not then listen to it, though years later he admitted that he regretted not taking my suggestion. Three years afterward I came back to this place with my own party and would then have executed my desire, but no trace of our former outfit remained except a hatch from one of the middle cabins, and the Major's chair. The latter I carried to Salt Lake, where I presented it to Cap, who was living there.

As before mentioned, the Colorado was so extremely high that the water backed up into the Kanab Canyon, and it was there that we left the boats, each tied to an oar stuck in the ground.[1] We could not get all the goods on the horses of the pack-train, and left a portion to be brought out later. Jack and Clem remained to make photographs, and taking a last look at the boats, with a good-bye to all, we turned our faces up the narrow chasm of the Kanab. A small stream ran in the bottom, and this formed large pools amongst numerous ponderous boulders that had fallen in from the top of the walls some three thousand feet above our heads, the bottom being hardly more than sixty to seventy-five feet wide. It was with considerable difficulty that we got the animals past some of these places, and in one or two the pools were so long and deep they had to swim a little. The prospectors the year

---

[1] Some men from Kanab afterwards came in, sawed one in two and made it shorter, and then tried to go up the canyon by towing. They did not get far, and the boat was abandoned. The floods then carried both down to destruction.

before had worked a trail to some extent, but here, where the floods ran high at times, changes occurred frequently. By five o'clock we had gone about eight miles up this slow, rough way, and arrived at a singular spring, where we went into camp. This we called Shower-Bath Spring. The water charged with lime had built out from the wall a semi-circular mass covered by ferns, which was cut away below by the floods till one could walk under in the sprinkling streams percolating through it. It was a very pretty place, but like all of its kind in the deep gorges it was a favourite resort for tarantulas, many of which we had seen in the depths of the Grand Canyon. These, with scorpions, rattlesnakes, and Gila-monsters, were the poisonous reptiles of the gorge.

The next morning, Tuesday, the 10th of September, our pack-train was early on the way. The walls grew somewhat lower, though still two thousand feet high, and the canyon was usually seventy-five to one hundred feet wide at the bottom. There were patches of alluvial deposit now along the sides of the watercourse, covered by fields of cactus loaded with "apples," the prickly leaves compelling us to keep the trail the prospectors had made by their passage to and from the ephemeral Eldorado. After a time we emerged from the lower canyon into a wider one in the way previously described; that is, like going from one floor to another by an incline between narrow walls. The little stream having vanished, a pool of rain-water helped us out for dinner, and while it was preparing Prof. and I climbed up to secure notes on the topography. A trifle before sunset we arrived at the cedar tree, a short distance below the mouth of the Shinumo Canyon, where our party had camped the previous March. The pockets were full of clear, fresh water, and we had plenty for horses as well as men. Not far off some human bones were found, old and bleached. We thought they must be the remains of one of the Navajo raiders who escaped wounded from the Mormon attack near this locality. The canyon bottom was quite wide at this point and comparatively level, covered by rushes and grass, and the horses were able to get a good meal.

During the day every time I dismounted to take compass

bearings on the trail I felt a sharp, peculiar pain shoot up my right leg from in front about half-way between ankle and knee. I could only discover a small red spot at the initial point, and concluded that I must have struck a sharp rock or cactus spine. Our party now again divided, the Major and Jones going up Shinumo Canyon to the Kaibab region, while Prof. and I rode on up the Kanab Canyon, starting at eight o'clock in the morning, Wednesday, September 11th, and riding steadily all day. As we had not expected to come out in this way saddles were scarce. Prof. and the Major had two of the three used by the packers, while the third was awarded to Jones, who was to have a long ride on the Kaibab trip. The rest of us had to make shift as we could, and I rigged up a "sawbuck" pack-saddle, with rope loops for stirrups and a blanket across it to sit on. This was not much better than, or as good perhaps as, bareback, and the horse was a very hard trotter. We wished to reach Kanab that night. We kept on at as rapid a gait as the canyon would permit, though it was easier than in March, when the numerous miners had not yet broken a way by their ingress and egress in search of the fabulous gold that was supposed to exist somewhere in the inaccessibility of the great chasm. The harder a locality is to arrive at the bigger the stories of its wealth, while often in the attempts to reach it the prospector treads heedlessly ground that holds fortunes up to his very eyes. We continued straight up Kanab Canyon, the walls running lower and lower, till there was nothing but rounded hills. Then we emerged on the summit, which was a valley bottom, about twenty miles from Kanab. Shortly after dark we halted for a bite to eat and a brief rest before striking for our old storehouse, a log cabin in Jacob's corral, where we arrived about eleven o'clock, having made about forty miles. I collected all the blankets I could find, and, throwing them on the inside of Jacob's garden fence, I was almost immediately asleep, and knew nothing till Jacob came along and said a "Good-morning." My ablutions over, I went to Sister Louisa's to breakfast with Prof. and Mrs. Thompson. The gardens were now yielding an abundance of fresh fruits, peaches, melons, etc., and I blessed the good management and foresight that directed the immediate planting of these things in a Mormon settlement. It seemed as if I could not get my fill.

Friday the 13th, the next day, was my birthday and Mrs. Thompson, who was always striving to do something to make our circumstances pleasant, prepared a large peach pie with her own hands in celebration. The Major and Jones having come in the night before, we passed most of the time that day in a large tent eating melons, the Major acting as carver of the fruit. When we had eaten a watermelon he would declare that he thought muskmelon far better. We all agreed. He would cut one only to find when we had eaten it that we had changed our minds and wanted watermelon, which see-saw opinions we kept up till all the melons were gone. It would be impossible for any one who had not had our canyon fare to appreciate the exhilarating effect of this fresh fruit.

My leg, which had developed the pain coming up the Kanab Canyon, now swelled till it was almost the same size throughout and any pressure made an imprint as in a piece of putty. No one knew what to make of it. I rode over to Johnson's, that person being the nearest to a doctor of any one in the country, though the Mormons do not much believe in medicines, and he gave me a liniment to apply. This did no good. In a few days the swelling disappeared except where the spot of keen pain was, and there a lump was left half as large as a man's fist, with two small red spots in the middle of it. I now concluded that these spots marked the bite of a tarantula that must have gotten in my blankets at Shower-Bath Spring. Suppuration set in at the spots where the flesh turned black and all the men said it was a bad-looking wound. They thought I would lose my leg. I concluded to poultice it to draw out any poison that remained, and kept bread-and-milk applied continuously. After a while it seemed to have a tendency to heal.

We ran the base line up through Kanab and at the head of it pitched a small observatory tent over a stone foundation on which Prof. set up a large transit instrument for stellar observations. He got in connection, by the telegraph, with Salt Lake City and made a series of close observations. I began an hourly set of barometrical readings and as soon as Clem came back he helped me to run them day and night for eight consecutive days. Jack meanwhile was preparing for a trip to the Moki Towns, the Major and Jones had gone off for some special work, and Andy started with a waggon for Beaver to bring down rations. Occasional bands of trading Navajos enlivened the days and I secured five good blankets in exchange for old Yawger, who was now about useless for our purposes. Prof. gave him to me to get what I could for him, and he also gave Clem another derelict for the same purpose. On the 9th of October Jack, Andy, and Clem, started with Jacob on his annual trip to the Mokis by way of Lee's Lonely Dell while Jones went north to Long Valley on the head of the Virgin, for topography. The Major on foot, with a Mormon companion and a Pai Ute, explored from Long Valley down the narrow canyon of the Virgin to Shunesburg, about 20 miles, a trip never before made.[1] The canyon is about two thousand feet deep and in places only twenty or thirty feet wide, twisting in such a way that the sky was not visible at times, and the stream often filled it from side to side so that they had to swim.

About eleven o'clock that night Prof. came to wake me up to say that a telegram had arrived stating that Najavos again had been raiding and had stolen seventy head of horses from Parowan. They were supposed to be making for El Vado and nobody in the absence of Jacob seemed to know just what to do about it. Prof. had advised them to organise a party and cut off the raiders, but they preferred to consult Jacob before doing anything. Prof. now asked me if I would be willing to ride at once to the Navajo Well where Jacob had expected to camp and notify him of the raid, no one else in town understanding where the well was, few besides ourselves and Jacob ever having travelled that way. I said I would go if I could have one companion. It was a lonely journey, and besides I might come on the Navajos before reaching the well. Charley Riggs, a splendid fellow whom I liked exceedingly, volunteered. Filling our overcoat pockets with cartridges, and each with a good Winchester across his saddle, we started about 12:30

[1] A description of this journey ascribed to September, 1870, occurs at page 108, et seq., in Powell's report on the *Exploration of the Colorado River of the West*, 1875.

under a fine moon and a clear sky. I knew the way perfectly, even by moonlight. We took no wrong turns, had no stops, and made excellent time toward the Navajo Well twenty miles away. On we went over the open country, skirting the Vermilion Cliffs on our left.

"Neck by neck, stride by stride, never changing our place," but not at the headlong gallop by which they brought the news over a first-class road to Aix, we rode steadily as fast as the ground would permit, sometimes on a gallop, sometimes on a trot. About two o'clock, as we neared a canyon where an old trail came down from the north which the raiders might follow, we slowed up and advanced with caution. Dimly we perceived what appeared to be a number of sleeping forms under the ordinary Navajo dark-blue and white striped service blanket. Throwing our guns up ready for action we rode ahead slowly to pass by a detour if not discovered. We then saw that the objects were nothing but peculiar bushes. With a feeling of sympathy for the dear Knight of La Mancha and his worthy Sancho we spurred forward. At half-past four by the watch dawn began to spread on the sky and we rode into the camp at the Navajo Well. A shout and our hoofbeats had roused the sleepers. I delivered my message to Jacob who immediately started for El Vado with Charley Riggs, intending to add several more men to his band at the Paria settlement which he would pass through; a route he had often before followed for a like purpose. My leg was by no means well and it would have been imprudent on this account for me to further lend my services. I let Jacob have my rifle and ammunition and returned to Kanab, Jack, Andy, and Clem going on to Lee's to wait. I reached the settlement before noon, when George Adair and Tom Stewart started heavily armed to join Jacob at the earliest moment. A Pai Ute later came in with a report that a fresh party of Navajos on a trading trip had recently come across the Colorado, and from this we concluded that the alarm was false, or that the culprits were Utes who went off into the Dirty Devil country. Prof. with Adams went out towards the Paria and then to the Kaibab to do some topographic work along the north rim of the Grand Canyon and I was left without any of our party in the village, it being deemed inadvisable for me to do much riding or walking till my wound, which was now doing well, had more nearly healed. I devoted my time to plotting up notes, finishing sketches, drawings of pictographs, etc., and took my meals at Sister Louisa's. I became much interested in the story of her experiences which she told us from time to time, especially as she was one of the women who had pushed a handcart across the plains. After a few days the Major came in from a trip accompanied by several Pai Utes, among whom was Chuarooumpeak, the young chief of the Kaibab band, usually called Frank by the settlers and Chuar by his own people. The Pai Utes having no "F" in their language prononnced his English name "Brank," just as they called me "Bred." Their usual name for me was Untokarowits, derived from the dark red colour of my hair. Frank was a remarkably good man. He had been constantly devoted to the safety and welfare of the whites. A most fluent speaker in his native tongue, he would address his people with long flights of uninterrupted rhetorical skill.

Old Patnish came in occasionally. Though he did not look particularly dangerous his eye was keen and his bearing positive. Nobody would have interfered with him unless prepared for a fight to the finish. One day I rode to Johnson by the trail and learned when I got back that Patnish had arrived at Kanab by the road, so I just missed an interview. The term "old" Patnish signifies "that scoundrel" Patnish, but when the people spoke of "old" Jacob the prefix was one of respect and affection — so contrary is the meaning that can be put into three letters. Charley Riggs and George Adair came back from El Vado saying that no raiding Navajos had been seen, so our opinion of the false alarm was confirmed.

On the 27th of October we had the first snow of the season, which lasted only a few hours, snow never being heavy at Kanab. The Major had planned another journey to the Uinkaret region and we started November 2d, taking with us three of the Kaibab band—Chuar, another called George, or, as they pronounced it, "Judge," and Waytoots; the Major desiring to talk to them in our camps to continue his vocabulary and the collection of other linguistic material which he had been gathering from them and others in and around Kanab at every opportunity. Our party proceeded to Pipe Spring, camping half a mile below the houses and striking the next day, Monday, November 4th, for the Wild Band Pocket. Finding no water there the natives led on toward a spring they knew of in a low line of cliffs. I was riding a broncho broken only a few weeks before, and at an unexpected moment I was suddenly deemed *persona non grata*, but I kept my seat and vanquished the beast after a vigorous circus, meeting thereafter with no further opposition. We saw a band of twenty wild horses spinning across the plain one behind another like a train of railway cars, a huge stallion playing locomotive. Perhaps my broncho felt the call of the band! Darkness dropped down on us before we could get to the spring. We had to make a camp that was not exactly dry, though there was no drinking water, for a drizzling rain, half snow, set in, the snow serving to hold the accompanying rain on the surface. We were wading in slush and it was a task to find a decent place for one's blankets. Jones and I bunked together. His side of the bed was a slight hollow, in consequence of which the melting slush formed under him a chilly pool that interfered seriously with his slumbers. I happened to be lying on a lump or ridge and kept fairly dry by never stirring the whole night.

The rain ceased by morning and all day Tuesday we travelled toward the Uinkaret Mountains over a comparatively level desert, but not going rapidly, as we had a waggon. The ground having been softened by the rain the wheels cut deeply, there being of course no road. A flock of antelope blew by. We did not give them a second glance, as they were too far off to be hunted. It was after dark when we arrived at the rocky pool where we had before camped in March, which we learned now from Chuar the natives called the Innupin (or Oonupin) Picavu, or Witch Water-pocket. They said the locality was a favourite haunt of witches. These were often troublesome and had to be driven away or they might hurt one. There was plenty of wood and we were soon comfortable, with a keen November wind to emphasise our blessings. The water in the

pocket was clear and pure, but it was full of small "wigglers."
We tried to dip up a pail which should be free from them.
The Major, seeing our efforts, took a cup and without looking
drank it down with the nonchalant remark, "I haven't seen
any wigglers." The Pai Utes had killed some rabbits, which
they now skinned and cooked. I say cooked, but perhaps I
should say warmed. Dexterously stripping off the skins they
slit open the abdomen, removed the entrails, and, after squeez-
ing out the contents by drawing between thumb and fingers,
they replaced the interminable string in the cavity, closing the
aperture with the ears, and stowed the carcass in the hot ashes
for a few minutes. Then they ate the whole thing with complete satisfaction. We preferred to fry ours, without the
entrails, in a pan with bacon fat. Frequently the Major gave
me little talks on science, as he was much interested in my
future career, and by the fire this evening he instructed me in
some of the fundamental principles of natural philosophy.
Chuar having had one of his men remove his shoes, which were
heavy "Mericats" ones, was reclining in a princely way smoking a cigarette on a bank near the fire. Suddenly he rose to
his feet, intently listening and peering anxiously out through
the enveloping gloom of the piñons and cedars. I asked him
what he heard. "Oonupits," he whispered solemnly, never
ceasing his watchful gaze. Then cautiously aiming his long
muzzle-loading rifle in the direction, he fired a shot and seemed
satisfied that the intruder was driven away or destroyed. He
described the noise of the Oonupits as a whistling sound. He
and his men had a habit of waking in the night in our various
camps and singing, first one beginning very low, the others
joining in one by one, and increasing the power as they did so
till all were singing in full voice. This woke us up. We threw
things at them, but with no effect. "What do you do it for?"
said I to Chuar. "To drive away the Oonupits," he answered. [1]

[1] Oonupits or Innupits is the singular, Innupin the plural. It may be translated
witch, elf, or goblin, with evil tendencies. On the other hand they did not fear a
spirit. When on the Kaibab in July with Chuar and several other Indians, Prof.
while riding along heard a cry something like an Indian halloo. "After we got
into camp," he said in his diary: "Chuar asked George Adair what he called that

In the morning, November 6th, the Major, Prof. and I went
off reconnoitring and did not get back to camp till after dark,
when we found there a short, fat, Uinkaret whom Chuar intro-
duced as Teemaroomtekai, chief.   In the settlements when he
ventured to go there he was known as Watermelon, according
to Frank Hamblin, who was with us.   Teemaroomtekai had a
companion and next day Prof. and the Major climbed Mt.
Trumbull with them.   Wishing to have a talk with the Shewits
we moved on the 9th around to Oak Spring, near which some
of them were encamped with their kinsmen the Uinkarets.   I
was interested to see what the slayers of the Howlands and
Dunn looked like.   Except for a wilder, more defiant aspect,
they differed little from other Pai Utes.   Their country being
so isolated and unvisited they were surly and independent.
The Uinkarets on the other hand were rather genial, more like
the Kaivavit band.   The Major traded for bags of food seeds,
baskets, spoons made from mountain sheep's horns, balls of
compressed cactus fruit from which the juice had been ex-
tracted for a kind of wine, rolls of oose-apple pulp, which they
ate like bread, etc., all for the Smithsonian Institution.

With the Shewits the Major and Prof. had a conference.
Prof. wished to make a reconnaissance through their region and
explained to them what he wanted to do.   An agreement was
reached by which he was to be permitted without molestation
of any kind to go anywhere and everywhere with two Shewits
for guides and one of our party as cook and helper, in order that
he could tell " Washington " about the country.   The helper,
however, was to stick to the trail and remain in camp, so that
he would know as little as possible, and should not tell that
little to the " Mormoni " whom the Shewits disliked.   Nathan
Adams, a Mormon, was the man to accompany Prof. and he
did not enjoy the prospect at all.   On Monday, November
11th, the Major, Prof., and Jones climbed Mount Logan for

---

which lived after the body died.   George replied, ' A spirit.'   ' Well,' said Chuar,
' that was what hallooed in the forest to-day.   It was the spirit of a dead Indian.
I have often heard it.   Sometimes it is near, sometimes far away.   When I was
here with Beaman I heard it call near me.   I answered, telling it to come to me.
It did not come nor reply, and I felt very much ashamed to think I had called.' "

more data and took a general survey of the country, while I
went out on foot, climbed, measured and located eight large
cinder-cones.   When they came down the Major said he had
seen a fine, isolated mountain to the west which he had called
after me, and I naturally felt much pleased with the honour of
having my name stamped on the map.

The next day, November 12th, our party divided into three.
Frank Hamblin went out to St. George with the waggon after
rations; Prof. with Nathan Adams, one Shewits, named Paantung, and our guide "Judge," who may have been a Shewits
also for all we could tell, prepared for the entrance into Shewits
land, while the Major, Jones, and I proceeded to the foot of
the Toroweap, to a water-pocket near the edge of the Grand
Canyon called by the Uinkarets Teram Picavu.   Chuar and
Waytoots went back to Kanab and we hired Uinkarets to carry
our goods nine miles down to the pocket, descending 1200
feet at one point over rough lava.   After some work at the
canyon we went back to the spring on the 14th, the Uinkarets
again acting as our pack-horses.   We had no salt left by this
time and very little food, but we killed some rabbits and cooked
them on hot coals, the adhering ashes making a substitute for
salt.   I reached the spring first and found little, round, beam-
ing, Teemaroomtekai, who knew our plans, already there with
a great big "Mericats" fire to welcome us, as well as a large
pile of wood for feeding it.   The Major got in soon after, but
Jones failed to come at all, which worried us.   Before we could
go in search of him in the morning he arrived.   His horse had
given out, compelling him to stay where he was all night.   We
had travelled hard up and down all kinds of hills, canyons, and
mountains, with seldom a trail, and it was wearing on the animals
living only on bunch grass.

I continued measuring and locating the oonagaritchets or
cinder-cones, of which there were more than sixty, and got in
four more on the 15th.   Then the Major decided to move to
another water-pocket the Uinkarets told about, farther east
across the lava, a pocket they called Tiravu Picavu or Pocket-
of-the-Plain.   It was on the edge of the basaltic table over-
looking what they termed the Wonsits Tiravu or Antelope

The Grand Canyon.
From North Side near Foot of Toroweap Valley, Uinkaret District.
Photograph by J. K. Hillers.

The Grand Canyon.
Storm Effect from South Rim.

Plain.   They said there was no water now, but as one declared
there was a little we decided to go. While the Major followed
a waggon-track leading to or from St. George, wishing to make
some special observations along it and expecting to meet and
stop Frank with the waggon now due, Jones and I struck across
on the moccasin trail, leaving our goods to be brought on by
the Uinkaret packers.   At sunset we rounded a clump of cinder-
cones studding a black, barren waste.   Far away across the
Wonsits Tiravu rose the red cliff land up and up to the eastern
sky; behind was the great bulk of Trumbull, together with
scores of the smooth, verdureless heaps of volcanic cinders.
Everywhere near was the desert of basalt, with nothing but the
faint trail to point the way and the night slowly enwrapping
us.   On we urged our stumbling, weary beasts, their iron clink-
ing on the metallic rocks; on till the thick blackness circled us
like a wall.   Then we halted and built a little brush fire, thinking to stay till dawn.   At the instant a weird cry from far back
fell leaden on the strangely heavy winter air.   Our packers saw
where we were and presently came to us.   They were in a rage,
pitching along in the dark under their heavy loads.   They were
cold, tired, famished, for the way had been long, the packs
heavy.   Frost was in the wind.   They now pretended not to
know where the end was.   I thought this was to see what we
would say or do.   We did not care; we said and did nothing
with all the nonchalance born of the feeling that the further we
went the worse it was.   Then one remembered.   The pocket
was near and he struck out for it, the rest following as best we
could through the thick night, the guide occasionally lighting
a torch of grass.   After a quarter of a mile he stopped in the
bottom of a deep basaltic gulch.   Here was the place.   The
Uinkarets threw down their loads and squatted glum and silent.
From the hill Jones and I scraped together an armful of brush
and got a small fire started in the bottom of the desolate hollow.
At the upper end of it on a sort of bench eight feet wide was a
depression covered with ice three or four inches thick.   With
some difficulty pounding a hole through this we found beneath
a small amount of thick, slimy water, full of green scum.   We
drank some, the Uinkarets drank some, but we could not see well

enough to get any out for the animals. We tied them to rocks to prevent them from leaving in the night. The Indians thawed a little under the influence of the fire, but they would barely speak when spoken to. They skinned a wildcat they had killed on the way and boiled the red meat briefly in our kettle and ate it like hungry wolves, while Jones and I, all the time wondering what had become of the Major, made a light lunch on some of our scanty supply. Then we climbed the hill, and getting together a little more brush Jones sat keeping a signal fire going as long as he had fuel. But the wind was keen and strong, wood limited, and he gave it up. Spreading our blankets we went to sleep. Morning came clear and sharp. I took my glasses and went up to scan the country for some sign of the Major or our waggon and I rejoiced to discover him not a quarter of a mile distant. He had headed for the fire, and losing it kept on by a star till he thought he was near us, when he made a small fire of his own, tied his mule, and waited for day. We had a bite together and thawed out some of the ice in our kettle, providing a diminutive drink for each horse; then leaving the natives in charge of the baggage we rode down into the plain to find our waggon, taking along our last bit of bread for lunch. In about ten miles we came to it and Frank Hamblin gave us the latest news, "Grant elected and Boston burned." After a lunch we turned back, making a camp at the foot of the basalt, thawing out more ice for the animals, and giving the Indians some food. About two o'clock the Major and I rode over to the Innupin Picavu while Jones and the waggon went around, as it could not cross the basalt. We arrived at seven, while the waggon did not come till half past eleven, when we prepared a good supper for all hands, turning in about three in the morning. Not a man awoke before ten, though the strong sun fell on our faces. The animals were used up and we did what we could on foot that day. I climbed four more cinder-cones, reaching camp at dark. Every day I climbed several of the cones, but some were so far away that I had to make a special camp from which to operate. The waggon was loaded with ice from the water-pocket, and a supply of provisions, and driven about seven miles to a basaltic gulch, in a well-wooded locality on the edge of a treeless valley, where the load was dropped and I was left with my horse. Before dark I gathered a lot of wood, made a good fire, and melted some of the ice that formed my water supply, in a brass kettle, watering my horse, which I then tethered with a long rope where there was good grass. I did not intend to waste time hunting my mount in the morning. After supper I spread my blankets near the fire and by the light of a bright piñon blaze I began to read *Great Expectations*, a paper edition with the last leaves gone having gotten into camp. As I read Pip's interview in the twilight with the convict on the dreary marshes I was in deep sympathy with the desperate hunger of the terrible man, and when Mrs. Joe buttered the end of the loaf and carved off the slices I myself was hungry enough to cook supper over again. Butter had now been absent from my bill of fare, with a few exceptions, for nearly two years. I was careful to place my fire where it would be well screened and not easily seen from a distance. I did not care to have any Shewits or even Uinkarets visit me and I hoped they were all in their own camps, though I sometimes had a feeling that one might be watching from the shadows of the great basaltic rocks. This, of course, was due to the circumstances and not to any probability, though I kept my Winchester near my hand. When I again got back to the main camp the Major told me that the first night of my absence several of the natives came in and, not seeing me around, inquired my whereabouts. He gave them an evasive answer, believing that it was quite as well not to apprise them of the situation.

The following day, Thursday, November 21st, I covered a wide territory, climbing five cinder-cones a great distance apart and each quite high. Several times I crossed recent moccasin tracks, but met no natives, and at nightfall I was still a long way from my camp. When the darkness became so dense that I could not see even faint outlines I took a star for guidance till clouds blotted it out. Then I was completely adrift in a sea of mountains. I could not tell one direction from another. Throwing the reins on the broncho's neck I sat back in my saddle to see what would come of it. Slowly, cautiously the animal plodded over broken, rocky ground succeeded by smoother footing, as I could tell by the motion, and in about an hour suddenly and quietly halted. I perceived that I was in the midst of cedars. A light spot appeared almost beneath. Dismounting I dropped to my hands and knees and found that it was the ashes of my fire. The broncho, the same that had tried to buck me off a few days before, had come back to the camp of a single night, about the best example of horse sense that I ever experienced. After another comfortable evening with Dickens I was prepared to go on with my special task, and finished it in this place by climbing the group of cones near the Tiravu Picavu the next day. About two in the afternoon I got back to my camp with a very tired mount, but I loaded all my traps on my saddle, the ice being almost exhausted, and started to find a new locality where I was to meet the Major. My pack was high, my broncho tired. While crossing a small open valley near sunset the poor beast suddenly lay down with me. There being no water anywhere in that locality, I was forced to use some brutality to get the animal up. Without further incident I came to the place agreed on and found the Major there in advance. We camped at the spot and the next day, Saturday, November 23d, I climbed five more cones, reaching the camp at sunset. Sunday the Major went on with his particular task while I added six more of the cones to my list, getting back to the side camp late in the day. The Major was to go in by himself when he was ready, so I took all the outfit on my horse again, reached the Oak Spring trail at sunset, and the main camp two hours after dark, glad enough to drop the load of pails, bags, blankets, etc., in which my broncho sympathised more deeply than could be expressed.

Monday morning, November 25th, we turned our faces toward Kanab, and I climbed four more cones on the way out, overtaking the waggon about an hour after dark. The night was very cold and I was ready to enjoy the warmth of a fire by the time I reached the camp. In the morning we had a visit from Lieutenant Dinwiddie of Lieut. Wheeler's survey. I rode over to the cinder-cone region again and climbed the remaining ones, seven or eight, reaching camp after dark, the days being very short at this time of year. The camp had been moved nearer to the spring in the low line of cliffs where we had halted coming out and the Major with his usual original ideas had caused the waggon to be lowered by ropes into a deep gulch. He had estimated that it was possible to go out through the cliffs that way instead of going all the way around. His geological knowledge did not lead him astray. There was no trouble whatever in taking the waggon up the gulch, and when we emerged we were many miles on the road to Pipe Spring, where the Major and I arrived in advance of the others. We had dinner and he then went on alone to Kanab, where the whole party arrived the next day—Thanksgiving Day. Prof. had come in on the 25th by way of St. George, having had a successful tour through the Shewits region, all agreements on both sides having been carried out to the letter. He had been two weeks in the wild country and Adams declared that to him the time was years, his only comfort being that he was wearing his "endowment garment," a sure protection from all evil. Prof. had climbed Mount Dellenbaugh, though the Shewits objected to Adams's going up and he remained on the trail. It was found to be a basaltic peak 6650 feet above sea-level, but only 1200 or 1500 above its base. On the summit were the ruins of a Shinumo building circular in shape, twenty feet in diameter, with walls remaining about two feet high. It was not far from the base of this mountain that the Howlands and Dunn were killed, Paantung, Prof.'s guide, saying it was done by some "no sense" Shewits. Prof. was of the opinion that the guide had been of the party himself.

All was preparation in our camp for the departure of the Major for Salt Lake and Washington. I had expected to go east at this time also, but both the Major and Prof. being desirous of having me remain a while longer, to help finish up the preliminary map, I agreed to do so and on the 30th of November all the original party set out but Prof., Mrs. Thompson, and myself. A new member, John Renshawe, had arrived a few days before to assist at the topography. When the party had been gone some time it was discovered that they had forgotten several things. I took a horse and rode over with the articles to the camp they intended to make at Johnson, where I remained till morning. The Major was so eager to get an early start that he had all hands up long before sunrise. When breakfast was eaten we had to sit by the fire three quarters of an hour before there was light enough for the men to trail the horses. Then I said good-bye; they went on and I went back. Jones and Andy I never saw again.

Prof. concluded to make winter headquarters in Kanab and a lot was rented for the purpose. On December 3d, we put up a large tent in one corner, with two small ones for rations and saddles. The next day we put up one in the other corner for Prof. and Mrs. Thompson, and at the back of the lot we arranged a corral for the horses or mules we might want to catch. The large tents were floored with pine boards and along the sides heavy cedar boughs were placed in crotches around which the guy ropes were passed before staking. The tents thus were dry inside and could not blow down. A conical iron stove on a boxing of earth heated the large tent like a furnace. In the middle of the general tent we placed a long drafting-table and were ready for work. Another tent, half boards, was erected near ours for kitchen and dining-room, and Riley, who had turned up again, hired as cook and master of this structure. Riley, who had spent his whole life in camp and saddle, was the best frontier or camp cook I ever saw. Scrupulously clean to the last detail of his pots and pans, he knew how to make to perfection all manner of eatables possible under the circumstances. Prof. arranged for a supply of potatoes, butter, meats, and everything within reason, so we lived very well, with an occasional dash of Dixie wine to add zest, while on Christmas Day Riley prepared a special feast. Though the sky was sombre the town was merry and there was a dance in the school-house, but I did not attend. Rainy weather set in on the 26th, and the old year welcomed the new in a steady downpour, making January 1, 1873, rather a dismal holiday. Even the mail which arrived this day was soaked. Toward evening the skies lifted somewhat and a four-horse waggon appeared, or rather two mules and two horses on a common freighting waggon, in which Lyman Hamblin and two others were playing, as nearly in unison as possible, a fiddle, a drum, and a fife. While we were admiring this feat we heard Jack's hearty shout and saw our waggon returning under his charge from Salt Lake with supplies, with a cook stove for our kitchen, and with a new suit of clothes for me accompanied by the compliments of Prof. and the Major.

Our camp in Kanab was now as complete and comfortable as any one might wish, and our work of preparing the map went forward rapidly. As soon as it could be finished I was to take it to Salt Lake, and send it by express to the Major in Washington, to show Congress what we had been doing and what a remarkable region it was that we had been investigating. In the evenings we visited our friends in the settlement or they visited us, or we read what books, papers, and magazines we could get hold of. John and I also amused ourselves by writing down all the songs that were sung around camp, to which I added a composition of my own to the tune of *Farewell to the Star Spangled Banner*, an abandoned rebel one. These words ran:

> Oh, boys, you remember the wild Colorado,
> Its rapids and its rocks will trouble us no more,

etc., with a mention in the various stanzas of each member of the party and his characteristics. The horses became high-spirited with nothing to do and plenty of good feed. One of our amusements was to corral several, and then, putting saddles on the most prancing specimens, mount and ride down on the plain, the horse running at top speed, with the impression that he was full master of the situation and expecting us to try to stop him. Instead we enjoyed the exhilaration of it, and let the charger alone till after a couple of miles he concluded the fun was all on our side and took a more moderate gait of his own accord. There were several horse races also, and the days flew by. On February 3d I finished plotting the river down to the Kanab Canyon, and as if to emphasise this point a snowstorm set in. By the 5th the snow was five inches deep, and we had word that the snow on the divide to the north over the culmination of the various lines of cliffs, where I would

have to pass to go to Salt Lake, was very heavy.   On the 7th
the mail rider failed to get through.   We learned also that an
epizoötic had come to Utah and many horses were laid up by
it, crippling the stage lines.   It had been planned that I should
go north with our own horses till I could connect with some
stage line, and then take that for the remainder of the distance
to the Utah Southern Railway, which then had been extended
south from Salt Lake as far as Lehi.

On the 16th of February, which was Sunday, I put the
last touches on the map, drawn from the original on a
large sheet of tracing cloth, rolled it carefully up, and placed
it in a long tin tube we had ordered from the local tinsmith.
This I carried on my back, as I did not mean to be separated
from it a minute till I gave it into the hands of Wells, Fargo &
Co.'s express in Salt Lake.   Jack was to go with me.   Saying
a last good-bye to Prof. and Mrs. Thompson, to John, and to
some of my Kanab friends who came to see the start, we left a
little after noon, with one pack on a broncho mule, Jack riding
a mule and I a favourite horse of mine called by the unusual
name of Billy.   The pack-mule always had to be blindfolded
before we could handle him, and if the blind should accidentally
slip off there was an instantaneous convulsion which had a most
disrupting effect.   Going straight up the canyon, we crossed
over finally into Long Valley, and were on the headwaters of
the Virgin.   At sunset we came to a little settlement called
Mt. Carmel, but continued to Glendale, where we arrived about
half-past seven, having come in all thirty miles.   At the bishop's
house we were welcomed and there got some supper, putting
our three animals in his corral.   We did not care to sleep in
the house, choosing for our resting-place the last remains of
a haystack, where we spread our blankets, covering the whole
with a paulin, as the sky looked threatening.   I never slept
more comfortably in my life, except that I was half-aroused in
the stillness by water trickling down my neck.   Half-asleep we
pulled the canvas clear up over our heads and were troubled
no more.   When we awoke in the morning a heaviness on top
of us we knew meant snow.   We were covered by a full foot of
it, soft and dry.   Valley, mountain, everything was a solid

expanse of white, the only dark spot being our red blankets as we threw back the paulin. The sky was grey and sullen. More snow was in the air. As soon as breakfast was eaten we slung our pack, saddled, and rode up the valley, following as well as we could the directions given by the bishop. Neither Jack nor I had been this way before. We could see the slight depression in the surface of the snow which indicated a waggon-rut beneath, and by that token continued up the ever-narrowing valley; the slopes sprinkled by large pine trees. Snow fell thickly. It was not always easy to see our way, but we went on. At a certain point we were to turn to the left up a side gulch, following it till we came to the divide, some eight thousand or nine thousand feet above sea-level, where we expected to go down to the head of the Sevier Valley, where Jack had before been by another route. At the gulch we deemed the correct one, no road or trail being visible, we turned late in the afternoon to the left and rapidly mounted higher, with the fresh snow growing correspondingly deeper till it was about two feet on the level. The going was slow and hard, the sky still dropping heavy flakes upon us. About five o'clock we found ourselves on the summit of a high bald knob topping the world. In every direction through the snow-mist similar bald knobs could be seen looming against the darkening sky. The old drifts were so deep that where a horse broke through the crust he went down to the end of his leg. This excited them, and they plunged wildly. I finally got them all three still and quiet, while Jack scanned the outlook intently. "See any landmark, Jack?" said I. "Not a damned thing I ever saw before!" answered Jack. At brief intervals the falling snow would cease, and we could see more clearly, except that the impending night began to cast over all a general obscurity.

There was a deep valley beyond to the right. While it was not possible to tell directions we felt that our course must lie there, and I led the way down a long treeless slope, breaking a path as well as I could, my horse following behind; the others urged on by Jack from the rear. The snow became shallower near the bottom. We mounted and I rode in the direction that Jack thought we ought to take to come to the road down the Sevier where he had before travelled. We crossed the valley in doing this, but at one point in the very bottom my horse wanted to turn to the left, which would have taken us down the deepening valley. I prevented his turning and we continued up a gulch a mile or two, where it narrowed till we could barely proceed. Jack then climbed up on a cliff and disappeared, endeavouring to see some familiar object, the falling snow having at last stopped. I stood in my tracks with the three animals and waited so long I began to be afraid that Jack had met with an accident. Just then I heard him descending. It was nearly dark. He could not see any sign of the region he had been in before. Snow and darkness puzzle one even in a familiar country. We then went back to the valley where the horse had wished to turn and followed it down, now believing that it might be the right way after all, for Billy had been over the road several times. Another example of horse sense, which seems to prove that horses know more than we think they do. We had expected to reach Asa's ranch before night and had not brought an axe, in consequence. Keeping down the valley till we came to a group of cedars, some of which were dead, and a tall pine tree, we camped, pulling branches from the cedars and bark from the pine for a fire, which quickly melted its way down to the ground, leaving a convenient seat all round about twenty inches high, upon which we laid blankets to sit on. Our pack contained enough food for supper; breakfast would have to take care of itself. We also had some grain, which we fed to the hungry animals and tied them under the cedars, where they were protected in a measure from the sharp wind though they were standing in deep snow. For ourselves we cut twigs from the green cedars and made a thick mattress on the snow with them. Our blankets on top of these made a bed fit for a king. The storm cleared entirely; a brilliant moon shone over all, causing the falling frost in the air to scintillate like diamonds.

In the morning, Tuesday, February 18th, we packed up at once, having nothing left to eat, and proceeded down the valley wondering if we were on the right road or not. The sky arched over with that deep tone that is almost black in winter in high altitudes, and the sun fell in a dazzling sheet upon the wide range of unbroken white. The surface was like a mirror; the eyes closed against the intense light instinctively. As we went on northwards and downwards a faint, double, continuous hollow began to appear on the snow—a waggon-track at the bottom. It became more and more distinct and we then felt sure that we were on the right road, though we were not positive till near noon when, approaching a rocky point, we suddenly heard the clear ring of an axe on the metallic air. A few moments later turning this we saw a large, swift stream flowing clear between snowy banks, and beyond a log cabin with blue smoke rising from the immense stone chimney. In front was a man chopping wood. His dog was barking. It was a welcome, a beautiful picture of frontier comfort. It was Asa's ranch. Asa was one of the men who helped the Major on his arrival at the mouth of the Virgin in 1869, now having changed his residence to this place. We were soon made welcome in the single large room of the cabin where all the family were, and while the horses were having a good feed an equally good one for us was prepared by Mrs. Asa on the fire burning snugly in the great chimney. Never did fried ham, boiled eggs, and hot coffee do better service. We could not have been more cordially received if these Mormons had been our own relatives.

We rested there till about three o'clock, when we bade them all good-bye and rode on down the valley, the snow continually lessening in depth, till, when we reached the much lower altitude of Panguitch at sunset, twenty-six miles from our night's camp, there were only three or four inches and the temperature was not nearly so low, though still very cold. According to custom we applied to the bishop for accomodation for ourselves and our stock and were again cordially received. We were quickly made comfortable before a bright fire on the hearth which illumed the whole room. While the good wife got supper, the bishop, an exceedingly pleasant man, brought out some Dixie wine he had recently received. He poured us out each a large goblet and took one himself. After a hearty supper Jack and I put down our blankets on the bishop's haystack and knew nothing more till sunrise. Leaving Panguitch we rode on down the Sevier, crossing it frequently, and made about forty miles, passing through Sevier Canyon and Circle Valley, where there were a number of deserted houses, and arrived for night at the ranch of a Gentile named Van Buren. By this time my eyes, which had been inflamed by the strong glare of the sun, began to feel as if they were full of sand, and presently I became aware that I was afflicted with that painful malady snowblindness. I could barely see, the pain in both eyes was extreme, and a river of tears poured forth continually. Other men whom we heard of as we went on were blinded worse than I. All I could do, having no goggles, was to keep my hat pulled down and cut off the glare as much as possible.[1] At Marysvale the stage had been abandoned. We kept on, finding as we advanced that all the stages were put out of business by the epizoötic. There was nothing for Jack to do but to go on with me to Nephi.

In riding through one village I saw a sign on the closed door of a store just off the road and my curiosity led me to ride up close enough to read it. I did not linger. The words I saw were "SMALL POX." That night we reached Nephi under the shadow of the superb Mount Nebo, where I tried again for a stage so that Jack could return. No stage arrived and the following morning we rode on northward over very muddy roads, finally reaching Spanish Fork, where a fresh snow-storm covered the country about a foot, making travelling still more difficult. Another day's journey put us as far as American Fork, only three miles from the end of the railway, a place called Lehi, for which we made a very early start the next day, Wednesday, February 25th, but when we arrived there through the mud and slush the train had taken its departure. Our pack mule was now very lame and travelled with difficulty, but we continued on toward Salt Lake. The train had become stalled in the immense snowdrifts at the Point-of-the-Mountain and there we overtook it. I was soon on board with my tin case and other baggage, but it was a considerable time before the

---

[1] For travelling across snow one should always be provided with smoked goggles. Failing to have them, lines of charcoal should be drawn below the eyes or a scarf tied so as to break the glare.

gang of men and a snow plough extricated the train. About
five o'clock we ran into the town. I went to the Walker House,
then the best hotel, and that night slept in a real room and a
real bed for the first time in nearly two years, but I opened the
windows as wide as they would go. In the morning I sent off
the map and then turned my attention to seeing the Mormon
capital. Cap. was now living there and it was Fennemore's
home. I also found Bonnemort and MacEntee in town, and
Jack came on up the remaining short distance in order to take
a fresh start for Kanab.

Nearly forty years have slipped away since the events
chronicled in this volume. Never was there a more faithful,
resolute band of explorers than ours. Many years afterward
Prof. said in a letter to me speaking of the men of the Second
Powell Expedition, " I have never seen since such zeal and courage displayed." From out the dark chasm of eternity comes the
hail, " Tirtaan Aigles dis wai!" and already many of that little
company have crossed to Killiloo. The Major and Prof. repose
in the sacred limits of Arlington. Strew their graves with roses
and forget them not. They did a great work in solving the
last geographical problem of the United States.

INDEX

A

Adair, George, 153, 241
Adams, Nathan, 241, 253; his endowment garment, 259
Agua Grande, Navajo chief, 147
Aigles, Tirtaan, slogan, 75, 267
Alcove Brook, 47
Altitude of Colorado River above sea, Black's Fork, 15; Junction Green and Grand, 114; Paria, 151, 217; Grand Wash, 217; Little Colorado, 223; Kanab Canyon, 241
American Fork, 266
Amerind, viii.
Andy, *see* Hattan
Aquarius Plateau, 200, 202
Arlington, Powell and Thompson buried there, 267
Arms, kind used, 12
Asa, ranch, 264, 265; assisted Powell, 265
Ashley, Wm. H., through Red Canyon, 2, 28, 95; name on rocks, 28
Ashley Falls, 26; portage at, 27
Ashtishkal, Navajo chief, 177
Aspen Lakes, 201
Averett, Elijah, grave of, 197
Azure Cliffs, 99

B

Baird, Professor Spencer, vi.
Bangs, Mount, climbed, 194
Barbenceta, principal chief of the Navajos, 168
Base line, 166, 173, 174
Basor, teamster, 68
Beadle, J. H., 215; under name of Hanson, 215

Beaman, E. O., place in boat, 11; duty of, 11; leaves party, 179; passes Paria on way to Moki Towns, 216; up from Kanab Canyon to Surprise Valley, 241
Beaver, ground, 77; shoot one, 78; steak cooked, 78; soup, 78
Berry's Spring, 188; arrive at, 191
Berthoud and Bridger lay out waggon road, 67
Best Expedition, place of starting, 95
Big Boulder Creek, 202
Bishop, Francis Marion (Cap.), place in boat, 11; duty of, 11; leaves party, 180
Bishop's Creek, 54
Bison, pictographs, 61; range on Green River, 61
Black Rock Canyon, 193
Black's Fork, 15
Boats of the Second Powell Expedition, the, 4; names of, 4; described, 5, 6; method of packing, 8; order of going, 11; crews of, 11; no iron on keels, 14; built to float when full of water, 25; reassignment of crews, 136, 215; *Cañonita* cached, 135; launched again, 209; crew for, 209; *Dean* cached, 154; *Nellie Powell* cached, 154; *Dean* discovered by Beadle, 215; *Nellie Powell* abandoned, 215; *Cañonita* and *Dean* abandoned, 244
Bonito Bend, 111
Bonnemort, John, 143; leaves party, 179; in Salt Lake City, 267
Boston burned, news of, received, 256
Bow-knot Bend, 108
Bread, kind used, 4

Bridger and Berthoud lay out waggon road, 67
Bridger, Jim, 95
Brigham Young, 170, 185
Bright Angel Creek, arrive at mouth of, 232; why so named, 232
Brown expedition, place of starting, 95
Brown's Hole, name changed to Brown's Park, 18, 30; arrive at, 30
Brush Creek, 54
Buckskin Mountain (Kaibab Plateau), 159
Buenaventura, Rio San, Escalante's name for Green River, 67
Buffalo *Express*, letters from F. S. Dellenbaugh to, vii.
Butte of the Cross, 110

C

Campbell, Richard, knew of ford El Vado de los Padres, 96
Camp moved to the Gap, 171
Cañonita, left behind, 135; reached overland, 209
Canyon of Desolation, enter it, 77; character and height of walls, 80, 84, 85; length of, 91
Canyon of Lodore, enter it, 34; declivity of, 43; length of, 48; fall of, 48
Canyons, for list of, with heights of walls, lengths, etc., see *The Romance of the Colorado River*, Appendix
Canyons not dark in daytime, 25
Cap., *see* Bishop
Capsize, of the *Cañonita*, 23; of the *Dean*, 235
Carleton, companion of Beaman, 216
Carson, Kit, 95
Cascade Creek, 43, 202
Cascades of rain, 105, 106, 132
Cataract Canyon, declivity compared, 43; beginning of, 115; height of walls, 116, 122, 126, 128, 129; we enter it, 118; declivity in, 118; boulders rolled by current, 118; width of river, 119; boat runs rapid alone, 121; stones rocked by current, 127; length of, 132; end of, 132; number of rapids, 132
Cataract Creek, 96, 202

Catastrophe Rapid, vi., 242, 243
Caves once occupied, 132
Chandler Falls, 87; Creek, 87
Chicago, burning of, first news, 157
Chicago *Tribune*, letters from Clement Powell to, v.
Chief Douglas, Major and Mrs. Powell winter near his camp, 172
Chocolate Cliffs, 166
Chuarooumpeak, chief of Kaibab band of Pai Utes, 250; shoots at Oonupits, 252; singing, 252; hears spirit call, 253; goes back to Kanab, 254
Circle Valley, pass through it, 266
Clarkson, Mormon settlement, 197
Clear or Spring Creek (Badger Creek), 158
Clem, *see* Powell
Clemente, Rio San, Escalante's name for White River, 67
Cliff-of-the-Harp named, 43
Coal Canyon, 91
Colob Plateau, 191
Colorado, from, into Utah, 56
Colorado River, accuracy of plat of course, vi., vii., 243; upper continuation of, 1; white salmon, 98; actual beginning of, 115; excessive high water, 244
Compass Creek, 24
Condition of party at end of first season's river work, 145
Course of the Colorado River, accuracy of, vi., vii., 243
Craggy Canyon, 57
Crater, recent, in Uinkaret country, 188
Creek, Sentinel, 149
Crescent Creek, 209
Crossing of the Fathers, the, *see* El Vado de los Padres

D

Dance, Mormon, 173
Davy Crockett, Fort, 30
Dean, the *Emma*, cached for the winter, 154; discovered by J. H. Beadle, 215
Deer, game, etc., 26
Dellenbaugh, Butte, 102, 104; Mount, named, 254; Thompson climbs it, 259
Dellenbaugh, F. S., joins party, 3; position in boat, 11; duty of, 11; letters from, to Buffalo *Express*, vii.

De Motte, Professor, 213
Denver, Colorado Canyon, and Pacific Railway, 119
Denver and Rio Grande Railway crossing of Green River, 95
Denver to Salt Lake, waggon road *via* Golden and Provo, and Robideau Crossing of Green River, 67
Descent, in feet of Green-Colorado River, from Union Pacific Railway to Black's Fork, 15; to Flaming Gorge, 17; in Red Canyon, 33; in Lodore, 48; in Whirlpool, 56; to the mouth of the Uinta, 71; from Wonsits Valley to Gunnison Crossing, 93; from the Union Pacific to Gunnison Crossing, 93; from Gunnison Crossing to junction of Green and Grand, 114; from Union Pacific to mouth of Grand River, 114; from mouth of Grand River to Dirty Devil, 134; from Union Pacific to Dirty Devil (Frémont), 135; from Union Pacific to Paria (Lee Ferry), 151; from Paria to Little Colorado, 223; from Little Colorado to Grand Wash, 223; from Little Colorado to Kanab, 241; from Paria to Kanab, 241
Desolation, Canyon of, enter it, 77; perforations in walls of, 82; width of river in, 83, 89; height of walls, 84, 85; natural arches in, 87, 88; end of, 91; length of, 91
Diamond Butte, how named, 192
Diamond Creek mouth astronomically determined, 95
Diary, of Professor Thompson, vii.; of John F. Steward, vii.; of F. S. Dellenbaugh, vii.; of Jack Summer, 7
Dinwiddie, Lieut., 258
Dirty Devil Mountains, *see* Unknown Mountains
Dirty Devil (Frémont) River, viii.; point of junction with Colorado, 3; failure to get to it overland, 70, 99; arrive at mouth by river, 133; overland trip to, 195; on head of, according to Dodds, 199; mistake discovered, 199, 200; reach mouth of, overland, 209
Disaster Falls, 39; dinner from wreckage of *No-name*, 40; fall of river at, 42

Distance, from Union Pacific Railway to Gate of Lodore, 33; to Echo Park, 48; to junction of Green and Grand, 114; to Dirty Devil, 135; Paria to Little Colorado, 223; Little Colorado to Kanab Canyon, 241; Wonsits Valley to Gunnison Crossing, 93. *See also* Appendix, *Romance of the Colorado River*
Dixie, name for Virgin Valley, 164
Dodds, Captain Pardyn, fails to reach Dirty Devil River, 70; meet him at El Vado, 143
Dog, Dandie Dinmont, of Mrs. Thompson, 166, 195
Douglas Boy, first meeting with, 64; comes to mouth of Uinta, 70; an eloper, 71; farewell to, 76
Dummy and his prophecy, 9
Dunn, William H., vi.; name carved in Music Temple, 141; killed by Shewits, 141, 259
Dunn's Cliff, 43
Dutch oven, 4
Dutton, Major, vii.

E

Echo, Cliff, 49; Park, 49; Rock, 53; Peaks, how named, 151
Eight Mile Spring, camp at, 165
El Vado de los Padres (Crossing of the Fathers), 7, 8, 41, 95, 96; first white man to ford after Escalante, 96; arrive at, 1871, 143; description of, 168; arrive at, 1872, 210; early known by Richard Campbell, 96
Emma, Sister, a wife of John D. Lee, 211
Endowment garment, Adams wears one, 259
Epizoötic visits Utah, 262
Escalante, his crossing of the Colorado, 7; Sierra, 43; of Green River, 67; his name for Green River, 67; for White River, 67; River, 210; river named by Professor Thompson, 210

F

Failure Creek, 129
Fennemore, joins party, 187; falls sick, 212; leaves party, 216; in Salt Lake, 267

Field, 5; arm-chair obtained from 8; breakfast at, 9
Flaming Gorge, 1, 2; height of walls, 17; Green River enters, 17; accessibility, 20; gateway to the series of canyons, 22
Frank, *see* Richardson
Frank, Pai Ute, *see* Chuarooum-peak
Frémont, River, 3; *see* Dirty Devil; General, 95;
First Granite Gorge of the Grand Canyon, declivity in, 43
First Powell Expedition, v.; plat of river by, vi., 2, 96; boats of, x.
Food supply exhausted, 141
Fort Davy Crockett, 30
Fort Defiance, Jacob Hamblin goes there, 143
Fort Pierce, 188
Fort Robideau, 67; only house on the river, 72
Fretwater Falls, 83
Fuzz, Mrs. Thompson's dog, 166, 195

G

Gate of Lodore, 32
Gentile frontier town compared with Mormon, 174
Gila monster, 245
Gilbert, G. K., vii., 136
Glen Canyon, beginning, 137; width of river in, 139; height of walls, 139, 143; end of, 151
Glencove, attempt to reach Dirty Devil River from, 99
Glendale, Mormon settlement, 262
Goblin City, journey to, 68; description of, 69
Gold, found on Colorado, 144; at mouth of Kanab, 174; miners go after, 185
Golden to Provo, waggon road, 67
Gosi-Utes, Gunnison killed by, 95
Gould's ranch, 190
Grand Canyon, Jacob Hamblin circumtours it, 96; Powell finds way in to the mouth of the Kanab, 174; Dodds and Jones get to it, 188; Whitmore describes a crossing, 188; Dodds and Johnson reach river, 189; Dodds and Dellenbaugh go to river at Lava Falls, 192; Marble division begins, 216; length of, including Marble Canyon, 217; beginning of, 223; enter it, 223
Grand River, 109

Grand Wash, 96; altitude of, 217
Granite, the, runs up, 225
Grant, news of election of, 256
Graves, ancient, discovered, 77
Gray Canyon, enter it, 91; colour, height, and character of walls, 91, 92; end of, 93; length of, 93
Gray Cliffs, 164
Great Basin, 164
Green River, points on, astronomically fixed before Powell, 19, 95
Green River City, arrive there, 3; described, 5; settlements below, 8
Green River Suck, 20
Green River Valley, 1, 2
Grizzly bears, 26
Gunnison, Captain, crossed Green River, 95; killed, 95
Gunnison Butte, 93, 99
Gunnison Crossing, Powell plans to rejoin his party there, 70
Gypsum Canyon, 127

H

Habasu (Havasu), 96
Haight, 153, 157
Hamblin, Frank, 254
Hamblin, Fred, 99
Hamblin, Jacob, scout and pioneer, 96; first after Escalante to cross at El Vado, 96; circumtours the Marble and Grand canyons, 96; arrives at Paria, 153; treaty with Navajos, 168; title of his book, 169; Indian engagements, 170; goes to Mt. Trumbull with Powell, 170; wives of, 174; hears plot to ambush, 243
Hamblin, Joseph, 156, 241
Hamblin, Lyman, 99
Hanson, name assumed by J. H. Beadle, 215
Harrell brothers, camp in Brown's Park, 30
Hastele, Navajo chief, 169
Hattan, Andrew, 4; place in boat, 11; his call to meals, 11; departure, 260
Headquarters, winter, of, 1872–73, 260
Hell's Half Mill, 44
Henry Mountains (Unknown Mts., *q. v.*), 207
Henry's Fork, mouth of, 17; astronomically fixed, 95
Henry, Professor Joseph, vi.
Henry (Azure) Cliffs, 99
Hidden Lakes, the, 201

High Plateaus of Utah, continuation of Wasatch Range, 95; end of, 164
Hillers, John K., joins party, 7; catches fish, 15; songs of, 52, 74; catches salmon, 98; photographer, 217; hurts his back, 225; trip to Moki towns, 248
Hog-backs, topographical feature described, 198
Hook, Theodore, drowned, 25; grave of, 25
Horse discovered, 90
Horse sense, 258, 264
Horseshoe Canyon, why so called, 21
Hotel Tovar, 232
House ruins, Shinumo, 112, 137, 138
House Rock Spring, 157, 160
House Rock Valley, 160, 175
Howland, Seneca, and O. G., 141
Howlands and Dunn, vi., vii.; why killed by Shewits, 171; left first party, 242; killed near Mt. Dellenbaugh, 259
Hurricane Hill, 190
Hurricane Ledge, 190

I

Illustrations in Powell's *Report*, x.
Innupin, definition of, 252
Innupin Picavu (Water-pocket), 251
Island Park, 56
Ives, comes up Colorado, 1858, 2; reconnoitres south of Grand Canyon, 96; names North Side Mountains, 186

J

Jack, *see* Hillers
Jacob, *see* Hamblin
Jacob's Pools, 159
Johnson, Will, 186; leaves party, 211
Johnson's, Mormon settlement 166
Jones, S. V., 10; place in boat, 11; falls ill, 152; leaves, 260
Julien, D., inscriptions by, 108, 113, 118
Junction, the, of the Grand and Green, 113; summit at, 116; trail to, 118

K

Kaibab (Buckskin Mountain), seen from Echo Peaks, 150; band of

Pai Utes, 177; trip to south-west corner of, 182; Point F established on, 184; seen from Marble Canyon, 222
Kanab, settlement of, 8; headquarters, 145; headquarters, winter of 1872–73, 260; description of, 166; base line near, 173; Christmas dance, 173
Canyon, journey up, 185, 244; supplies to be brought in there, 224
Kapurats, Pai Ute name for Major Powell, 171
Kettle Creek, 24
Killiloo, refrain, 75, 81, 226, 267
Kingfisher Canyon, 22; why so called, 22
Kingfisher Creek, 21
Kit Carson, 95
Koneco, Navajo chief, 154

L

Labyrinth Canyon, enter it, 105; end of, 110; length of, 110
La Sal, Sierra, 103, 109, 127
Latter-Day Saints, 212
Lava Falls, Dodds and Dellenbaugh climb to river there, 192
Leaping Brook, 46
Lee, John Doyle, 195; settles at Paria, 210; meet him, 210; wife Rachel, 210; wife Emma (his XVIII.), 210; called Naguts, 211; executed, 211
Lee Ferry, 215
Lehi, Mormon town, 262, 266
Let-down, 26; method of accomplishing a, 90
Letters from Clement Powell to the Chicago *Tribune*, v.; from F. S. Dellenbaugh to the Buffalo *Express*, vii.
Life preservers, 8; indispensable, 237
Light, the controversy of the, 63
Lighthouse Rock, 80
Lignite Canyon, 91
Line portage, 26
Little Brown's Hole, 29; name changed to Red Canyon Park, 29
Little Canyon, 31
Little Colorado, canyon of, forms division between Marble and Grand Canyons, 217; mouth of, 222; altitude of mouth, 223
Little White, or Price River, 92
Little Zion Valley, 190
Lodore Canyon, party goes through on the ice, 2; gate of, 32; why

Lodore Canyon—(*Continued*)
so called, 32; we enter it, 34;
width of river in, 35, 42, 43;
velocity of current in, 35, 42;
sunlight in, 36; wreckage found
in, 41; height of walls, 42, 43, 46;
character of 42; declivity in, 43;
end of, 48; length of, 48
Logan, Mt., 188
Log-cabin Cliff, 84
Lonely Dell, 211
Long Valley, route *via*, 262
Lost Creek (Crescent Creek), 209
Louisa, a wife of Jacob Hamblin,
174, 195, 250
Lower Disaster Falls, 42

M

MacEntee, 166; leaves party, 179;
in Salt Lake, 267
Mackenzie, General, ix., map A,
facing page 95
Macomb, 95
"Major, The" viii., *see* Powell,
John Wesley
Mangum, Joseph, 153; the lost
guide, 155, 157
Manti, Mormon settlement, 99, 174
Map, accuracy of plat of Colorado
River, vi., vii., 243; sheets giv-
ing Colorado River, viii.; prelimi-
nary, finished, 262; sent to Wash-
ington, 267
Marble Canyon, 150; miners wrecked
in, 195, 217; enter it, 216; total
length with Grand Canyon, 217;
height of walls, 216, 217–222;
end of 222; descent in, 223;
number of rapids in, 223
Markargunt Plateau, 191
Meek, Joseph, goes through Lodore
on the ice, 95
Melvin Falls, 86
Millecrag Bend, 129, 132
Moki (Hopi) ruin, 79
Monument built 1869 by Powell,
78
Mookoontoweap or Little Zion
Valley, 190
Mormon, settlements, 96; method
of pioneering, 167, 174; dance,
173
Mt. Carmel, Mormon settlement,
262
Mount Dellenbaugh, named, 254;
altitude, 259; Shinumo remains
on, 259
Mount Ellen, Henry Mountains, 208

Mount Hillers, Henry Mountains,
208
Mount Logan, 188, 253
Mount Nebo, 266
Mount Pennell, Henry Mountains,
207, 208
Mount Seneca Howland (Navajo
Mt.), 141
Mountain Meadows massacre, 195;
Lee's version, 211
Music Temple, grotto, 141, 210

N

Narrow Canyon, 3, 133
Natural arches in Canyon of Deso-
lation, 87, 88
Navajos, agency, 143; meet with,
146; afraid of our boats, 153;
dance with, 154; ceremonial, 177
Navajo Creek, 149
Navajo Mountain, 139, 141, 201
Navajo Well, 175, 248
Nephi, 266
New Year's Day, 1872, 174; 1873,
260
No-name, boat, wreck of, 38
North Side Mountains (Uinkaret
Mts.), 186

O

Oak Spring, 187, 188, 191
Old Jacob, *see* Jacob Hamblin
Old Spanish Trail, 95, 246
Oonupits, sound made by, 252; de-
scribed, 252; Indian shoots at,
252
Orange Cliffs, 110
Order of going, 11, 72, 136, 215
Overland Stage Co. road, Salt Lake
to Denver *via* Provo, Robideau
Crossing, and Golden, 67

P

Paantung, Thompson's Shewits
guide, 259
Painted Desert, 150
Pai Ute women, Jacob Hamblin,
sealed to, 174; language without
an "F," 250; name for Major
Powell, 250; name for Professor
Thompson, 250; name for Dellen-
baugh, 250; George, Waytoots,
Chuar, 250; *see also* Chuarooum-
peak; method of cooking rabbits,
252
Pai Utes, despised by Navajos, 170;
Kaibab band of, 177; wickiups,

Pia Utes—(*Continued*)
177; arms, 178; rabbit skin robe, 178; fire obtained by drill, 178; ceremonial, 178; songs, 178, 179; stone arrowhead making, 178
Panguitch, arrive at, 265
Paria, 95, 151, 197; up cliffs at, 155; settlement, 166
Parowan, 248
Patnish, chief of renegades, 8, 167, 250
Photographic outfit, 6, 58
Pictographs, 61
Pierce, Fort, 188, 191
Pine Valley Mountains, 189, 190
Pink Cliffs, 164
Pipe Spring, 185; Wash, 185
Plateau Province, the, 109
Point F, 184
Portage, line, 26; method of making, 40
Potato Valley, 199
Powell, Clement, letters from to Chicago *Tribune*, v.; place in boat, 11; duties of, 11; leaves party, 259
Powell, Emma Dean (Mrs. J. W.), 7; and infant daughter, 165; in Middle Park, 172; leaves for Washington, 179
Powell, John Wesley (The Major), the conqueror of the Colorado, 2; title in Volunteer Army, 2; first descent of Colorado; v., 3, 96, no right arm, 8; titles of reports, v., vi., position in boat, 11; duty of, 11; goes up Yampa, 50; on Yampa River 1868, 50; goes ahead to Uinta, 56; to Salt Lake, 67, 70, 99, 144, 179, 259, 266; songs of, 73; rejoins party, 98; fails to reach Dirty Devil overland, 99; leaves for Washington, 179, 259; reports through Smithsonian Institution, vi.; runs course of river, vii; buried at Arlington, 267
Price River, 92
"Prof.," viii., *see* Thompson, A. H.
Provo to Golden, waggon road, 67
Putnam's Magazine, copy found, 43

R

Rabbits, Pai Ute method of cooking, 252
Rain cascades, 105, 106, 132
Rapid, the first, 21; method of running, 35, 36; tails of, 36;

eddys at, 36; Catastrophe, vi., 242, 243
Rations, 4, 111, 119
Red Canyon, 2; entrance of, 22; upset of *Nellie Powell* in, 23; width of river in, 24; speed of current, 24; height of cliffs, 24, 28; end of, 30
Red Canyon Park, 29
Red Cliff, 176
Red Lake Utes, Jacob pacifies them, 170; meet with band of, 204
Regiment marches from Salt Lake to Denver, 68
Renshawe, John, joins party, 259
Richardson, Frank C. A., 10; position in boats, 11; skill in dressing deer, 16; leaves party, 31
Riggs, 157
Riggs, Charley, 248
Riley, George, 143; head of pack train, 156; cook, 260
Rio, San Buenaventura, 67; San Clemente, 67; San Rafael, 95, 103; San Juan, 140, 210
Robideau, crossing of Green River, 67; Fort, 67
Rocking stones in current, 127
Roundy, Lorenzo W., 153
Rudder useless on the Colorado, x.

S

Sag, the, at Disaster Falls, 38
St. George, Mormon settlement, 194
Salmon, white, caught, 98
Salt Lake City, 7, 17; the major goes to, 67, 70, 99, 144, 179, 259, 265
Salt Lake to Denver, waggon road, *via* Provo and Golden, 67
San Clemente, Rio, Escalante's name for White River, 67
San Francisco Mts., seen from Mt. Trumbull, 187; from Echo Peaks, 250
San Juan River, mouth of, 140; pass it, 1872, 210
San Rafael River, 95; arrive at, 103
Santa Fé and Los Angeles trail, 94
Santa Fé Railway to the Grand Canyon, x.
Scorpions, 132
Second Powell expedition, the, vi., 3; material used for report on first expedition, vi.; supplies of, 4; method of sacking rations, 6; ready to start, 8; personnel of, 11

Selden, 95
Sentinel Rock and Sentinel Creek, 149
Sevier Canyon, 266
Sharp Mountain Falls, 91
Shewits, killed Powell's men, vii. 96; territory of, 186; afraid of us, 191; plan to ambush us, 243; meet us, 253; conference and agreement, 253; Thompson's guide, 259
Shinumo, the, 112, 149; trail, 113, 145; caves, 132; Canyon, 184; ruin on Mt. Dellenbaugh, 259
Shower Bath Spring, 245
Shunesburg, Powell descends Virgin River to, 248
Sierra, Escalante, 43; La Lal, 103; Abajo, 127
Simpson, Captain, 95
Sinav-to-weap, 117
Sister Emma, 211
Sister Louisa, 174
Smithsonian Institution, Powell reported through, vi.
Snowblind, 266
Soap Creek, 159; Frank M. Brown, drowned near mouth of, 159, 217; Rapid, 217
" Sockdologer, of the World," 222; rapid, 226
Songs of the camp, 73, 74
Sorghum molasses, 172
Spanish Fork, 266
Spanish Trail, Old, 95
Split Mountain Canyon, 57; enter it, 58; end of, 60; length of, 60
Springs in river bottom, 103
Stanton, R. B., proves the White story incorrect, v.; completed Brown expedition, ix.; Canyon Railway project, x
Steward, John F., place in boat, 11; duty of, 11; on a raft, 16; discovers gigantic fossil, 20; determines nature of Unknown Mts., 136; ill, 146; recovers, 152; leaves party, 160
Stewart, Bishop, of Kanab, 167; saw-mill of, on Kaibab, 181
Stewart, John, goes with Powell to Grand Canyon, 172; returns with news of gold find, 174
Stillwater Canyon, beginning of, 110; nature of walls, 111, 113; house ruins in, 112; width, 113; end of, 113; length, 114
Summit Valley, 164
Sumner Amphitheatre, 79
Sumner, Jack, 7

Supplies, nature of, 4; to be brought in at three places, 7
Surprise Valley, 241
Swallow Canyon, 31
Swallow Park, 197

T

Table Mountain, 198
Tapeats Creek, 240
Tavaputs Plateau, 80
Teemaroomtekai, Uinkaret chief, 253
Teram Picavu, 254
Thompson, Professor Alvin Harris, vi., vii., ix., 7; place in boat, 11; duty of, 11; first white man to explore Shewits country, 254; to climb Mt. Dellenbaugh, 259; buried at Arlington, 267
Thompson, Mrs. Ellen Powell, 7, 165, 166, 172, 181, 195, 216, 259
Tiravu Picavu, 254
Tirtaan Aigles, slogan, 75, 267
Tokerville, Mormon settlement, 190
Tom, Pai Ute guide, 197; leaves party, 199
Toroweap Valley, 192
Trachyte Creek, 208
Trail up cliffs of Paria, 155
Tribune, Chicago, letters to, from Clement Powell, v.
Trin Alcove, 107
Triplet Falls, 43
Trumbull, Mt., why so called, 186; climbed, 187, 192; height of, 187
Trumbull, Senator, 186
Tuba, a Moki (Hopi), goes home with Jacob, 169; ceremony on crossing Colorado River, 169

U

Uinkaret, Indians, 186; region, 186; plateau, 190; chief, 253
Uinta, Indian Agency, 7, 8, 71
Uinta Mountains, 1; first view of from river, 15
Uinta River, pass mouth of, 76; arrival at, 66; Powell goes ahead to, 56; mouth astronomically determined, 95
Uinta Utes, 61
Undine Springs, 103
Union Pacific Railway, crossing of Green River, 3; see Descent and Distance
Unknown country, the, 95, 96, 199, 200, 201, 202